# ACROSS THE SEVEN SEAS
## AN IMMIGRANT'S MEMORIES

By Al Lohn

Published by Pen It! Publications, LLC
812-371-4128   www.penitpublications.com

Published in the United States of America by Pen It! Publications, LLC

ISBN: 978-1-949609-22-6

# Contents

Contents.................................................................................. 3
Dedication ............................................................................... i
Chapter 1 ............................................................................... 1
Chapter 2 ............................................................................... 3
Chapter 3 ............................................................................... 5
Chapter 4 ............................................................................... 9
Chapter 5 ............................................................................. 15
Chapter 6 ............................................................................. 25
Chapter 7 ............................................................................. 31
Chapter 8 ............................................................................. 35
Chapter 9 ............................................................................. 39
Chapter 10 ........................................................................... 43
Chapter 11 ........................................................................... 47
Chapter 12 ........................................................................... 51
Chapter 13 ........................................................................... 57
Chapter 14 ........................................................................... 61
Chapter 15 ........................................................................... 65
Chapter 16 ........................................................................... 69
Chapter 17 ........................................................................... 73
Chapter 18 ........................................................................... 77
Chapter 19 ........................................................................... 81
Chapter 20 ........................................................................... 89
Chapter 21 ........................................................................... 93
Chapter 22 ........................................................................... 97
Chapter 23 ......................................................................... 101
Chapter 24 ......................................................................... 105
Chapter 25 ......................................................................... 109

Chapter 26 ......................................................................... 111
Chapter 27 ......................................................................... 117
Chapter 28 ......................................................................... 119
Chapter 29 ......................................................................... 121
Chapter 30 ......................................................................... 125
Chapter 31 ......................................................................... 127
Chapter 32 ......................................................................... 131
Chapter 33 ......................................................................... 135
Chapter 34 ......................................................................... 137
Chapter 35 ......................................................................... 139
Chapter 36 ......................................................................... 143
Chapter 37 ......................................................................... 145
Chapter 38 ......................................................................... 149
Chapter 39 ......................................................................... 153
Chapter 40 ......................................................................... 161
Chapter 41 ......................................................................... 165
Chapter 42 ......................................................................... 167
Chapter 43 ......................................................................... 167
Chapter 44 ......................................................................... 173
Chapter 45 ......................................................................... 177
Chapter 46 ......................................................................... 181
Chapter 47 ......................................................................... 185
Chapter 48 ......................................................................... 189
Chapter 49 ......................................................................... 193
Chapter 50 ......................................................................... 199
Chapter 51 ......................................................................... 207
Chapter 52 ......................................................................... 213
Chapter 53 ......................................................................... 217
Chapter 54 ......................................................................... 223
Chapter 55 ......................................................................... 227
Chapter 56 ......................................................................... 231

Chapter 57 ..................................................................... 235
Chapter 58 ..................................................................... 239
Chapter 59 ..................................................................... 241
Chapter 60 ..................................................................... 247
Chapter 61 ..................................................................... 257
Chapter 62 ..................................................................... 261
Chapter 63 ..................................................................... 263
Chapter 64 ..................................................................... 265
Chapter 65 ..................................................................... 269
Chapter 66 ..................................................................... 273
Chapter 67 ..................................................................... 275
Chapter 68 ..................................................................... 279
Chapter 69 ..................................................................... 283
Chapter 70 ..................................................................... 285
Chapter 71 ..................................................................... 289
Chapter 72 ..................................................................... 293
Chapter 73 ..................................................................... 299
Chapter 74 ..................................................................... 305
Chapter 75 ..................................................................... 307
Chapter 76 ..................................................................... 315
Chapter 77 ..................................................................... 323
Chapter 78 ..................................................................... 327
Chapter 79 ..................................................................... 331
Chapter 80 ..................................................................... 335
Chapter 81 ..................................................................... 337
Chapter 82 ..................................................................... 339
Chapter 83 ..................................................................... 347
Chapter 84 ..................................................................... 353
Chapter 85 ..................................................................... 357
Chapter 86 ..................................................................... 361
Chapter 87 ..................................................................... 369
Chapter 88 ..................................................................... 375

Chapter 89 ...............................................................................381
Chapter 90 ...............................................................................389
Chapter 91 ...............................................................................397
Chapter 92 ...............................................................................403
Chapter 93 ...............................................................................411
Chapter 94 ...............................................................................417
Chapter 96 ...............................................................................427
Chapter 97 ...............................................................................437

# Dedication

This book is dedicated to our ancestors, and descendants, so they may know and cherish what their ancestors left for them to build upon.

# Chapter 1

In the kitchen on the second floor of a brownstone, a young expectant father paced from wall to wall to the window overlooking hundred-year-old oak trees in seasonal plumage. He admired the colors to overcome his anxieties. It was a mix of glowing gold, bronze, and deep brown. It was a beautiful sunny day. Brown, bushy tailed squirrels, ran up and down the trees, rustling the fallen leaves. Aroma of fresh roasted coffee permeated the air from the coffee roastery down the street. From there you could overlook a valley of vast farmland. A river, called the *Dhünn*, divided fields of vegetables and golden wheat.

The young expectant father heard the pain filled cries from the room next door. The nineteen-year-old Wlhelmine, affectionately called *Miensche*, labored in the final throes of childbirth. Wlhelmine Theodora (Schneider) Lohn was the wife of Alois Johann Lohn. The three-story brownstone was located at *Bahnhof Strasse 280 Leverkusen Schlebusch, Germany* and was the property of my paternal grandparents, Josef and Maria Lohn.

After hours of suffering under labor pain, and the anxious pacing of the young father, the lusty cries of the couple's first-born child sounded through the home to the joy and relief of all. The midwife opened the door and said to the young father, "Come and admire your son." Dad was overjoyed and united with his loving wife. Together they examined and admired the miracle of their first-born son. Thus, began my journey in this world as Alois Josef Lohn.

After hours of anxious waiting, Dad needed to steady his nerves. Out of cigarettes, he left his small family to some much-needed rest. He went across the street to the grocery store to buy a pack of cigarettes. He was dressed in lounge around clothes, slippers, and unshaven. Since he was an immaculate dresser, who would go to the beach in a suit, tie, and hat, this was unheard of. But then, he was only picking up a pack of cigarettes.

# Chapter 2

Leverkusen Schlebusch, where I was born, was a small town on the outskirts of Cologne, Germany. Looking down from my paternal Grandparent's house into the valley, you could watch the rapidly flowing river turning the large water wheel of a gristmill. A forest in full autumn splendor bordered the river to the left. Adjacent to the forest sat the idyllic Game Warden's House with its thatched roof. In the valley straight across the river and just beyond the swaying amber grain fields, was the house of my maternal grandparents. Next-door, to the right of that, was the home of my lifelong friend, Gerhard.

\*\*\*\*

As it is typical in small towns everywhere, the people know each other and are friends. Naturally, news of the newborn baby boy had to be celebrated. A *prosit* to the new baby was in order. Out came a bottle of Witzeller's corn schnapps, the area's favored drink. Of course, the good news needed propagating. The proprietor, Albrecht, called dad's best friend, Otto Marx. A few minutes later, Otto entered the store and joined in the toasting to the new father. The toasting continued to make the rounds. First, a toast to the baby, then to the daddy, and of course mommy, and whatever else they could think off. Each person present, called for another toast. Moreover, every customer entering the store became an additional well-wisher; and you guessed it, a toast accompanied each wish.

It did not take long before the group, now sizeable in numbers, decided to spread the good news throughout the town. Mr. and Mrs. Albrecht locked up their store and the happy-go-lucky bunch went off to the closest tavern called Zum *Lemmer*. It was a favorite watering hole where the townspeople regularly wet their whistles. Of course, the good news was a welcome occasion to further the celebration by all. Each toast to the new father was now schnapps with a beer chaser; and they kept coming and coming.

After spreading the word via song and drink at all the taverns in town, the now large assembly was feeling no pain. Collectively they decided to march to our home and serenade the young mother and her newborn son. They promptly loaded Dad into an old baby carriage. With his legs dangling over the side of the baby coach, they pushed him through every street in town accompanied with loud singing and laughter. This was to the chagrin of the now awakened neighborhoods and to my grandparent's embarrassment.

Otto Marx, a 6'3" tall giant weighing 300 pounds and my dad, a 5'4" skinny, short guy of only 130 pounds, made quite an interesting pair standing in front of my grandparent's house holding each other up. They sang as loud as they could their version of *Die Blauen Dragoner* (An old army tune from the Kaiser's era) *Sie künnen uns all jet driesse hell zu den Hügeln empor.* (Liberally translated it means to *hell with all of them!* Only the phrase was a lot more colorful when sang in the Cologne dialect). This is how my first day in this world drew to a rousing close.

# Chapter 3

Dad, Alois Johann Lohn, was born on June 8, 1907. He grew into a slender built man with brown eyes, dark curly hair and physically strong. He was a determined man but with a heart of gold. Under the pretense of being a tough and commanding person, he was soft as butter when it came to the needs of others. If he could help someone in need, he would part with the shirt off his back. Dad was a very spiritual, devoted Catholic and always said, "Never let anyone walk away hungry as long as you have food to share."

Having grown up as one of seven children during hard times, he knew the meaning of hunger. However, he was also keen in teaching people to earn their keep.

Dad had a tailor shop. Beggars would come often and ask for handouts. The first question dad always asked was, "Did you eat today? Are you hungry? "If they answered *yes* to the latter, he took them into the kitchen and had my mom feed them. However, if they said *no*, he would get a broom and tell them "Go sweep the street and I will pay you for it." If they refused, he felt they did not need the money.

As a young man of eighteen, Dad learned the trade of tailoring in the town of Euskirchen. After finishing his apprenticeship, he went on *die Wanderschaft*. As it was customary back then, young tailors and other Journeymen fresh out of training would go from town to town throughout the land. They worked for many different shops to learn variations of the many tricks of the trade. Food and lodging were the pay for traveling

Journeymen. After a few weeks in one place, the travel fever would grab them again and off they went in search of new adventures. Dad was one of those Journeymen.

I remember him telling stories of how he captured the hearts of fair-haired maidens in small towns where strangers were a novelty. He told stories of eating the puddings and cakes that were cooling off on windowsills, left by busy housewives in preparation for the Sunday dinner. He would tell these stories with a twinkle in his eye accompanied by a slight shrug of his shoulder and a mischievous crooked smile. My favorite stories were about his experiences in the smallest of villages like *Willoch*.

The town was a village made up of seven farms and a tavern, nestled in a snug valley surrounded by rolling hills. In the summer, the dirt road through *Willoch* was hot and dusty and in the winter, snow and ice covered the road. Other than walking, transportation consisted of horse or oxen drawn carts and occasionally a bicycle or two. On Sundays, the local farmers and their families, dressed in their best clothing, would set out on a five-kilometer pilgrimage past whitewashed Tudor homes to the neighboring town that had a church.

After returning from the Sunday service, the men were very thirsty and went to the local tavern to wash down the dust. The women went faithfully home and prepared the big traditional Sunday dinner. These meals usually consisted of soup, salad, meat, potatoes, pudding, and a cake for the four o'clock coffee.

The tavern was the most important building in town. It served as the grocery store, the tailor shop, and the beer hall. The bartender was the tailor and the grocer. The owner, besides drawing beer and appraising the customers of the daily news, was also the local dentist. Sunday mornings after church, anyone with a toothache got a shot of schnapps, and by hook or crook got his tooth pulled by the rusty pliers wielding *Gastwirt* (the tavern owner).

Dad was hungry, thirsty, and in search of food and work as he walked down the dirt road of *Willoch*. The wonderful aromas of the roasting dinners entered his nostrils and told his brain that it was time to eat. Looking from whence the wonderful smells came; Dad noticed the puddings and cakes cooling on the windowsills. He picked out the most delicious looking cake and pudding, grabbed them and retreated into the forest on the outskirts of town. The cake and pudding provided a delicious meal and the clear running little stream the drink.

Upon hearing a noise outside her window, the farmer's wife went to look what the noise was all about. What she saw was a young man dressed in a dusty suit, a tie, and a haversack slung over his shoulder. He had a pudding in one hand and a cake in the other running for the woods. The generous woman, familiar with the customs of wandering tradesmen, smiled and said, "I hope he likes my cake." She was not too worried because she knew there was plenty of time to make another pudding and cake before her husband would come home for the Sunday dinner.

Another story Dad used to tell was about a certain young lady in a different little village. At the tavern, frequently patronized by the young folks in town, was a girl a bit older than Dad. She loved to flirt with naïve young men, especially strangers from out of town. Young men that had seen a bit of the world rarely came through the village. When they did, it was a special attraction for the homegrown girls. Taking cigarettes from younger men and hiding them in her bra, was this girl's favorite game. When they wanted to smoke, she enjoyed teaching them how to *fish for a cigarette*. That was circa 1925. I guess the farmer's villages were ahead of their time.

Traveling the country on foot taught them many valuable lessons, but also fostered enough memories to last a lifetime. They matured from the experience and it enabled them to master what lie ahead.

# Chapter 4

Mom was a blond, 4'4" tall, blue-eyed beauty. She married Dad at the age of eighteen despite her parent's disapproval. Her mom and stepfather thought Dad enjoyed his beer and drinking friends too much; and their daughter was too young, while Dad was too old for her. He was seven years her senior. When the age was mentioned as an objection, my father promptly responded," She can age with me."

Mom, a stubborn young girl, typical of so many young people, did not heed the advice of her parents. She insisted on getting married, which turned out to be a long and successful bond. As you will find out, marrying younger women and being determined suitors, is an inherent trait in the Lohn clan.

My parents met when Mom went with Dad's best friend to a dance. As usual, all the young people in town were there including Dad. Known for his love of beer and a good time, Dad enjoyed himself with a bunch of friends at the bar. After a while, he noticed the pretty girl with whom one of his friends was dancing.

*Die Karre ausspannen* (unhitch the wagon) was a game the young men in town loved to play. It meant to snitch away the girl from the young man. This, in most cases ended in a fight. Dad moved in on his friend and began dancing with the pretty girl who was to become my mom. Dismayed, his friend had to watch while *his* date danced the rest of the night with his friend. In the process, Dad fell in love. The arrow of cupid had hit him hard.

The next day, he announced to his friend, "I am going to marry that girl." His friend, surprised, disappointed, and hurt, immediately broke off the friendship with Dad. However, he did not fight with him. Dad could stand his ground and could defend himself.

Mom had different ideas. She wanted no part of the drinking, carousing young man. However, Dad was both persistent and determined and finally managed to get her to say the big word, "YES." Less than a year later, they were married.

Mom and Heinrich, her older brother would have had a protected and much cared for childhood had it not been that they were born out of wedlock. Back then, the self-righteous citizens in town considered it shameful and barbarically reminded the two siblings of their substandard status in life whenever they could. This left a life-long scar on Mom that she never managed to overcome.

Grandma was a very loving mother and Grandpa, an honorable man with high standards. He loved his adopted children as if they were of his own blood. The Reidenbach family, my mother's mom's side, and her stepfather's family, the Schneider's, were large families and provided lots of uncles, aunts, and cousins that made up a loving and supporting clan. They helped to shield Mom and her brother from many of the poisonous tongues in town.

Mom's grandfather, my great-grandfather, Adam Reidenbach, had been widowed three times in his life. My maternal grandmother was the daughter of Adam Reidenbach's first wife. During my mother's childhood, he was married to his third wife. Unfortunately, I do not know her name as Mom always referred to her as her grossmutter (grandmother). She ran a restaurant for the executives of a steel mill called Wupperman. Great-grandpa Reidenbach worked at Wupperman's until his retirement at the age of seventy-two.

As both, manager and chef of the restaurant, Great-grandmother Reidenbach had a substantial income and loved to shower her little granddaughter with clothes and toys. She also had a flare for the finer things in life. She enrolled Mom, in an arts and craft school, as well as the local theater group, when she was still a small child. Many times, Mom told of crocheting tablecloths and of the plays in which she performed.

Mom's grandmother loved to take the trolley car into the big city of Cologne where she would meet with her wealthy friends for coffee, cake, and gossip. Afterwards she would attend a show at one of the many theaters, or a concert at the symphony. On those occasions, Grandmother wanted to show off her beautiful granddaughter. She would send a message to my grandmother to have little Wlhelmine ready in the morning dressed in one of the many outfits she had purchased. She always specified precisely the way she wanted her dressed so the little girl could attend the theater, show, or café in Cologne with Grandmother and friends. Everything had to be perfectly coordinated from the dress, to her hair band, stockings, and shoes. Since my mom had a flare for the theatrics, it gave her grandmother great pleasure to introduce her granddaughter to the finer things in life. She had no children of her own. I do not know whether her marriage to Great-grandfather was her first, or not. She died several years before Mom got married.

As a child, I loved Mom's stories. Especially the one she used to tell about her first communion. At that time in Germany, first communions bore a close resemblance to a wedding. Evidently, the entire family was present at the celebration, including all the children. There were many cousins. After the church ceremony, there was always a wonderful feast with plenty of delicious food and cakes prepared and served by the women in the neighborhood. Everyone was dressed in his or her best Sunday clothes for the occasion. Per the dress code of that day, the boys wore shorts extending below the knee and white sailor shirts. The girls wore cute frilly white dresses with white bloomers. Naturally, they all were told, "Play carefully and stay clean."

Typical of children's selective hearing, they heard the word *play*, but not the word *clean*. Using a sandy hill as a slide was a lot of fun. However, it did little for the cleanliness of the young fellow's shorts, or the white bloomers of the cutely dressed little girls.

As if that were not enough to make the grownups cringe, troublemaker cousin Hans, a few years Mom's senior, had some mischief up his sleeve. Followed by the whole entourage of kids, he loaded Mom into a wheel barrel, still dressed in her white communion dress. Then he organized a parade. The children lined up and marched behind cousin Hans pushing the wheel barrel. No events like this take place in Germany without some marching song accompanying the deed. Marching along the children sang a reworded old folk song (Who God wants to shower with favors, he sends into the wonderful wide world). Only in this case the words used by the children were, "Who God wants to shower with favors, he sends into the *butcher shop.*"

One must remember that in those times stuffed sausages were a treat that children very seldom got. The butcher-shop was like a candy store for the children.

The highlight of the parade was when cousin Hans happily wheeled her over to the manure pit and dumped her into the unspeakable mess.

I can just picture Mom covered with manure and the rest of the kids with sandy bottoms looking shamefully down at their shoes while their outraged mothers loudly lectured their offspring. However, the fathers looked at things differently. They quietly laughed and continued enjoying their beer.

At the age of fourteen, Mom started her apprenticeship as a sales person. At the time, it was customary for children at the age of fourteen to either start working in a factory, on a farm, or if their parents could afford it, learn a trade. Post World War I Germany was economically devastated. After the Reparations payments, there was nothing left to rebuild the country. Naturally, jobs were scarce and so were places that were willing to take in an apprentice. Mom had wanted very badly to become a hairdresser, but at the time, there just were no apprentice positions available. Waiting for an opening, doing nothing was unheard of. As providence would have it and after lots of prayers, an opening in sales became available at Isaac's Department Store in the city of Leverkusen.

To become a certified *Verkäuferinn*, (salesgirl) you had to work as an apprentice for three years, go to trade school one day a week, take a test every six months, and take your exam for the Journeymen's Papers at the end of the three years. Mom became Mr. and Mrs. Isaac's favorite sales girl. They treated her as if she were an adopted daughter. On her wedding day, an Isaac's department store van delivered a full load of porcelain and house wares. It was a wonderful wedding present from Mr. & Mrs. Isaac.

However, by then the dark cloud of the emerging *Regime of Tyrants* was forming on the horizon. The Storm Troopers, with their brown shirts, two story hats, swat stickers, and nightsticks, ran rampant with anti-Semitism. I recall mom talking about the day the Storm Troopers rampaged through the store yelling *Dirty Jews!* Breaking everything in sight and closing the store. They yelled at Mom, "Get out of here, you daughter of a lousy Marxist working for a Jew!"

Mr. Isaac, with tears running down his face said to the Nazis, "I don't understand? What did I do to you? I fought in the German Army during the War against the same enemies as you did. I am German just like you."

However, his exclamation had no effect on the rampaging hoodlums. This was the beginning of the darkest time in Germany's history.

# Chapter 5

My paternal grandparents were Opa Josef (Josef Lohn) and Oma Maria (Maria Klünker Lohn). Opa Sheng (Johann Schneider) and Oma Mimmi (Wilhelmine Reidenbach Schneider) were my mother's parents. Both sides of my grandparents were very loving. Despite coming from different backgrounds and mindsets, they pursued the same goals. They were all hard working, devoted to their families, and set high standards for life's values; which they passed on to their children and grandchildren.

Opa Josef, the oldest of twelve siblings was a stocky built man with a broad smile, big strong hard-working hands, and a Groucho Marx-type mustache. He was born and raised in Brachtendorf, a small farming village in the soft rolling mountains of the Eiffel. The region was close to the famous Mosel Delta known for their *Riesling Wines*. His family was very impoverished and considered one of the poorest in town. Although, his mom was the daughter of a wealthy gristmill owner by the name of Bantes, Opa Josef's mom broke the golden rule when she married the son of a sheepherder. Under the golden rule, it was common practice for money to marry money and the poor to marry the poor. In those times, parents disowned and left disobedient children out in the cold.

When Opa Josef was twenty years old, his mother became pregnant with her twelfth child. With so many mouths to feed, Johann Lohn, my grandfather's father, became distraught and depressed. Not knowing how to feed his still growing family, he committed suicide by hanging.

Tragedy, bereavement, and hopelessness led to the adoption of the twelfth child by Mr. and Mrs. Klöckner. The Klöckners were childless but well-to-do farmers in the neighboring town of Roes. That is how Dad's Uncle Jacob's last name became Klöckner instead of Lohn. Even though there was a large age difference between the brothers, the two enjoyed a very close relationship throughout their lives.

Grief and despair led Opa to drinking. Wine was cheap and plentiful in the region. When he got very sick one day from drinking, he swore off alcohol. His trust in God gave him the strength to stay sober. As long as I can remember, Opa Josef drank only an occasional glass of wine or beer and never more than one.

After his father committed suicide, his Grandfather Bantes thought it was time to get back into the act. Several years later, he tried to marry Opa off to a wealthy farmer's daughter. Opa, being disgusted with his grandfather's heartless behavior to his mother and his meddling ways, had enough. He took his meager belongings and left for the big city of Cologne. It was not an easy task for a poor farm boy to adjust to the life in a large metropolitan city. Because of his knowledge and experience handling horses, he became the Beer Coachman for a big brewery. He delivered beer to the many taverns in the city maneuvering a six-horse drawn wagon through the cobblestone streets and alleys of Cologne. The old-fashioned beer wagons were like the Anhäuser Busch six horse-wagon often seen in television advertisements, or at the Anhäuser Busch Gardens.

One day, the lonely twenty-eight-year-old man sat in a beer garden having lunch. While eating, he noticed a very attractive young woman sitting with a man at a table a few feet away. Since he did not see any rings on their fingers, he concluded they were not husband and wife. Upon closer observation, it also seemed that they resembled one another. He figured they might be related.

16

As mentioned earlier, the men in the Lohn clan wasted little time and were determined suitors.

He worked his way over to the table and started a conversation with the couple. He found out that the fellow chaperoning the young girl, Maria Klünker, was her brother Josef Klünker. Josef was a tailor by trade.

Opa Josef was a principled and spiritual young man of the Catholic faith. Despite cupid's extra-ordinary job making him fall head-over-heels in love, he wanted to make sure that his newfound love was an honorable young lady of good standing. Opa was an excellent dancer and loved to swirl the girls around on the dance floor. However, this beautiful girl did not know how to dance. Therefore, he had no choice but to continue to make small talk.

They exchanged information about their hometowns, the likes, and dislikes of the city etc. Somehow, Opa Josef needed to get his self-devised test into the conversation. He began naming places of questionable repute and invited them to go there. Both brother and sister promptly declined this. After a short while, the brother countered Opa's requests by an outburst of outrage. Oma's brother reprimanded Opa, "What do you mean by asking us to go to places like that? We are decent God-fearing people of the Catholic faith. We do not patronize places like that. Please leave this table!"

This was exactly what Opa Josef wanted to hear. The young girl and her brother had passed his test. Now he had some explaining to do. He must have said the right words because six weeks later they were married in the big city of Cologne. Maria Klünker became Maria Lohn and Josef Lohn, Dad's uncle, referred to as Josef the Tailor.

A few years and several children later, they moved to Schlebusch where Opa got a job at the Maschinenbau Firma Eumuko as a tool and die maker. Hard working and frugal he managed to buy half of a three-story duplex with a wonderful large garden. He retired from Eumuko at the age of seventy-four.

Opa Josef, much like Dad, could be stubborn and pig-headed; always ready to prove his point when he thought he was correct. I remember a heated discussion between Dad and my grandfather about being able to push a fully loaded wheel barrel with coal down the basement steps and then turn it in a small space at a 90-degree angle. Dad said, "It can't be done!"

Opa pulled out a five mark bill and said, "Fine, put your money where your mouth is."

Dad pulled out five marks as well and said, "Show me."

Opa, at the age of seventy, took the wheel barrel full of coal, rolled it down the steep steps, turned the barrel, and wheeled it into the next room proving his point much to Dad's chagrin.

The basement was a typical cellar, with a dirt floor and brick walled vaulted ceilings. It was a dark, below ground level labyrinth with no lights. Some small openings on the top of the wall served as basement windows for air circulation. There was no means to shut the windows. During the cold winter days, they were closed off by stuffing hay-filled burlap bags into the holes. It minimized the bitter cold temperatures from entering the cellar.

Cold winters were typical of that region in Germany. To support the building, there were several walled off rooms that served as foundation for the structure. Dirt-floor common cellars in older homes were the norm. They stored coal, potatoes, carrots, fruits, and if you could afford it, wine in there. During severe winters, when the water pipes froze along the ceiling, Opa would defrost them with a blowtorch. Fruits and vegetables stored in those cellars used to freeze in the wintertime. One cannot compare Veggies frozen in that fashion with today's frozen foods. They tasted horrible. Especially the potatoes, they tasted sickeningly sweet. Regardless, everything was eaten because it could not be replaced.

As a child, I was deeply touched and impressed by this strong, principled, resolve-oriented man that humbled himself every night on his knees praying the rosary with Oma Maria. Opa Josef was a member of the Catholic Workers Association and a member of the CDU, Christian Democratic Union, during the struggling Weimarer Republic. With strong spiritual convictions and values, he wanted to be part of rebuilding the country into a democracy during the post World War I era.

After the German Kaiser abdicated and fled into exile, Opa Josef, like many of his companions, dreamed of creating a society that recognized values, human and worker's rights instead of being ruled and used by the aristocracy. Unfortunately, the hungry-bellied German citizens fell prey to the false promises and games of the upcoming murdering criminals, thus ending a short-lived democracy. This conviction to values and principles did not endear him with the new rulers of Germany's Third Reich.

****

Oma Maria had an unshakable, almost child-like faith in God. Without complaining, she endured the pain of losing two of her children, one at the age of fourteen, and another at the age of six months. Neither did the hardship of raising her remaining five children on my grandfather's meager income steer her off course during very difficult times.

Oma Maria had been born and raised on a farm in the rolling forested hills of Westphalia. Her family struggled for survival on their small farm. During that time, she learned how to grow vegetables and to raise animals. It was common for poor children from small farms to leave their homes when they became of age. Small farms could not support large families. Therefore, Oma Maria went to Cologne and worked as a maid. Josef the Tailor, her brother, was already in Cologne and as mentioned before, took on the role as her chaperone. Because of her experience on the farm, she worked their large garden, raised chickens, and goats, which supplied most, if not all the food needed for her family.

Oma Maria, a slender petite woman was a simple, clean-cut country girl that was into hardy, heavy cooking, and heavy-duty scrubbing. She did not have much time or patience for fine delicate cooking or cleaning. Nevertheless, I loved her apple-pan cakes. What I hated was the goat milk and her buttermilk pan-fried potatoes.

My cousins and I used to love the winter evenings. With the flickering coal fire in the stove lighting up the room and creating jumping shadows on the walls, Oma would sit in the dark and warm her feet in front of the open door from the baking oven. We clustered around her on the floor listening to the stories of Snow White and the seven Dwarfs, Red Riding Hood, and many ghost stories. Oma was a wonderful storyteller. She had the ability to keep us listening to every one of her words.

Weeks before Christmas, we would sing carols and imagined St. Nick stamping through the frozen snow watching all the children. On the sixth of December was the feast of St. Nickolaus. He was a bishop known as the Saint of Giving. He had helped the poor in his time. We children believed that he would bring gifts to deserving kids that behaved. As a prelude to Christmas, St. Nick dressed in bishop's attire and was accompanied by the devil's helper, Knecht Ruprecht. He was a fearsome looking character dressed in burlap-rags dragging chains behind him. He would visit families with children, checking their behavior and reporting it to the Christ child. If the report was good, St. Nick would hand out cookies and a small toy. If the children had been naughty, Knecht Ruprecht would put them into a burlap sack and carry them off to hell, or so we thought. This was an old German tradition, which I think was an invention to keep the children in line before Christmas. Excitement used to come to a crescendo when Christmas came closer. After St. Nick's appearance, until Christmas, Oma would tell the story of the first Christmas. She always managed to turn the story into enough segments to last until Christmas Eve.

As children, we never got to see the decorated Christmas tree prior to Christmas Eve. In my hometown, everyone celebrated not only Christmas Eve, but also two days of Christmas. We celebrated Christmas Eve at our home. After attending the midnight mass, Mom's parents would take me to their house where the Christ-child came during the night and brought more toys and sweets.

The first day of Christmas was always celebrated at my mother's parents and the second at dad's parents. Until the age of fifteen, I was the only grandchild in my mother's family enjoying undivided attention on Christmas. But it was different at my dad's parents. We were nine cousins. I loved the excitement we created while we waited for the Christ Child to decorate the tree and set up the presents. At least this is what we children believed was going on behind the closed doors of the living room. The grownups would wet their whistle during the decorating of the Christmas tree.

Oma Maria's living room was off limits until the evening on the second day of Christmas. That is when all my dad's family gathered at the house of my grandparents Lohn. Impatient and excited, we sang carols and told stories while Oma, Opa, and our Parents *helped* the Christ-Child. The fear of being caught by the Christ-child doing something wrong was the best babysitter.

When the doors finally opened we marched single file into the living room; youngest child first, oldest last. That's when we saw the beautifully decorated tree for the first time illuminated by real wax candles. The candles were the only illumination in the room. It never failed to put us in a state of awe watching the dancing shadows in the dimly lit room. The presents were displayed in full view, not wrapped up and in boxes. By today's standards, there were very few presents. For the most part they were additions to toys we already had. But seeing my castle from previous years, wonderfully displayed with the added hand-poured led soldiers created by my grandfather, was overwhelming.

Home baked cookies, apples, nuts, and chocolates on beautifully printed paper Christmas plates, richly decorated with artificial snow, and Christmas scenes, were a rare treat. All the little smiling faces with shining eyes brought pleasure to the Christ Child's helpers. This is a pleasure I can fully appreciate today as a grandfather when I watch our grandchildren unwrapping the presents.

On Sundays, we would meet at Oma Maria's together with my uncles, aunts, and cousins for a friendly card game and later coffee and cake. The card players, consisting of Opa Josef, my dad, his two brothers, his two brothers-in-law along with Aunt Veronica. She was the only female that played cards. Aunt Veronica never joined the women-folk doing handy crafts, gossiping, and baking cakes. She was addicted to card games. The card games were played for pennies but were as heated as any high-stakes game. My Aunt Veronica pounded the table as hard as the guys and made the towers of pennies that my cousins and I had built, tumble.

By the volume of the voices my grandma knew when it was time to intervene and prepare the table for the coffee and cake. Sooner or later the game of the hotheaded players would get overheated. It always finished with my grandpa saying, *Genug, schluss, pasta!* (Enough, the end, basta!). He then collected the cards and promised never to play again, which lasted only until the next family gathering.

When the card game closed, the women set up the table. However, Oma Maria was banned from making coffee. All of dad's siblings agreed on one thing, Grandma's coffee tastes like dishwater. The saying was, "She does not know how to make coffee!" Therefore, according to the joined consensus of the family, grandma was not to make the coffee; it had to be done by Dad, Aunt Veronica, or Aunt Anna. The aroma of the coffee and the delicious looking fruit tarts changed the dispositions of the hotheaded players in a jiffy. Now the afternoon continued with jokes, funny stories, and laughter much to the relief of us children who always thought a fight would break out but it never did. However, World War II started to show its ugly face and ended these simple pleasures. But life goes on as it always does.

# Chapter 6

Opa Sheng, my mother's Dad, was a stern looking, stocky built man with an erect posture. He had a big handlebar mustache and boldly wore his head shaved. He was filled with values, principles, logic, and wisdom. He was a wonderful grandpa to me.

Opa Sheng was one of seven siblings. He had three brothers and three sisters. They were all raised by a widowed mother. He learned to appreciate even the smallest of favors. "Waste not, want not" was his motto especially when it came to food. To him, letting leftover food spoil was the greatest sin you could commit.

If the doorbell rang during eating, Opa Sheng would hide the lunchmeat in the table drawer. He would say, "You never know whether the friend that comes in is as fortunate as we are. Do not make them suffer over wanting and not having."

Opa Sheng's many wise sayings during the early impressionable years of my life helped to form my convictions and values. Some of his phrases were: "Son, you are neither superior nor inferior."---"Treat everyone with respect and demand the same."---"Think first and then act; and you will be more right than wrong."---"Humble yourself and your greatness will shine."---"Actions not words are what people will remember."---"Respect is not free, you must earn it."---"Honor is the greatness in a man, dishonor the downfall."---"Stand up for what you believe and never waiver."---Those were some of the values he believed and lived by.

Because of a knee injury as a child, that had been improperly treated by an incompetent backwards physician, Opa Sheng was handicapped. His right leg was a foot shorter than his left. After the injury, his leg stopped growing from the knee down. Thus, his foot on that leg was the same size as that of a child's. To compensate for that Opa wore a heavy brace in which his foot rested and extended below to even out both legs. He always walked with a cane. However, it did not deter Opa Sheng from enjoying a normal life.

He was a weaver by trade and worked in the local textile mill. From the time I can remember, Opa Sheng was retired but spoke often about his work.

He belonged to an all men's choir called the Lorelei; he loved to sing, travel and hike despite his handicap. Always meticulously dressed in a suit, heavily starched white shirt, a navy polka dot tie and his shoes were always polished like a mirror. He was a sight to behold. My dad used to tailor his suits from the same fabric Opa used to weave. He always got the fabric from the mill gratis.

His meticulous attention to detail commanded respect. It was Opa Sheng's trademark. He was a stickler about polished shoes and always cleaned them himself. Opa used to say, "I will not reduce anyone to be my shoeshine boy." When he worked in the garden, or did chores around the house, he wore indigo blue linen overalls. His finicky precise ways carried through even in menial work. The vegetables in his garden where planted in straight rows with none being out of line and planted in exact equal distance. There was no more than a millimeter tolerance.

In fact, he would line up a string along the rows when planting. When he harvested, the carrots would be placed in a sandbox in the basement for use during the winter months. All of them were perfectly lined up and spaced. Briquettes, pressed coal shaped like bricks which was our heating fuel, were perfectly stacked in the basement like a series of brick walls. Even an experienced bricklayer would have had a hard time to top the perfection. Opa would cut old newspaper in precisely 6X 8 inch sheets to be used as toilet paper. All the sheets measured the same to the millimeter. Picking fruit from the trees before all of them were ripe would make him angry. He could not understand people without patience and squandering was against all his principals.

As a child, I loved raw carrots and so did my friends. My friends used to urge me to get some of Opa's meticulously stored carrots from the basement. When I asked Opa for a carrot, his answer was always, "Okay, but only one," which literally meant only one. I would hand out the carrots through the basement window for my friends. Then I would parade one carrot in front of him and say, "See Opa only one."

With a smile on his face he would respond, "Good boy." He knew very well that I had passed carrots out through the basement window. In my lack of wisdom, it did not dawn on me that he would find out when even one carrot was missing from his perfectly set up army. Unshakable commitment to values, principles, and honor were his life.

Opa was also a man full of pranks and humor. He often told funny stories about his encounters like the Buttermarkt story. Oma Mimmi and Opa's sister were wondering what the Buttermarkt was all about. The Buttermarkt was one of the red-light districts in Cologne. The street was filled with bordellos like the famous Raperbahn in Hamburg. Prostitution was and still is legal in Germany. Opa Sheng and Uncle Johann said, "We'll take you there and show you."

Here I must explain that my Opa's sister was married to Johann Fiedler. The act of engaging with a prostitute was called Fidele in the Cologne dialect.

On a sunny afternoon the four took the trolley car to Cologne. After having the traditional coffee and a piece of cake at the Café Ritz, they marched off to the Buttermarkt. Due to my grandfather's handicap and my grandmother's heart condition, they walked slowly to the famous street. The Butter- market was lined with pimps in front of the bordellos advertising *their merchandise*. Flaunting streetwalkers were calling out to the men, "Wills de mal." (Would you like to?) Bare-breasted women were hanging out of the windows and laughing at the slow walking couples waving them to come up.

Several ladies of the night called out, "Kumm ens rupp fidele" (Come up fidele). Can you guess what's coming?

Yes, my Aunt Gretchen started beating my uncle up saying, "What have you been up to? All these women know you here."

I am sure you can well imagine the fun the Buttermarkt had at my poor Uncle Johann's expense. Innocent as a lamb and always faithful to his wife, it took a lot of explaining by the men to convince Aunt Gretchen of the difference between *fidele and Fiedler*. For many years this story brought tears of laughter to the eyes of the listeners at family gatherings.

Before retiring, Opa Sheng was the union's shop-steward at the weaving mill. He was highly respected by the workers and management alike for his fair and principled representation of the workers. Like my other grandfather, he also dreamed of being part in building a new Germany under the Weimar Republic where human rights and the rights of the working class were honored and respected. Opa Sheng was joined in this endeavor by his stepson Heinrich, my mom's brother. He shared the same values as grandpa did.

Uncle Heinrich was also a weaver who with only an elementary education had worked his way up to become the factory-manager at the age of twenty-seven. It took a genius in those days to move up the ladder that quickly; especially when one was born on the wrong-side-of-the-tracks and without proper credentials. Both Uncle Heinrich and Opa Sheng belonged to the SPD (Social Democratic Party), one of Germany's political parties that based its philosophy on that of Karl Marx, equality for all.

Both were outspoken defenders of their beliefs and a thorn in the side of the Nazis who at that time were about to come to power. They continued to speak out even after the Nazi Party's take over. I remember them saying, "These lying hoodlums cannot last forever. Some day we will get the country back.

After a motorcycle accident, Uncle Heinrich died at the age of twenty-eight of heart failure. More than likely, his untimely death spared him from being arrested for his controversial views and outspokenness.

Opa Sheng died of stomach cancer during the war. He never raised his hand in the Nazi salute or gave homage in words to the monster, Adolf Hitler. He was convinced that the Third Reich was doomed. On his open grave, Director Hass from the textile mill delivered the eulogy and said, "Mr. Schneider stayed the man he always was, a man with high values and never wavered in his beliefs."

Opa Sheng and Opa Josef strived for the same goals but differed in their philosophies. While Opa Josef strongly believed in God, state, and the Catholic Church, Opa Sheng did not believe in the institutional church. He only went to church on the high holidays, weddings, and first communions. But he made sure that in my dad's absence I went to church and was educated in the Catholic Faith.

# Chapter 7

Oma Mimmi, my maternal Grandmother, was the oldest of many children. Her father had remarried after his first wife died. She literally became the Cinderella in her family. After her mother had died, it became her duty to clean, cook and care for the younger siblings while my great-grandpa Reidenbach was at work. But it was her stepmother's oldest son, from a previous marriage, who gave her the most grief. Ironically, he went to the USA before World War II and later became the Reidenbach clan's greatest benefactor during the post-World War II years.

However, Oma Mimmi managed to get out of the house and began working as a sales girl in a general store in Schlebusch. But, her troubles were not over. She fell in love with a factory worker by the name of Wilhelm Rötzel. This was much to the annoyance of Wilhelm's brother who was a successful inventor and wanted my grandmother for himself. This brought her a lot of grief.

Young and innocent she became pregnant with Uncle Heinrich. But before they could make any marriage plans, Wilhelm's conniving brother, whose name escapes me, managed to maneuver him into the Royal Hussars. To get into the Hussars you needed to have your own horse. His brother bought a horse and then bribed Wilhelm's superiors to confiscate all mail from both directions. After his training they sent him to a garrison in East Prussia, which was far away from home.

As fate would have it, he came home on leave after my uncle was born and impregnated my Oma Mimmi again. Supposedly, more bribes where paid by his brother to keep them apart. After his release from the army he found my grandma married to my mother's stepfather, Johann Schneider. At least this is the story Wilhelm Rötzel told. However, I am not certain that his story washes. I believe he took advantage of my grandma's naiveté.

After that, there was no contact between him and my mom's family. However, several sisters and his brother Gustav Rötzel stayed friends with my grandparents.

Wilhelm Rötzel did pay child support, which my proud grandfather refused to use and instead deposited in a trust account for my mom and her brother. The money could only be withdrawn by mom or her brother at the age of twenty-one. By the time they became of age, with the inflation and devaluation after World War I, their account was wiped out.

During World War I food and clothing became scarce. Otherwise the effects of the war, unlike World War II, were not felt in small towns like Schlebusch. Except if a member of the family was in the military but no one in Mom's family was in the service during WWI.

My grandparents managed better than most. Opa raised rabbits for meat, grew vegetables and fruits, gathered wild berries, hazelnuts and they used wild nettles to cook like spinach. Since Opa Sheng worked in the textile mill he was able to get fabrics and had Oma Mimmi turned them into garments.

After Germany capitulated, allied occupation forces moved into the region bringing with them tough times. Though food and other merchandise became available again, unbelievable inflation made it almost impossible to buy anything. I remember both my grandparents telling stories of receiving their weekly pay in the morning and by the afternoon it was devalued to the cost of a loaf of bread. The women would wait at the factory gates for their husbands pay and immediately spend it for fear of having worthless money in their pockets by evening.

The British military was quartered in private homes throughout the town. My grandparents had a British officer staying with them who took a liking to my mom and her brother. They were, at that time, small children. Many times, he sent his aid with a burlap sack full of food. He deposited the food with a twinkle in his eye, announcing, "For the rabbits." Writing this brings memories back of my childhood after World War II, and later my time as a GI stationed in Germany.

Oma Mimmi was a short full-figured lady. She wore her hair in a bun and had the warmest smile. She was the most loving grandma a child could have. I was her *one and only* and nothing had been denied me, providing it could be had, or could be done. Some of my fondest memories were the trips as a small child into Cologne before Christmas. Oma would take me through the festively decorated city and into the department stores. The store windows were decorated with Christmas scenes and toys. Scenes of St. Nick stomping through the frozen snow on a white horse pulling a sled full of all kinds of wonderful things. I used to drool over the beautiful toys hoping that the Christ Child would remember to bring them. Oma would tell me, "I told the Christ child what you would like." Christmas would come, and the Christ Child always remembered my wish list. Of course, that was before WWII.

Since I was afraid of the dark, like most children, Oma Mimmi would lay down with me until I went off into dreamland. My wife Heide reminds me a lot of my Oma. She is loving, watching, protecting, and spoiling our little munchkins today.

Oma Mimmi was a great cook and knew all my favorite meals. Having no sense of smell, which my mom never believed, I would only eat what looked appetizing to me. So, Oma made sure the presentation was to my liking.

Sunday afternoons used to be a real treat at Oma's house. Dinners were served at noontime with wonderful vanilla pudding covered with raspberry or strawberry syrup for dessert. At four o clock in the afternoon, she would serve coffee and her home baked cake. Those wonderful fruit tarts with whipped cream, or the butter cream cakes went well with my hot chocolate. Yes, Oma knew just how to tickle the fancy of my palate.

Oma Mimmi was never one to sit idle. She was very good at knitting, crocheting, and handicrafts. It seemed she was constantly knitting sweaters and socks. Although they looked nice, I hated the ruff scratchy wool. Especially bad were the long stockings that I had to wear with shorts when it got cold. As soon as I was out of mom's watchful eyes I rolled them down no matter how cold it was.

My beloved Oma Mimmi, who read me stories, taught me prayers, children's songs, and rhymes, died when I was about nine years old. A stroke took her life a couple of weeks before Christmas at the age of fifty.

# Chapter 8

Schlebusch, along with several other towns like, Manfort, Wiesdorf, Küppersteg, Uppersberg, Edelrath, Bürrig and others, formed the city of Leverkusen. It was and still is an industrial city. Factories are still abundant like the ones my grandfathers and great-grandfather worked in, plus an English-owned asbestos factory called Textar and a Dynamite Factory. But by far the largest was IG Farben known as the Bayer Werke. The Bayer Werke was a pharmaceutical and chemical factory internationally known for its Bayer Aspirin. Prior to World War II the company employed twenty-five thousand employees. It was in Leverkusen-Wiesdorf.

The Bayer company, which later became an even larger conglomerate by acquiring Farbwerke Hoechst, has an interesting beginning. The surrounding area of Leverkusen was mainly a farming area in the late eighteenth and the early nineteenth century. One of the main vegetables grown in our area was flax, the fiber used to make linen fabric.

Farmers and factory workers alike wore overalls, jackets, and trousers as well as coats made from indigo-dyed linen. It was big business, keeping farmers, spinners, dye workers, and weavers working. At the time, indigo dye was imported from India. During the early nineteenth-century the trade route was constantly being interrupted by warring factions. Thus, making it difficult to obtain the indigo dye.

A pharmacist by the name of Dr. Karl Leverkus owned a pharmacy near Wiesdorf. He invented a synthetic indigo dye and started to manufacture dyestuffs. Henceforth, the city was named after him. Later his sons sold the business to Friederich Bayer of Friederich Bayer et comp. It was the forerunner of IG Farben AG.

The town of Schlebusch lay nestled at the foothills of *Dem Bergischen Land* (the mountain land). It was a favorite spot for the city folks of Cologne to spend their Sundays. The town is quaint, rich in history, and has many stories to tell. Divided by a small river, the Dhünn, Schlebusch has a low-lying area bordering the hills with soil of heavy clay, and a higher lying sandy half on the other side of the river that bordered the city of Cologne.

My paternal grandparents and my parents lived on the high lying sandy half while my maternal grandparents lived on the lower half. The river's rapid clear flowing water was flanked by wonderful meadows on the outskirts of town. As you moved along the water the meadows gave way to cow pastures on one side and grain and vegetable fields on the other. On the east side the river flowed through a beautiful mixed forest of evergreens and leaf trees. The forests were meticulously kept clean of underbrush or trash by the forestry service. It was a pleasure to walk the hiking trails along the river.

On the end of the trolley line, coming in from Cologne, started an all-time favorite trail for the city folks to the village of Edelrath. The trail led through beautiful woods on hilly grounds down to the river. Following along the water's edge under a canopy of hundred years-old oak trees, the trail crossed the Dhünn and led up a steep hill to the little farm village called Edelrath.

From the little farm village on the top of the hill one could overlook an array of meadows, forests and the river. The main attraction in town was a butcher shop with a restaurant and tavern owned and operated by the Gerver family. It was a great place to take a rest, wet your whistle, have dinner and or cake, and coffee. Sitting on an outside table on a clear day, one could watch the big twin towers of the Cologne Cathedral in the far distance. An Um-

Pa-Pa band entertained the guests with old fashion music on weekends. If so inclined, couples could swing a leg.

****

The Main Street of Schlebusch was a cobblestone road connecting Paris with Berlin. Napoleon built the road to move his troops into Russia during Napoleon's Russian Campaign in 1812. In town, the street was lined with historically protected, whitewashed Tudor homes, small stores, and the twin-towered St. Andreas Catholic Church. In the center of town, the townspeople did their daily grocery shopping, praying, and gossiping. The thirsty men folk would hoist their beers in the many taverns during Frühschoppen, (a gathering of men shooting the bull in the morning over a glass of beer). People used to congregate on the street corners talking about the latest events in town. During my childhood, cars were rare. Horse-drawn wagons, some tractors from the more affluent farmers, and bicycles were still the transportation of the time. On the west end of town, the road rose rapidly up into the mountains. Forests, farmland, and little homes with slate sidings, also historically protected, would line the road through the hills. It was an obvious change of architecture.

****

State Route 1 the main road through town was Napoleon's approach to Russia. It reminds me of a story that had been passed down through generations about a company of Napoleon's Cavalry.

When the Napoleonic Army moved through the region they left a company behind in the town of Schlebusch. Plundering soldiers were harassing and relieving the farmers of their food, the town's people of their valuables, and violating the lady folk. The town's angry men banded together and armed with whatever they could find on the farms; sickles, clubs, spates, knives, and a few flintlocks, battled the well-equipped soldiers and drove them out of town never to be seen again.

It was incidents like this and others that started the formation of the *Schützen Vereine* (like the Minute Men) throughout the country for the protection of the towns. In later years, these organizations converted to local rifle clubs belonging to a national association. One of them was the *St. Sebastianer Schützen Bruderschaft*, a Catholic rifle club. The organization elected *St. Sebastian* as their patron and was involved in charitable deeds like a Lions Club.

# Chapter 9

Through the generosity of the Baron Freiherr Von Diergart, Opa Sheng and three other handicapped neighbors; Mr. Weinrich, Mr. Engstenberg, and Mr. Carl, my lifelong friend's dad, were each awarded a piece of property upon which to build. Baron Von Diergart was a local aristocrat who owned ninety-nine estates with farmland. Many aristocrats owned ninety-nine estates because during the Kaiser's reign, if you owned one hundred or more, it was mandatory to keep and support an army. One of the Baron's estates was within ten minutes walking distance from my grandparent's house. Baron Von Diergart was a down-to-earth man that would ride his bicycle through my grandparent's street on his way to *Schloss Mossbroich,* his moat-surrounded château. If any of the neighbors were out on the street, he would stop and chat.

****

Life in Schlebusch was tranquil. Families and friends would stroll together on the weekends along the many hiking trails through the woods. Afterwards, they would stop at a tavern, or at one of their homes for coffee and cake, or for a Schnapps and a beer-chaser.

I used to love those Sunday afternoons. It was a real treat. After enjoying Oma's wonderful Sunday dinner at noontime and the leisurely stroll was over, the ladies would sit together knitting and crocheting while the men played cards, drank beer and a couple of schnapps. Watching the card game, and listening to the story telling, was fascinating for me. At promptly three-thirty the game and the knitting stopped. The table was cleaned off and coffee and cake were served.

My grandparent's house, a stucco duplex, was located at Von Diergart Strasse 79. Oma's kitchen was a combination of kitchen, dining, and living room. When you came through the door, straight ahead in front of the window was a rectangular kitchen table with chairs and a sofa under the window. The table was used for both preparing meals and dining. To the right of the kitchen table was a small table flanked by high-backed chairs. Next to it stood a coal-burning stove that heated the room in the wintertime and served as cook top and oven all year around. To the left of the kitchen table was a breakfront that held all the china, silverware, cooking utensils, and tablecloths, and also served as the pantry. Next to the door was a sink with a cabinet and one of those old washbasins. The sink was used in the morning for shaving and washing, and at meal times for cleaning vegetables and washing dishes. In my mind's eye I can still see the house. My grandparents occupied the lower floor while the upper floor was rented to a family by the name of Schommer, who had a boy my age.

Opa Sheng loved to smoke his pipe sitting next to the stove in the high back chair. As a little boy I was deathly afraid of thunderstorms. During the lightning and thunder, Opa would take my head into his lap, closed my eyes and ears with his hands, and calmed me down. When I grew older, I loved to sit in Opa's chair with a book and read.

After Oma had died and my mom did the cooking, she would tell me, "Watch the food so it does not burn." However, engrossed in my book I would forget the pot on the stove. When mom came in the room and smelled the burned meal, she would smack me saying, "Did you not smell the food burning?" Since I could not smell, I honestly said *No*. This just earned me another smack with the comment, "Don't lie to me. Everybody can smell."

"No Mom, not everybody, not I." But that got lost in the anger until I was ten and a doctor agreed with me.

****

A five-minute walk from the Schloss, on the end of a Chestnut-tree lined dirt road, was a little quaint chapel dedicated to a local saint, St. Gezelinus. On one side the chapel was flanked by wheat fields and on the other three sides by a forest of exceptionally tall, hundreds-of-years-old Beechnut trees. There was not a spec of underbrush or weed under the trees, but wonderfully sweet little strawberries grew below them.

The water of the spring on the outside of the chapel was supposed to cure eye ailments. Legend has it that St. Gezelinus, a very prayerful saintly sheepherder, would graze his sheep in the meadows where now the chapel stands. When a drought befell the region, people and animals suffered from lack of water. Meadows and fields turned brown and sheep and people died from dehydration. After weeks of intense prayers, the saintly shepherd was guided by divine intervention to poke his staff into the ground. A spring of wonderful clear water started to flow from the earth where now the chapel is located. Both sheep and people where saved.

More good deeds were recorded of this saintly man. After his beatification, the grateful citizens of Schlebusch erected and dedicated the chapel to St. Gezelinus. Every autumn the town celebrated a whole week in prayer, with processions, masses, and prayer services in honor of St. Gezelinus. People from surrounding towns set out on pilgrimages to attend the festivities. The week would start with a prayerful procession carrying the relics of St. Gezelinus from the parish church to the chapel. After displaying the relics for adoration for a week, they were returned to the parish church. Masses and prayer services with lengthy sermons were held in the open air under the wonderful tall trees.

For us kids, the most enjoyable part of the festivities started in the afternoon when the prayers ended. As was the case at all festivals, vendors with their hardy seasoned bratwurst and sauerkraut filled the air with aromas that made us hungry. I remember the stands with little toys, the wonderful tasting gingerbread hearts, large pretzels to hang around your neck, and the great tasting sugarcoated roasted almonds. Enjoying the goodies, playing catch and hide and seek with friends, while our parents sat under the trees watching their offspring with pride, was one of the highlights of the year.

# Chapter 10

Weekend bicycle tours were always big events as well. I would get to sit on a little saddle mounted on the crossbar of my dad's bicycle. Mom, Dad, me, and often friends or family members, armed with picnic baskets full of goodies, would set out on a bike ride. The most favorite spots were Altenberg, about ten kilometers away, and Schloss Burg, about fifteen kilometers away. Altenberg was a lovely little town surrounded by forests. A monastery with a cathedral occupied the center, and to the joy of the children, a fairyland was erected inside the forest. All the Grimm's Fairytales were represented in animated settings. No matter how often we visited the place the big bad wolf with his big teeth and mouth open in the Little Red Riding Hood scene, would scare the wits out of me. I loved the story of Snow White. But I could not help calling out to Snow White, "Don't eat that apple."

High on a mountaintop sat Schloss Burg. It was a well-preserved old castle that was turned into a museum. The rooms were fully furnished with antiques and tapestries. Old armors, weapons, and antique paintings were displayed throughout the rooms and halls. The dark dungeons in the basement, filled with torture tools like stretching racks, branding irons, and leather whips with led balls and hooks, would give me the shivers. Surrounding the castle were plenty of cafés, taverns and restaurants. The view from there, overlooking the hills and valleys with hundreds of acres of forest, was breathtaking. As always, after being a good boy the reward was a ginger bread heart, or a very large sweet pretzel on a ribbon to hang around my neck.

After one of those outings, on our way home, a car passed by us and hit a pigeon in flight. This had to be the one car-of-the-month that passed through our town. Since pigeons were a delicacy in Germany, dad picked up the bird, butchered it at home, and mom roasted it for dinner. Nothing was wasted.

Dad also loved smoked eel. Which reminds me of one of dad's many escapades. He belonged to a tradesmen association of self-employed tailors. They had a monthly meeting discussing business and mutual interests. The meetings ran for several hours. But tailors were also known for loving a good time and a beer. After the meeting ended, they would reassemble in the *Ratskeller*. This was a tavern in the basement of City Hall. Of course, that part of the meeting lasted several hours longer than the business meeting. Jokes were told, brats were eaten and flushed down with plenty of beer.

On this night, dad had proudly shown off a brand-new suit he had made for himself. However, he felt no pain when it was time to bicycle home. Coming out of the tavern singing, he noticed a street vendor selling smoked eel. Loving the delicacy, he bought several of them. Not knowing where to put them, he tied the eels together, hung them around his neck, and happily bicycled home. The greasy smoked eels did a job on his brand-new suit. When he walked through the door, his suit no longer looked brand new. It looked more like a hobo's greasy suit. Of course, the suit was ruined. For a week the menu in our house existed of *Kalte hundeschnauze* (a cold dog's snout). It was an expression used for, *Mom is not on speaking terms with Dad.*

Life at the time of my early years in Schlebusch was simple. Choirs, brass bands, and a movie theater dominated the great cultural scene. The entertainment for the young men consisted of bowling, drinking, dancing, and to dream up as many pranks as they could. As in all escapades, there were instigators and there were victims. My dad was among the instigators and Karl Kierdorf, a midget, was the prime victim. Karl loved to drink. One night, a bunch of young fellows were buying drinks for Karl. He was completely inebriated and needed to discharge his beer. Before the poor guy could make it to the bathroom, some wise guy stuck a hot dog in the button fly of his pants. Karl came back with his pants soaked in urine. Yes, I think you can figure it out.

# Chapter 11

Young couples living in the same house with one set of parents, can have its problems. So, it was in our family. We moved from my paternal grandparents' house into an apartment ten minutes away. The street, Linienstrasse, was a new development in town. There were homes on one side of the street and rhubarb fields on the other. Beyond the rhubarb fields were a couple acres of heide, the German version of a desert. It was sandy land covered with heather. When the heather was in bloom, it looked like a big carpet of little pink flowers.

Since Dad kept his tailor shop on first floor of my grandparent's house, where my mom worked with him, I played a lot with my cousins, Käthe and Marianne. Respectively, they were one and three years older than I and lived upstairs above my dad's shop. We would play in the backyard, and if it rained, in my dad's shop. Dad would give the three of us ten pennies each to buy candy or in the summer ice cream. Ice cream was sold in little rectangular waffle boats. A big ice for ten pennies was about three inches long and a small one for five pennies, was about one and a halve inches long.

Marianne and I spent the entire ten pennies at once while Käthe would spend halve and save the rest. The two of us big spenders were able to eat the ten-penny candy or ice quicker than Käthe could eat the five-penny treasure. Conniving as the two of us were, we always somehow were able to talk her into sharing what was left of her smaller halve. We were so nasty and she was so nice.

Next to my grandparent's house was the home of the family Thevas. Mr. Thevas, a high school principal, and Mrs. Thevas, a former kindergarten teacher, had two boys about ten and fifteen years older than I. Taking a liking to me, Mrs. Thevas would call me in and feed me brown rock candy. I noticed a beautiful real fur-covered rocking horse standing in the corner of the living room. Oh, did I love that horse. Knowing this she would sit me on it and let me rock to my heart's content.

One day, I discovered her son's working model steam turbine. My eyes and mouth were wide open in admiration of this wonderful and fascinating steam turbine. Mrs. Thevas fired it up and let me play with it while her sons were in school. It almost became a daily routine for me to sneak over for rock candy and to play with the steam turbine.

When my mom did not go to Dad's shop, she would bring me to her parents where I would play with the neighborhood children. There were four, Bernhard next door who was two years older, my life-long friend Gerhard nine month older than I, Peter who was the same age as I, and Norbert also the same age.

Norbert lived in the apartment above my grandparents. He was always able to convince his mom that any misdeeds of his were committed by me. She steadfastly believed it. That is, until one day when it all changed. You see, he made the big mistake of trying to convince his mom that I was the one who had messed in his pants. That's when the lights went on in his mom's head. Henceforth, I was no longer in trouble.

Mom's parents lived on a dirt road lined with beautiful large, mature Chestnut trees. In the autumn, a skinny little old man by the name of Fritz would come, sweep the leaves into heaps, and burn the piles. He could tell the wildest stories of owning elephants and tigers that not even we kids would believe. In fact, Mom told me he had been telling these wild stories even when she was a child.

After the fire was hot enough, Fritz showed us how to roast potatoes and chestnuts. I remember one-time Mom calling me to come home for dinner. However, I was not going to miss my roasted potato. Trying to bite into the still halve-raw potato, I managed to lose my *famous first front tooth*.

Starting first grade was a very special and festive day. I felt grown up entering school with a leather backpack full of schoolbooks and a little black board and chalk. However, by far, the best part was the fancy, inspiringly painted, cone-shaped cardboard container full of cookies and candies. Parents and grandparents created a lot of fuss on our first school day. After receiving my cookie-filled cone, I was sent off with tear-filled eyes from the Omas and Opas, hugs and kisses from Dad.

With pride, yet sad that her blond, blue-eyed little boy was now embarking on his first responsibility, Mom brought me to school. After a five-minute walk from home, we arrived at the eight-room schoolhouse. Most of the teachers, who had taught my mom, were still teaching; including my first-grade teacher Fräulein Weber. Mom's teacher, now my first-grade teacher, greeted Mom with a big hello. I could see she really liked Mom. I figured I had it made. Listening happily to the conversation of, "How are you? You look wonderful. Is this your little boy?" However, then came the cold shower. Miss Weber turned to me with a very stern look, and said, "Your mother was an excellent student. You had better study as hard as she did."

Very timidly, I nodded my head and thought to myself, *so much for having, it made,* and with that, I entered the world of real responsibilities.

# Chapter 12

One year before I was born, in 1933, started the darkest era in German history. Hitler became Chancellor of Germany. Soon thereafter, he took over the absolute and dictatorial power of the country. Hitler's cohorts, the brown shirted Storm Troopers referred to as SA, the feared black uniformed SS, his secret police called Gestapo, or the murderous gangs, crooks, and criminals as my dad called them, ruled Germany. In conjunction with Dr. Paul Josef Goebbels' propaganda machine, the brainwashing and intimidation that had started before the takeover intensified.

Hitler's rabble-rousing anti-Semitic speeches, or those of his Propaganda Minister, designed to push Germany into the worst ethnic cleansing epoch, were a daily event. Before every movie, moviegoers had to sing the national anthem with their arms raised in the Nazi salute. Instead of previews, a newsreel was shown of Hitler, or Goebbels, in a rage with their fists raised, pounding the podium proclaiming their doctrine. In the well-documented *Kristal Nacht*, (The night of broken glass), the homes and stores of Jews were ransacked, windows and unwanted items were smashed, and German's of Jewish faith were beaten up, arrested, and simply disappeared. People, who had different views, were outspoken, or people that were considered interfering, were arrested and taken away as well. Nazi officials even disposed of people they disliked for personal reasons, or wives they no longer wanted.

Dad spoke of a case that happened before Hitler's official takeover. One of the storm troopers murdered a man in cold blood in our town because he stood up for his Marxist beliefs. The hoodlum who did this was rightfully convicted and sent to jail by a Jury of the Weimarer Republic. However, he was immediately released and promoted after the Nazis took over.

Life started to turn ugly despite the pomp and circumstance of colorful parades, big brass bands, goose-stepping SS, military, SA, and Hitler Youth trying to instill national pride. Religion was frowned upon and the people were discouraged from practicing spirituality—especially Catholics. Old Germanic heathen ceremonies as initiations into the Germanic cult of the third Reich, were stressed to replace baptisms. Nazi followers started to replace Christmas trees with an earthen pyramidal Germanic symbol topped with a candle and covered with swat stickers and other old Germanic pagan signs. Nazi fanatics replaced Christian worship and other religious services with heathen glorification services to Hitler. This was to emphasize loyalty to the, quote unquote, *Nazi Third Reich, a Cleansed Arian Thousand Year Empire.*

Resorts were built to entertain loyal Nazi members and decorated soldiers. Young women, especially blond-haired blue-eyed ones, were brainwashed to bear a child as a gift for Hitler. They were sent to the resorts for the pleasure of Nazis and decorated soldiers. Mothers were rewarded with money for having children as a monthly support. If you had enough children, you could literally live off the income. It was an effort to build the true *Arian Thousand Year Reich,* or as people would call it secretly, *cannon fodder.*

Torture and murder were the tools to build their Arian Reich. It turned Germany into a sick, decadent society. The Gestapo watched churches and took names of those that attended, but the faithful only became stronger in their Christian beliefs. However, too many Germans joined the Nazi cult for misguided beliefs or profiteering from *The Superior Arian Race circus.*

Hitler turned on the war machine; building weapons, planes, tanks, and roads to move troops. Consequently, this created work. The depression that had been ravaging Germany since WWI slowly began to disappear. Unfortunately, the uneducated masses, and the profiteers started to march to the drummer—*See no evil— speak no evil—hear no evil—*as did the Global Profiteers.

The *Murder Incorporated* regime in the meantime continued their unspeakable evil deeds. Those with value and opposing views began to fear for their lives or their families' safety. One never knew whom you could trust, other than close family or friends. Parents were afraid to speak openly in front of their children for fear that they might accidentally repeat opposing views in the wrong places. The Hitler Youth brainwashed to report all negative comments they heard to their leaders. Many times, it got children's parents arrested. Most ordinary citizens did not know what happened after the arrests, but they did know people were not coming back.

I don't remember how old I was when mom and I were at my grandparent's house. I was a small boy, probably age four or five when the doorbell rang. A friend of my grandparents came in with tears streaming down her face crying uncontrollably.

Aunt Levi, as I called her, was catholic. But she had married a German of Jewish faith. I heard Opa Sheng mutter, "those bastards!"

On questioning my mom, "Why is Aunt Levy crying?" She told me; "Uncle Levy was very ill and died." Having overheard something about ashes, I was still puzzled and further inquired, "But why did they burn him and send the ashes?"

Being very careful not to have me repeating politically incorrect views, mom said, "Uncle Levi had to go into a sanatorium because he was very ill. When he died, they had to burn his body so no one else could catch the disease."

I felt very sorry for Aunt Levy, but now I understood why she had received only the ashes. Well, I still believed in the Santa Claus.

It was also then, when some people began to understand what was happening in the places from where no one ever returned, and everyone was afraid to talk about. However, we did not know the full extent of the horror until the war was over.

After Hitler had taken over Austria, Sudetenland, and Czechoslovakia, he invaded Poland in September 1939 and after a short campaign, defeated and occupied the country. France was next. In 1940, tanks and troops started to run through Belgium, Holland, France, Norway, and Denmark with record speed, occupying each of those countries.

I am not a qualified historian and therefore will not elaborate on events other than to convey the feelings and affect it had on friends, family, and myself.

At first, all that we felt about the war were notices of soldiers wounded or killed. The propaganda machine of Hitler and Goebbels was too busy pumping out information of victorious heroic soldiers over-running the enemy, and highly decorated navel captains sinking enemy ships in mass. Patriotic music, proclaiming the victories in the air, land, and sea interrupted the radio programs. Feldmarschall Goering bragged about the invincible German Air Force that owned the skies of Europe. He said on the radio, "If one single enemy airplane crosses the German border you can call me Meier."

In 1940, after Great Britain rejected Hitler's ludicrous peace offer, Germany started to bomb England. However, it was not long thereafter when my parents and I watched the first dog fight between an RAF Spitfire and a German Messerschmitt in the skies over Schlebusch. Dad said bitterly, "Herr Meier, it is starting."

Hitler went on the radio and newsreels pounding the podium in an unprecedented rage proclaiming, "Ich werde ihre

Städte ausradieren!" *(I will erase their cities).* However, that year the worst nightmare the German people had ever experienced, began.

# Chapter 13

The first of May was Germany's Labor Day; it was also the month and day Catholics dedicated to St. Mary. The faithful walked in procession from the church along a predetermined route in song and prayer. They stopped at dedicated altars, beautifully decorated with spring flowers, for special prayers, songs, and blessings. Every house had a little altar dedicated to St. Mary. People would try to outdo each other with the floral decorations. The church assemblies carried their banners and flags and walked as groups. After the procession, the celebrations started around the *May-tree* in the town's centers.

A May-tree consisted of a tall pine trunk cleared of all branches and decorated with a wreath and streamers. A brass band provides the music and the town's folk would enjoy brats, beer, and dancing. Young men would go the night before and cut birch trees down, the symbol of spring, and place them in front of their sweetheart's home. It was always an event to behold—but all of that ended when the Nazis took the country captive.

The Nazis abolished religious processions and replaced them with elaborate fanfare parades, and pomp and circumstance. Highflying flags, military bands, and the whole array of political and military organizations in uniforms and swat sticker armbands paraded through town. I must admit, as a child I was impressed and proudly watched the pomp and circumstance, speeches, and troops bellowing out *Heil Hitler or Sieg Heil* with their arms raised in the Nazi salute. Operation Brainwash accomplished what it was designed to do— seduce the children to believe in the proud clean

Arian Super Race. They replaced the beautiful alters on May Day with decorated pictures of Hitler. It was a mandate to pay homage to the Führer. If you owned a store, you were required to decorate your window glorifying the Great Third Reich. Disgusted with the whole shit and shebang, Dad did not do it. In fact, he never ever owned a picture of the murdering bastard.

One thing the Nazis did not abolish was the drinking and dancing. On May 1, 1940, Mom, Dad, friends of theirs, and I, were in Ferger's Tavern. Everybody enjoyed the wine and beer. Being about six-years-old, mine was the nonalcoholic kind.

Time passed and Dad, full of the golden nectar, was feeling no pain. One of the brown shirted Nazis approached him. He harassed Dad for not decorating his storefront with Hitler's picture. At first, he kept his cool and ignored the Nazi. As more Nazis joined in, and Dad with his senses dulled, had enough. He blurted out, "Get away! You dirty murdering swine. You all belong in jail!"

The noisy place suddenly hushed and became quiet. So quiet, that you could hear a pin fall. After staring at him the brown shirts returned to their corner and continued drinking.

The hours passed and the place started to empty out. With Dad, not too steady on his feet, we left to go home. Once we got outside, the Nazis came and formed a circle around us. The guy that had harassed Dad, accompanied by the loud laughter of his accomplices, pulled out his Luger, held it against my father's temple, saying, "Okay, wise guy, would you like to repeat what you said in there?"

In the interim, people gathered in the street and started to murmur. Hearing a child bitterly crying, and Mom's pleading to let her husband go, pointing out that he was drunk and did not know what he was saying.

After some more harassing, prodding Dad to make more negative comments, the Nazi that started the harassing, said with a flamboyant gesture, "Should I put a bullet through his head?"

However, the other brown shirts noticed the people gathering, said to him, "No, let him go. This is the wrong place and time. He is not going anywhere, we will get him later." Therefore, by the grace of God, Dad's live was spared.

# Chapter 14

Two months later, Dad was drafted and had to report for basic training in Landshut Bavaria. After completing his training, he was assigned as the company's tailor to an outfit called, Landes Schützen. (Homeland Security) The unit was comprised of older guys not usually inducted into the army. Landes Schützen were supposed to protect the home front and guard POW camps. Dad ended up stationed in a town called Moosburg in Bavaria. He was there among guys that shared the same views. They were not in the army by choice or conviction. That was his luck. He was able to express himself without fear of being sent off to a concentration camp, which would have happened had he stayed at home.

My father had always been his own boss and was not suited for military life. Away from his beloved family, he would often drown his sorrows in alcohol, which got him into trouble. Company punishment and even days in the stockade, were not uncommon for him. Dad, and his friend the company shoemaker, who shared the workshop with Dad, got promoted and demoted all in the same month. Consequently, neither one of them ever made rank above corporal.

Food in Germany had become scarce. But Bavaria, a heavy agricultural region, still had plenty. Dad made friends with some local townspeople whose relatives had farms. He would make clothes for the farmers who in turn would give him smoked meat and other none perishable groceries that he would send home. Those packages were lifesavers for us.

The POW's were even worse off than we were. Their food rations were just enough to prevent them from starving. My compassionate Dad, having experienced hunger as a child, would smuggle food into the compound. This was an extremely dangerous undertaking. Had he had been caught, it would have meant the firing squad. In appreciation, a French POW asked Dad to bring him canvas, paint, and brushes so he could paint a painting for him. This painting still hangs in our home today. It has a great deal of sentimental value for me.

Mom, pained by the separation from Dad, moved with me to her parent's without relinquishing the apartment on Linienstrasse. By then, all able-bodied women had to start working, taking men's places in the factories. She had to work in a place about a half-hour away by train milling nuts and bolts. While working there, Mom befriended a young woman by the name of Frieda. She was about Mom's age. Her parents had a strawberry farm in the same town where the factory was located. We used to go there to pick strawberries. There were always more berries in my stomach than in the basket.

Some French soldiers from a nearby POW camp worked in their fields. The guards watching them were regular German army. The parents of Mom's girlfriend were members of the Communist Party and as anti-Nazi as one could be. They treated the POW's and soldiers the same. They invited them in the house for lunch and coffee brakes. The soldiers, who were draftees and not Nazi friendly, closed their eyes if they did not lose anyone.

Mom's girlfriend, Frieda, fell in love with a French officer from Algiers. That was a dangerous game. If it became public, she would have been arrested. Her parents worried daily about their safety. They begged her not to enter a relationship with the officer, but she did it anyway. Luckily, the German guards looked the other way.

After the war ended, they got married. On their wedding day, the French officer revealed that he was the son of a very wealthy plantation owner in Algiers. Aunt Frieda, as I called her, was shocked by the news, as was her family. Assuring her that all would be okay, and that his parents would love her. He told her that as soon as he was discharged from the army, he would bring her to Algiers.

The young officer was repatriated. After a few weeks of letter writing, the letters suddenly stopped. A month later, an official of the French Government showed up with annulment papers. The young woman was stunned and inquired, "Why?" She was arrogantly informed that the young lieutenant's father was an official of the French Government. Who would not allow his son to marry a *German Nazi Woman*. And so, ended the French Cinderella story.

# Chapter 15

Earlier during the war, air raid bunkers had been built on every street corner and daytime raids were on the increase. The neighbors in my Grandparent's street got together to build a bunker on their own initiative. Mr. Martien, a neighbor who had a lumberyard provided the supplies. Since he had the expertise as well, he managed the project. The rest of the neighbors and children supplied the workforce and that is how we managed to get our bunker.

So far, our small town and the other surrounding villages had escaped the bombing. This changed one night. The air raid sirens suddenly sounded off in the middle of the night. All of us hurried to the bunker expecting the planes to fly over and bomb Cologne. However, this time it was different. We heard the noise of exploding bombs. For the first time we experienced the earth trembling without an earthquake and thunder rambled in the air above us from exploding bombs. Residue from the cement walls and ceiling crumbled down on us. Mothers panicking, held tightly onto their screaming children. When we emerged from the bunker, after the all-clear, we saw flames shooting out of the windows from Mr. Martien's house and the roof was ablaze. The house, adjacent to the bunker, was hit by an incendiary device. Neighbors ran to help, saving their belongings. They formed a chain passing buckets of water toward the fire.

Now, the real fear began. We children expected our house to be next. Horror stories of the big city bombings passed around.

We heard how whole sections of Cologne had been reduced to rubble, and people had been buried alive for days.

After another heavy bombing raid on Cologne all transportations had ceased and all telephone lines to the city were down. My great-grandfather, to whom Opa Sheng and Oma Mimmi bowed to in respect and I looked up to like he was a king, walked, at the age of 85, thirty miles on foot to his daughter, Else. He wanted to assure himself that she and his grandchildren were unharmed. They had been lucky, they had survived the ordeal unharmed.

He was a wiry, small skinny man with gold-rimmed spectacles. He always dressed in a three-piece dark gray suit adorned by a white kerchief in his breast pocket. Urgrossopa Adam accessorized his suit with a white shirt that had a detachable heavy starched collar, a Windsor knotted navy and silver striped tie, a wide brimmed hat, and a gold pocket watch with a gold chain crossing his vest. He always walked briskly carrying a beautifully carved walking cane. Urgrossopa Adam died two years later at the age of eighty-seven.

The daytime bombing raids intensified and so did the nighttime bombing. At that time the bombing raids had become a 24/7 event. In the night you could see the blood red sky over the burning city of Cologne. The thunder of exploding bombs filled the night air while the ground shook as if an earthquake were in process. Air raid sirens would sound the alarm night and day. We always slept with our clothes on and sometimes even our shoes. Several times during the night and day we would run for our lives to the bunker, while waves of roaring, flying fortresses passed over us. Powerful floodlights searched the skies and the Anti Air Craft Guns exploded; firing their projectiles into the air lighting up the sky like fireworks.

Reports about Dresden and the destruction of other cities like the city of Barmen, put the fear of God into us. Barmen, a city divided by a river and surrounded by low-lying mountains, was especially hit hard. In the middle of the night Barmen was bombarded with heavy explosive ordinance and phosphor bombs that turned the city into a blazing inferno. We were told that iron fences and gutters melted from the heat. The bricks and cement in the rubble, covered with phosphor, were red hot and burned. Men, women, and children ablaze, jumped into the river but to no avail. The phosphor did not yield to water. In the aftermath, the city was nothing but a pile of smoldering rubble. The streets were littered with bodies shriveled to half their original size and unrecognizably burned to a crisp. "Oh, God, have you forsaken us?" the people cried.

# Chapter 16

Children, being children continued playing despite the war. All the boys in my grandparent's street would gather at my friend Gerhard's house. They had a big back yard and an empty garage that made for a perfect playground. Wartime kids played wartime games and we were no exception. The garage roof became an airplane, and umbrellas became parachutes. We were now paratroopers.

Scared to death of what was going on around us, we felt we had to prove our courage. Without the knowledge of our parents, we jumped off the garage roof until Gerhard hurt his leg.

Now that we were barred from jumping off the roof, we were no longer paratroopers; we became submariners. The inside of the garage had a loft with hay and we pretended to be submerged, hiding in the hay. Gerhard's older brother and his friend became the destroyers trying to sink our submarine. An old inner tube from a bicycle set on fire became their depth charges. Dripping the burning rubber through a ventilation pipe into the hay, made us scramble to put out the fires; and that ended our career as submariners.

However, we were always able to dream up new adventures. Gerhard's brother had a chemistry set and made black powder. One day, when no one was at home, Gerhard and the rest of us wanted to see firsthand the power of black powder. Traugott, Gerhard's brother had shown us how black powder explodes with a swoosh. Trying to experience the power of black powder, we took some, put it in the stove, and lit it. The stove had an opening that was covered with rings to adjust the size for different pots. When we saw the rings pop up from the power of the exploding black powder, we were fascinated. Wanting to test how high we could make the rings pop, we kept adding more and more black powder until we added a little too much. Consequently, the rings popped high off the stove and its door burst open discharging fire and soot. Not only the entire kitchen, but also, we little scientists were black with soot and smoke. This time, Gerhard's mom caught us while we were desperately trying to clean the soot from the kitchen. House arrest for a week cooled us off.

****

To get me away from the dangerous games in which I had become involved, Opa Sheng, still fond of the weaving mill, took me there to visit. On the premises of the factory grounds was also the director's villa. In those days, OSHA enforced no safety rules. The son of the director and I became friends and watched the workers weave and finish the fabrics. We were fascinated watching the shuttle on the looms fly back and forth. Our favorite pastime was jumping on bails of fabric or playing with the big electric train. The setup ran through several rooms and had three trains running on the tracks at the same time. What a wonderful setup it was.

Of course, not all the playtime was filled with dangerous games. Playing soccer and other ball games filled much of our time. The winters were severe and we had lots of snow that was especially great fun. Building snowmen, lying down in the snow creating eagles, and having snowball fights from behind igloo-type snow bunkers were fantastic winter games.

School curriculum consisted of Nazi propaganda more than writing, reading, and arithmetic. Most of the teachers had no choice. However, some of the party followers taught it because they believed in that nonsense. Having been brought up with values and fairness, to this day I have not forgotten, nor have I forgiven the one teacher, Fräulein Kassenberg, who was deeply ingrained with Nazi ideology. The schools instituted collecting items made from metal and copper to melt down for the war effort. Herbs, growing in the wild and bones were also sought-after items. Since we had no meat to eat, I had no bones to bring to school. Fräulein Kassenberg would not accept my reason why I had not brought bones to school. She punished me with hours of detention and extra homework. This really ruffled my invisible fair-haired feathers. I was happy when she got fired after the war.

In the year 1943, a few weeks before Christmas, my beloved Oma Mimmi died of a stroke and only seven months later, my wise Opa Sheng died from stomach cancer. In a way I think of it as a blessing as they were spared the worst, that was yet to come. After that, my mom and I moved back into our apartment.

# Chapter 17

When dad heard of the dangerous bombing's raids at home, he rented a room from the friends in Moosburg and had us join him there. For the next half-year, we were safe—no air raids, no bombings, life almost seemed normal. Dad would come and see us when he was off duty, and we would go on hiking and biking trips. We went with our friends to their relatives and helped in the fields. For that we got plenty of food and the wonderful black-smoked Bavarian ham.

Having seen very little meat at home and no eggs, Easter with the family my parents had befriended, was a big surprise. My eyes almost popped out of my head when I saw dozens of colored eggs, a great roast with the wonderful Bavarian dumplings, and several cakes. My parent's friends, the Mosers, whom I called Tante Anni and Onkel Simon, were childless. I became the child they never had. They spoiled me wherever they could.

Dad's unit was quartered in a school located next to an orphanage run by wonderful and compassionate nuns. I spent many hours playing with the kids after school. Climbing up the fence we could watch the soldier's parade around, including my Dad.

Mom and Tante Anni had done a lot of work at the church and for this, a loving priest, Father Raubing, rewarded us with a week at his family-owned cottage high in the Alps. Accompanied by his sister and niece, we enjoyed climbing the mountains and walked through the fields of beautiful red Alpine Roses. The sounds of the cow bells, from the grazing cattle up on high and the wonderful voices of the two ladies singing alpine folk songs, was a delight to hear. The cow herders up in the mountains made wonderful homemade cheese and hearty bread that they graciously shared.

But all this came crashing down when dad's battalion commander decided that the wives of the soldiers were a bad influence on the discipline of the troops and therefore ordered them to leave. Each soldier had to report in writing that his family had left the area and had gone home. Dad was very bitter about having to send us back into the bombing raids and promptly wrote, *I hereby certify, that by the order of the commander, Colonel Von Roebel, my wife and child have left the area to return to the endangered bomb raided city of Leverkusen.*

Dad was asked three times to take the document back but he stubbornly refused and was promptly transferred to an artillery unit in France as punishment—France was considered a combat zone.

By the time my mom and I were back home, the nightmarish air raids had gotten worse. Our town and the city of Leverkusen were no longer spared. Back in the apartment on Linienstrasse, we were only a quarter of a mile away from a dynamite factory. And an 8.8 anti-aircraft battery was in the Heide across from our apartment. These installations heightened the fear in us of being carpet-bombed. Since day and nighttime raids were a constant occurrence, we did not undress at night for fear of not getting to the air raid shelter fast enough.

Many times, we saw the bombs falling from the planes as we ran toward the air raid shelter before the sirens sounded the alarm. It seemed that after the all clear, you hardly were back in bed when the next wave of flying Fortresses or double-bodied Lightenings would approach. When we jumped out of bed in the middle of the night and ran toward the bunker. We saw the flare markers overhead. We called them Christmas Trees because the corners of the bomb runs were marked with groups of flares shaped like the lights on a Christmas Tree. They announced that we were in a bombing run square. Hearing the wailing sirens, loud droning airplanes, whistling bombs already falling, explosions and having to pass burning buildings on the way to the bunker, made the run seem like a marathon. It is impossible to imagine the fear unless you have experienced it. When we finally arrived at the bunker, we had to pass through two airtight doors into a tube of steel reinforced concrete. Once inside, you felt the earth shake. You heard the thunder of exploding bombs, measured by a flapping lid on a valve. Cement trickling from the wall down the back of our neck made us wonder when it would become our coffin. It was a nightmare I hope no one will ever have to experience again. But as we know, the world still has not learned to live in peace.

Food became increasingly scarce. Even the small rations allotted to us were hard to find. People waiting in long lines to buy groceries often had to run for cover because of air raids. After the all-clear, they had to start all over again only to find out that the items they wanted were sold out by the time it was their turn.

For clothing and shoes, you needed special allocation certificates. These you had to request at city hall. Since our family was blacklisted, every time Mom went there, she was told, "There are no allocations for enemies of the Reich."

When Opa Sheng was still alive, he always found a way to rejuvenate old shoes, tools, my schoolbag etc. Mom took cloth from grandpa and dad and remade them into pants, shirts, and jackets for me.

Since dad was stationed in France and the allied forces had landed in Normandy, we did not know whether he was dead or alive. Dad, hearing about the air raids and destruction in our area, never knew whether we had survived another bombing run.

The separation and the raging fury of the war left its mark on the people. Children grew up into adults over night. Parents spent many nights awake, crying in fear for their loved ones. Organizing, the expression of the time, meant gathering something to eat by hook or crook, had children going by night into the fields, guarded by farmers or police with weapons, steeling potatoes, rhubarb, or whatever eatables they could find.

Hence, on Easter morning 1944, instead of colorful eggs, we had five little potatoes that Mom boiled and we ate. My Aunt Elli, the wife of grandma's youngest stepbrother, had a dairy store and always managed to have some extra food. So, off we went to the neighboring town of Manfort to my aunt. On arrival, Aunt Elli said, "Sit down and have something to eat." Out came the eggs, butter, and freshly home-baked raisin bread. I thought I had died and gone to heaven. Overwhelmed, Mom started to sob uncontrollably. Tante Elli, trying to comfort her, joined in the crying. Her husband and oldest son, only seventeen-years-old at the time, had been drafted into the army and were somewhere in harm's way. Only God knew whether they were alive or dead. But at least, that Easter we went home with a full belly.

# Chapter 18

Enduring the endless raging bombing raids with little sleep and fear for our lives, Mom accepted the invitation from my Aunt and Uncle Rasquin to stay with them on their little farm. There was nothing to bomb except fruit trees and farmland. It was considered a safe area. Tante Anna was Oma Mimmi's sister, and Uncle Josef her husband, was the local Gendarme. He was the only police officer in the village and the adjacent towns. Fifteen small farms, surrounded by fields and forest, and set among rolling hills made up the village. They had two daughters and one son. Tante Gretchen was married to an automobile mechanic away in the Army; Tante Anna (the other daughter) was married to an accountant who also away in the military; and Uncle Josef Yr. was unmarried and in the military.

Life was quiet in this small town. One could almost forget the war, had it not been for husbands and fathers being away in harm's way. Growing their own vegetables, fruits, raising chickens, pigs, and a couple of cows, food was always available at my aunt's. They loved Mom and me and tried to do what they could for us. My aunt would make me my favorite homemade waffles. My uncle, after coming home from work, would ask, "Boy, would you like some Wurst?" I was always in the mood for sausage, especially blood and liver sausage. So, he would go off to his friend, the local butcher. After a few beers and a couple of Schnapps, he would come home with some sausage for me. Had it not been for the fact that we did not know whether our house was still standing, or dad and other family members were still alive, life on the farm was good.

On a beautiful midsummer's hot and sunny day, without a cloud in the sky, we stood outside and heard the distant roar of flying Fortresses approach. Naturally, afraid, I was ready to run for the basement. It was a typical dirt floor cellar with bricked walls and vaulted ceiling. But, my uncle said, "Don't worry, boy, they are just on the way to bomb Cologne again."

All of us watched the approach of the unopposed bombers. By that time the German Air Force and anti-aircraft batteries were already history.

An armored unit had camped in the forest the day before. However, they had moved out early in the morning. Suddenly, as we were watching the planes, we saw bombs falling from the lead plane. Under the bomb's whistling sound, we ran for cover into the basement. We prayed and cried aloud, "Jesus, help! Jesus have mercy!" as we lay face down on the floor covering our ears. Only my uncle, a six-foot three-hundred-pound giant, sat straight as a statue on a chair trying to look composed. But the earth shook so hard that he tumbled over with the chair and our stomachs hurt from the trembling ground.

With the sound of roaring planes, the whistling of the falling bombs, and the noise of the explosions closing in, it felt and seemed as if the world was ending. In our minds the question was not would we die, but rather how many minutes or seconds did we have left to live.

The carpet-bombing lasted about ten minutes, but it felt like an eternity. After we emerged from the cellar the sunny day had turned dark as night from all the smoke that filled the air. High explosive bombs, and thousands of incendiary devices had demolished and set afire the little village. We stepped over unexploded bombs and dead animals to put out fires and rescued the animals from the burning barns.

78

As we tried to get some frightened, screaming animals out of my uncle's barn, we noticed that a bomb had hit the manure pit directly outside the cellar wall where we had survived the attack. Had the bomb hit a half yard to the left, it would have been a direct hit on the cellar. So, by the grace of God, I am here to tell the story.

# Chapter 19

Now that we knew there was no real safety anywhere, Mom and I went back to our apartment. The house was still standing, but there was a hole in the roof where a slab of cement had crashed through the ceiling onto the bed-couch on which I usually slept. But for the time being, we were alive.

It was extremely difficult for parents and grandparents to educate their children in their religious beliefs, the correct values, and right from wrong. During the years of death and destruction, the Nazi propaganda machine was in full swing trying to brainwash people—especially the young. Every boy and girl at a certain age was forced into the Hitler Youth. By the end of the war, children the age of fourteen and fifteen were being taken from the Hitler Youth meetings and sent directly into combat. When I became old enough to join the Hitler Youth, Germany was already in such a chaotic state that my mom was able to keep me out of it.

****

Despite all the turmoil, my grandparents and my mom did not despair and succeeded in teaching me the right values. In first grade, barely able to read, I became an altar boy along with my next-door friend. Grandpa's wisdom and grandma's love, along with my mom's, kept me turned in the right direction. I never forgot the values of religion and my grandfather's wise sayings about respect, honor, equality, humbleness, and to never waiver from what you believe.

The raging fury of the war was nearing its end. The allied forces had liberated France, Belgium, the Netherlands, and after Italy, moved into Germany. Soon they captured the left side of the Rhein region. Remagen and Cologne fell into the Allie's hands.

Although, heavy bombardment from the air, artillery shelling and low flying machine gunning airplanes added chaos to the nightmare. Despite obvious defeat hanging in the air, Goebbel's propaganda machine was still declaring victory. Even after Cologne had fallen to the Allies, he went on the radio threatening the citizens of Cologne with execution for surrendering to the enemy.

The Ortsgruppen Führer was the local commander of the SA, and a fanatic loyalist to the cause, fortified the town with tank barricades made from five-foot thick double-walls, build from railroad ties and filled with rocks and sand. He rigged the bridge that crossed the river separating the town with dynamite. It was to be blown when the allied troops advanced into Schlebusch. All major utilities, gas, water, telephone, and electricity led through conduits in the bridge. But under the cover of darkness, my dad's friend, Florentine Goldman, courageously snuck up under the bridge and disarmed the explosives. Therefore, he not only prevented the destruction of the only bridge into town, but also saved the town's utility system.

However, the fanatic commander was still determined to defend Schlebusch at all costs. With the American Army only fifteen kilometers away, he rounded up all party members regardless of age, and all members of the Hitler Youth fourteen years and older who were not already drafted into the army. The Ortsgruppen Führer marched them off into the forest east of town to fend off the advancing American troops. Armed with rifles and whatever hand grenades were available, they were to face the incoming American tanks.

Still in fear of bombardment, as well as the wrath of the Nazis, we lived for several weeks in the basement and prayed for the war to be over soon. Since we had not heard from Dad, we had no idea whether he was dead or alive.

One night, a heavy barrage of artillery fire landed in the sandy hills of the heide across from our apartment. Looking out of the basement windows, we saw solders running across the sandy hills, backlit by a red wall of exploding bombs and artillery shells. The soldiers were retreating German infantry. The exploding shells started to walk closer to our street. When they reached within twenty feet across the street, the bombardment suddenly stopped. Five minutes later they started anew. Only now the shells passed over us and landed in the hills outside of our town. When we went upstairs to look, we could see the fiery glow of the heavy guns going off in the far distance. In the luminosity of the exploding flares, we saw more soldiers running across the sandy dunes of the heide throwing away their weapons. Several weeks later, we found out the reason for the shift of the shelling.

In Uppersberg, a town up in the hills past our town, was a German gun emplacement of howitzers. The soldiers that manned the guns had fled and gone home. However, the Orts Bauern Führer, a local leader of a Nazi organized farmer's group, and a fanatic loyalist, had taken over the howitzers and started to fire in the direction of the advancing Americans. Not knowing what he was doing, the shells fell harmlessly into the fields but not without drawing fire from the advancing Americans. The local farmers subdued the Orts Bauern Führer and put an end to the firefight.

When we woke up the next morning, we realized that we had fallen sound asleep. There was no artillery firing deadly shells, and no bombs exploding—there was an eerie quiet. We went out to look. Word was coming down the line, "The Americans are coming!" Minutes later, we saw the first American tank turn into our street. Not knowing whether they were going to start shooting or not, we lay on the floor peaking around the corner of the building. Those big tanks, with the heavy guns, coming toward us was a scary sight. Someone said, "Let's hang white bed sheets out the windows. Let's show them that we surrender, and so we did. The tanks, guns pointing up the street, stopped and sat there. But still, they were a fearsome sight. An hour later, they pulled out of the street and left. It was March 15, 1945, the war was finally over for our town.

The next day, we realized that the American soldiers, other than using able-bodied civilians to help remove the tank barricades, meant us no harm. People started to search for their loved ones. Word had it that the group of Nazis and children, led by the fanatic Ortsgruppen Führer to defend the town were all dead except for a few wounded. Wives and mothers flocked to the woods to find their husbands and children. The stench of death and rotting flesh invaded town. It was a nightmare to witness the sobbing mothers stumbling between fallen trees and bomb craters searching for their children among the dismembered, blown apart bodies crawling with flies and worms. The Nazis got what they deserved; but the poor children, forced into this madness by ruthless fanatic animals, was the ultimate horror.

****

In the meantime, my father was facing the invasion in France. Allied troops advanced with overpowering forces and equipment. Their outfit had been annihilated. A handful of survivors tried to escape the heavy artillery barrage. Shrapnel hit Dad's friend William in his backside. Loading his wounded friend onto a horse-drawn cannon carriage, Dad drove him through heavy bombardment and gunfire to safety.

The German lines had become chaotic. Dad ended up in Holland. He and a small group from different outfits, were ordered to stay and hold the line. Only armed with rifles and low on ammunitions, it was impossible to stop the incoming tanks. Trying to fall back, they were deliberately shot at by the SS who were dug in behind them. Dad, shot in the back of his head, bandaged by his friends, tried to make it back to safety.

The lines where breaking down. Every first-aid station they came upon, was on the run. With blood-soaked bandages around his head, and a sweater stiff from dried blood, Dad stumbled over the smallest of pebles. After two days, he finally found a field hospital that accepted him. The doctors operated on him as best they could but left two small pieces of shrapnel still inside of his head, which he lived with for the rest of his life.

Again, the hospital packed up and fled from the approaching allied troops. Dad was transported clear across the country to Burg by Magdeburg in the eastern sector of Germany. He did not know whether anyone of his family had survived the air raids. The postal service had totally broken down.

The Russian troops started to move in on Burg where dad was hospitalized. Heavy gunfire heard in the distance moved closer in by the hour. Then the shells began to drop into the city. The town was under siege by the Russians.

Wanting to get out of the threatened area, Dad went to the commanding officer, a high-ranking doctor, and requested official travel orders to go to Moosburg in Bavaria where he could stay with our friends and recuperate. If he would be caught without those papers by the German Military Police, he would have been executed on the spot as a deserter.

The commanding officer looked at him, and said, "I gladly issue you travel orders, but I don't know if you can make it out of the city. Do you know that the city is surrounded by Russian troops and is totally isolated?"

"Yes Sir, but I like to try."

"Okay, good luck." He handed Dad his travel orders.

With proper papers in hand, Dad, still with bandages wrapped around his head, set out on foot to cross the Russian lines, and travel the 360 miles cross country to Moosburg. A military currier on a motorcycle stopped and asked him, "Where are you going?"

My dad replied, "I have traveling orders giving me permission to try and make it to Bavaria. Hopefully my wife and son made it out of Cologne and went there to stay with friends."

The motorcycle currier said, "Hop on, I think I still know a way out of here."

With grenades bursting and gunfire everywhere, they managed to ride the gauntlet through the Russian lines unharmed. Wishing each other good luck, they went their separate ways.

Through the valley of death and destruction he walked, hitchhiked, and sometimes caught a train towards Bavaria. Along the way he dodged bombs and cannon fire from strafing airplanes. Dad met refugees and soldiers tired of the war fleeing from the advancing Russians. He crossed through towns and cities in rubble with dead soldiers and civilians lying around like discards. It was chaos of epidemic proportion. When Hitler came to power he proclaimed; "Give me ten years and you shall not recognize Germany."

This was surely true; but not what the Germans had expected. After traveling four weeks through a country in ruins resembling Death Valley, he arrived in Moosburg at our friend's doorstep. Against all odds, he had made it alive. However, he was disappointed that we were not there. Our friends did not have any news about us either. Mail service was non-existent. Fearful of the worst, they all prayed for our safety.

Staying with our friends, Dad went daily for treatment to the military hospital in town. With the American troops approaching the area, the Army doctors and medics deserted the hospital and ran for home. His friend, Simon, who was about the same size as my Dad, said, "Take your uniform and dump it in the outhouse. Here, put on some of my clothes."

He did that and was now a soldier in civilian clothes. A few days after the Americans occupied the region, they posted proclamations, saying, "All military personnel in the area must report to the local allied command for screening."

Dad did not want to get into trouble. So, he went to the local US military command office where they wrote down his personal information, the address where he was staying, and sent him back to his friends saying, "We will call you."

When Germany capitulated a week later, and the war was officially over, MPs came knocking on the door and took my Dad away. He was then transported into a POW camp in Nürnberg where he was fingerprinted, interrogated, deloused, fed, and sent on his way home with a crew cut. After years of fear, death and destruction, the war finally ended.

# Chapter 20

Total chaos replaced the war. All kinds of weapons, thrown away by fleeing German soldiers, were lying around in the fields, woods, wasteland, and even backyards. Utilities worked off and on at best, and stores were out of everything. The German people were angry with the Nazis for having brought upon Germany destruction and the hungry bellies that they had promised to fill. Lowlife characters, seeing an opportunity for looting, stole everything in sight. It was unfortunate that these same people did not, or could not, see the road this tyrannical Nazi Regime would take before they got into power.

Had the profiteers and the, *see no evil, speak no evil, hear no evil,* German citizens taken a stand against the wrongs committed by the Nazis at the onset, millions of men, women and children around the world would have been spared from the terror of war and the concentration camps.

I can relate to the reports on television about the chaos in Iraq. In the first four weeks, after Germany capitulated, I saw the people pulling and pushing carts and wagons with stolen goods down the street. They broke into deserted homes and stole everything that they could carry away. Public facilities, military installations, stores, and warehouses were stripped of all their inventories. Even my Aunt Veronica helped herself to a piano from the anti-aircraft site. Since no one had food and clothing it was understandable for people to help themselves to merchandise from government and military buildings. However, there were no excuses for the looting of private homes, stores, and warehouses.

During the ransacking of the local party headquarters, a paper was found listing the Enemies of the Third Reich. Topping the list were the names of our family and extended family. I can easily imagine what might have happened if the Nazis would have been victorious.

My Reidenbach cousin and I, 11 years old at the time, went to an army warehouse in a nearby town. Two GI's, guarding the front door, stopped us, and said something. Not being able to understand English, we assumed they were asking us what we wanted. So, in sign language we pointed at our clothes and let them know, *we have no clothes, and would like to get some from the warehouse.* The two soldiers nodded and said "Okay." One of them took us into a large room full of new and used uniforms, shoes, boots, shirts, and sweaters. We learned our first English words, *good stuff, take.*

We were at awe over the amount of merchandise piled up on the floor. We began looking for items we could use. First, we looked to replace our worn-out cardboard shoes with soles full of holes. The boots were intriguing. We tried on the smallest ones that we could find. We must have looked like marching Puss in Boots. The soldiers got a kick out of that, laughed, and said, "Looking good."

We carried out as much stuff as we could carry. Because Mom was very handy in making new garments out of old ones. With shoes tied together and hung around our necks, and arms full of clothes, we marched home. Munching on chewing gum and chocolate, given to us by the Americans, we were jumping for joy in our new boots and enjoyed the treasures we had found.

To the amusement of the soldiers we learned two more English words, *come back,* which we did several times. We had fun with our newfound friends who always had some goodies for us.

Of course, word got around. It was not long before the place was empty.

Mom chuckled as she watched me stumble around in boots that reached above my knees. But when she looked at the garments, she said, "That is great, now I can make new cloths for you.

Mom and I took the garments apart and dyed the pieces in the washing machine navy blue and black. Those were the best colors to re-dye the field gray military uniforms. Very masterfully, my Mother made the dyed parts into new shirts, pants, jackets, coats, and sweaters. I was happy. I had new clothes. I was rich and I was the one who had provided the means.

# Chapter 21

Next to our church was a catholic hospital staffed by nuns. The Americans had set up shop in there to treat the wounded, both friend and foe. Some of the wounded Nazi survivors from the last stand in the woods, were also in there. Two American soldiers were placed as guards in front of the hospital.

Encouraged by our previous experience at the military warehouse, a couple of my friends and I watched from a distance and slowly but carefully closed in on the two soldiers. They sat on chairs smoking cigarettes and drinking coffee. Their rifles were hung across the back rests and their helmets placed on top as they talked, they did not look that scary to us.

We moved in closer. When the two guards became aware of us, they called out, "Come," and waved us over. *Come*--was a word we had learned from our friends at the warehouse. Hesitantly we walked over. They said, "Hi," and extended their hands in greeting. We shook hands and learned the new word, *hi* which we assumed meant, *Guten Tag*.

The sign language took over from there. After sharing chocolate with us, the soldiers noticed our dirty hands. One of the guards took out a sheet of yellow paper and tore it into four equal-sized squares. They motioned for us to hold out our hands. Placing a piece of that paper in each of our palms and poured water on the paper from his canteen. Then they made a hand washing motion. We rubbed our hands and behold, it turned into soap! Our excitement over the discovery amused our new friends. It made a welcome entertainment for the solders. They gave each of us several sheets of this soap paper, which we proudly took home.

When I showed Mom this newfound miracle, she was astonished. We had forgotten soap existed. All through the war we had only sand soap as we called it. It was a bar of composite that mostly felt like sand. Many times, we had used sand to clean our hands. After that day, a visit to the hospital became our daily ritual.

Then we found out that an American infantry unit was stationed at the textile mill. That smelled like a new adventure for us playing pals, the curious clan from the Von Diergart Strasse. Like fearless explorers, we made our way over to the mill. First, we watched from a distance and saw a bunch of soldiers in front of the factory. After observing them for a while, we noticed they had no weapons but were playing a silly ball game that made no sense to us. They threw the ball from one person to another and caught it with a leather glove. We could not figure out any kind of game rules, but they seemed to be having fun because they were yelling and laughing a lot.

We decided that maybe these soldiers were not as bad as we had been told during the war years in school. After all, they had treated us kindly, and had given us chocolate, chewing gum, and soap. Encouraged, we moved in closer. Upon seeing us, they waved us over. The usual sign language came into play. But we did say, "Hi, Joe," which was a greeting we had picked up. That aroused loud laughter from the troops. After a round of, "Me Tarzan, You Jane," we had mutually exchanged our names.

A soldier put his leather glove on my hand and said, "Catch," while he threw the ball to me. Of course, it took a few rounds before I finally got the hang of it. After that, they clapped their hands in applause and yelled, "Yea, good catch!" We surmised the game was called, *good catch*. I still thought it was boring to just pass the ball back and forth, but we had made new friends and they had taught us an American ball game.

Naturally we had asked the age-old question, "Chocolate Joe?" and pointed to our mouths. As always, we were rewarded with pockets full of goodies.

The next day we went back to teach the soldiers a real ball game, fussball (soccer). To the laughter of the troops we had fun running circles around the men. In those days, soccer was not a game known to Americans unless they were of European descent. We also found out, *good catch* was not the name of the American ballgame. It was called, baseball, a new word we easily added to our growing English vocabulary.

C & K rations, the much frowned upon combat food of the American troops, were pleasing meals to us. The soldiers had fun watching us eating their combat rations with an enthusiastic appetite. At the time, German ice was not like American ice cream. It was more a mix between soft ice cream and Italian water ice. We thought we had died and gone to heaven when the soldiers generously shared their ice cream with us. Much to our despair, our new friends left after a few weeks and moved on. American troops were replaced with British forces that were not as much fun as our old friends the *G.I. Joes.*

# Chapter 22

Other than SS or other Nazi members held for interrogation, the captured German soldiers were released by the American, British, and French forces and sent home. One of those returnees was my Dad. About eight weeks after the war was over, a friend of my parents came by on a bicycle and rang the doorbell. When I answered the door, he announced, "Tell your mom I just passed your dad coming home from the train station. He is on his way, but people talking to him are slowing him down."

I yelled upstairs, "Mom, Dad is alive! He is on his way home from the train station, I am running to meet him!"

Without waiting for an answer, I ran off towards the train station. Which was about three or four kilometers away. Halfway there, I saw him coming down the road with a shaved head dressed in strange clothes. I remembered my dad only dressed in his beautifully custom-tailored suits, or in a uniform. It was indeed an unusual sight, seeing him in a poorly fitting outfit and a shaved head. When I caught up with him, I jumped up and grabbed him around the neck. I received the biggest hug ever. Dad was home and now all would be well.

****

Rebuilding a country in disarray is not as easy as the Phoenix rising from the ashes. From the end of the war until the reform of the German monetary system in 1948, little food and no merchandise to speak of was available except on the black market.

One pound of butter on the black market sold for 150-Reichsmark, which was the forerunner of the Deutch-Mark. A single cigarette sold for 7-Reichsmark, a pound of meat for 500-Reichsmark and so forth. For comparison, Dad in his tailor shop would charge 150-Reichsmark to create a custom-tailored suit that took forty hours to make. In other words, for a pound of butter you had to work a whole week and a pound of meat three weeks.

To rebuild his business, Dad did not want to charge black market prizes. He knew eventually the country would normalize and a loyal customer base was essential for a healthy business. However, we needed to eat, and air raid damages had to be repaired on my grandparent's house where Dad's tailor shop was located. Food, building materials, and other essentials were only available on the illegal black market that was running on all cylinders. Bartering became a way of life and wherever possible, Dad would ask for food or building materials as pay instead of money.

Men's and ladies suits were created from used clothing of deceased parents or other family members. The largest source of fabric came from American Army/Navy surplus like OD sleeping bags. Fabrics from wool-blanket-sleeping-bags became a thought of material for overcoats and ladies winter coats. The sleeping bags were available on allocations as well as on the black market. Ripping the seams on the sleeping bags became my job. The material was then dyed dark brown, navy blue, dark green, or black. Dyestuffs had to be bought at high prices or bartered for with people working at the Bayer factory, which manufactured synthetic dyes.

As time went on, inferior fabrics started to become available at the wholesalers for black market prices. Fabric for a suit was available at the cost of 1500-Reich-Mark. Thus, dad would sell the completed suit for 3000-Reichmark. This started to bring in some money for building materials and other essentials. My Dad, a very frugal man, knew how to cut suits most economically. From the leftover fabric he made children's shorts that he traded for food at the farmers.

I remember, one time he had received 100 pounds of barley. We ate that stuff day in day out. After weeks and weeks of eating nothing but barley, it turned me off to the extent that to this day I still get repulsed when anything reeks or looks like it contains barley. Another time he had bought 10 pounds of butter. That was like gold. To celebrate Mom baked a butter-cream cake. It tasted wonderful. But the whole family was plagued by *Montezuma's Revenge*. After haven't had fat for a long time, the sudden enjoyment of real butter became a curse.

On a different occasion, Dad very happily brought home several pounds of meat he had purchased for a high price on the black market. All of us ate hearty, it tasted great. However, days later Mom found out that the guy had sold Dad a butchered dog. Well, it did not affect me. But I cannot say the same for my parents, *Montezuma* returned.

Demand for my father's work grew rapidly. He hired three tailors. The space of the workroom became too small. My Opa Josef, Dad, and a retired bricklayer by the name of Jan started building an addition onto the back of the house. We hauled off old bricks in carts from bombed out buildings and brought them into our backyard. We cleaned the cement off the bricks with chisels and hammers until they were usable. The work was day and night including me. Child labor was not a term we understood.

Dad bartered with the heir apparent to Baron von Diergart a suit for oak trees. The Baron took us to his forest and marked some nice tall trees that we could chop down. After harvesting them, we lugged them off to a sawmill where they were transformed into building materials. We eventually finished our addition, which became the new workroom and turned the old tailor shop into a store and fitting room. Later, when times normalized it became a Haberdashery store.

# Chapter 23

Slowly, some cars, mostly old rebuilt or converted military vehicles began appearing on the streets. Most all privately-owned vehicles were confiscated by the military during the war. Besides military automobiles like Volkswagens and trucks, a couple of old DKW models from Auto Union, the forerunner of Audi, appeared on the streets. Those DKW models had a two-cylinder motor and wooden body covered with leather or wax cloths. Hitler, during his reign, established a savings program for all citizens to own a Volkswagen. The name given to the car meant, *the peoples car.* However, the money was not used to build cars for the people. Instead it became part of the war machine. The first *Volkswagen* were army vehicles.

Gasoline was in short supply and only available on the black market. German engineers, faced with *'necessity is the mother of invention,'* invented a steam boiler conversion for gasoline-powered trucks. The boiler, about five feet tall, mounted on the side of the truck, was fired by charcoal. Since it was a chore to start the vehicles, they were always left running unless parked for several hours. Towards the bottom of the boiler was a round hole to feed the burning charcoal with oxygen. The opening was two inches in diameter and was covered by a flopping disc.

It did not take us kids long to discover that closing off the oxygen feed to the boiler would stop the motor. Mischievous boys that we were, it became part of our favorite pastime. We learned to run next to the slow-moving trucks and covered the holes with a block of wood, or even cardboard. It worked every time. With a few choice words, the drivers would exit the cab and started the truck up again by cranking the starter in the front. To the annoyance of the driver, but to the amusement of us kids, this process took about five to six minutes.

There were no bicycles to be had, so Dad made one for me from parts he could find. My bike was put together from an old rusty black frame, a strange long brown leather saddle that made my butt sore every time I rode it, one black and one blue wheel, and a funny looking handle bar like the ones that were used in the old silent movies.

Uncle Peter, Dad's brother, who was very handy with fixing vehicles, made money by re-building motorbikes much the same way and sold them on the black market. He collected frames, tanks, engines parts, wheels, and tires until he had what he needed to build a bike. After he put the parts together, he had the ability to make them work. A friend of his, very good at painting, gave the bikes color and even decals. It is amazing how resourceful people can become during lean times.

To hold on to his tailors, who did not have much to eat, Dad had to organize food for them as well. Uncle Peter was a butcher by trade but was driving a mail truck for the postal office. Black marketeering was illegal and punished severely if you were caught. However, in all the years from the end of the war until 1948 we did not hear of any convictions; it had become a way of life.

Until Dad started his business, there had been a butcher shop in my grandparent's house. In the basement was a smoke room for meat. In the laundry room was a large boiler to cook the sausage. Uncle Peter, accompanied by his friend, a police officer, picked up several live cows and pigs in the mail truck, which Dad had purchased from a farmer. Since this was an illegal black-market activity, it had to be done in the dark of night. With a police officer in uniform riding shotgun in a sealed mail truck, the chances of being stopped and checked were nil. My uncle butchered the animals in the large garage on our property. They buried the hides in the backyard. The meat was cut and the ham was smoked in the smoke room; but by far the best part for us kids was the wonderful sausage and lunchmeat that was cooked in the huge caldron. The broth, with a couple of busted sausages, made for a great soup. The meat and sausage were then divided up between family, the police officer, and the tailors. Mom canned the meat and sausages in glass jars. That kept us supplied with meat for a couple of months.

# Chapter 24

One day, out of the blue, a package arrived full of groceries, sweets, and a rubber ball for me. We felt like Christmas had come early. Every item my Mom took out of the package was accompanied with Mom's "Oooh look at this! Coffee, and look at this, chocolate for you!" and on and on. It was from Mom's uncle, Oma's stepbrother in America and was marked, *Care Package*. The packages came in regular intervals. Mom's uncle kept records to make sure all the Reidenbach families were getting their equal share. This generosity, extended to the family, was a godsend.

Under the Marshal Plan, food aid started to arrive into Germany. Bakers received tons of corn flour. However, bakers did not know how to use it. In our region corn was not grown for human consumption, it had only been used for animal feed. Recipes either did not come with it or the bakers couldn't read English. The bakeries used their wheat bread recipes to bake the corn flour bread. Maisbrot, as we called the new bread, was hard as a rock and created heartburn to no end.

*The School Lunch Program* was another food aid. Schools received boxed pea soup, biscuit soup, and other soups, which were cooked in large German Army mobile kitchens called the goulash cannons. These kitchens were the size of a horse drawn gun carriage. The mobile kitchens were coal or wood fired and had a stovepipe; therefore, the nickname, *goulash cannon.*

For many children, the lunch program was the only full meal of the day. In a rotating fashion, we would draw kitchen duty.

As a reward for working with the housemaster on the meals, we could take the leftovers home. That was always a big treat.

Also, part of the aid program were the surplus C & K rations. The rations were distributed through grocery wholesale distributors. Several neighborhood kids and I got a job at my dad's friend's distribution center sorting C & K rations. Spam went in one box, cookies in another and so forth. For pay we could eat as much as we wanted; but we couldn't take anything home. Therefore, we filled our tummies with power bars, candies, chocolate, and canned Spam.

Like all war and post-war children, we grew up fast and learned to fend for ourselves. The sight of scrawny kids dressed in rags who ran around looking for food instead of playing. It always forms a sad picture of the innocent victims of war.

Not all of our fun was innocent and safe. With all the weapons and ammunition lying around in the sand dunes, we played some extremely dangerous games.

Close to our apartment was a deep rock-quarry. One of our favorite games was laying at the edge of the quarry, shouldering an anti-tank recoilless launcher. The pre-fitted launcher had a shape-charged warhead packed with octogen, and a black powder filled launching tube.

With our finger on the trigger we aimed the launcher at one of the boulders on the bottom of the quarry. When we thought we had the launcher lined up, we pulled the trigger. Fire shot out of the back forcing the warhead out and on its way. Watching the warhead travel to its target and explode was a lot of fun but a deadly game for children. The shape charge warhead was designed to burn its way through the tanks armor. If the rock you had called as the target got hit and exploded, you were the winner.

Another game we played was no less dangerous. We gathered the heavy caliber anti-aircraft ammunition that was left behind at the abandoned antiaircraft emplacement. We broke off the bullets from the 20 mm Ammo of the quadruple-barrel anti-aircraft guns. Then we poured out the black powder from the cartridges and pile it up in heaps. Lighting the heaps and watching the black powder explode was fun but extremely dangerous. The big, explosive-filled, anti-aircraft bullets, which we had broken off from the shells, became the basis of a whole new game, trying to throw the bullets into the rock quarry so the point hit a rock and exploded, was the rule of the game. He, who got the most bullets to explode, won the game.

My cousins from the Reidenbach clan and I, all boys, heard that hand grenades made good fishing tools. We went off to a little lake with our pockets full of hand grenades shaped like an egg instead of the German potato mashers. To activate the grenades, you had to pull out a small button attached with a string. One by one we pulled the pin on the grenades, counted to three, and then threw them into the pond. The exploding grenades created geysers which was fun to watch. Much to our surprise, the surface of the lake was covered with dead fish. We quickly scooped them up, divided them between us, and took them home. We did not tell anyone how we had gotten the fish. There was no evidence of shrapnel in the fish. Having watched our grandfathers butcher rabbits and chickens, we had an idea how to clean the fish.

In hindsight, we were extremely lucky that none of us had gotten hurt by those insane games. Every day the newspapers reported that children got hurt or killed from playing with explosives, weapons, unexploded bombs, or landmines. In the forest, near the chapel, three boys got killed and two lost limbs while playing with mines.

One day, as I was on the way to see my Reidenbach cousins, I passed a backyard and heard an explosion followed by a rising puff of smoke. Seconds later, a woman cried out, "Oh, my God, no! Oh, no!" Running over to the fence I saw a wailing mother holding the lifeless, blood-covered, and shredded body of her ten-year-old son.

That sobered me up and did slow down my involvement in the weapons games—but not altogether. We still thought we knew more than those other kids about handling military ordinances. Luckily for us, not long afterwards, most of the weaponry was collected and secured. However, in areas where big battles had been fought, some minefields did not get cleared until several years later.

# Chapter 25

When the schools reopened, parents as well as teachers tried to face the task of trying to fix the damage done by years of Nazi brainwashing. Centers were set up with picture stories of concentration camps and torture devices that had been repeatedly used. They took us on a field trip to a center where we heard a lecture on the horrors of the concentration camps. We had a tough time believing and understanding that the SS soldiers, who had been held up to us in school as heroes for the past several years, could have committed such atrocities.

It was not until we were taken into the exhibit and saw the actual photos that we began to realize the magnitude of the lies we had been fed. Seeing the gruesome pictures showing men, women, and children's bodies piled up in heaps and burning, while SS men stood around and laughed, stunned me. I stared at the photos unable to move. The movies and pictures that had been taken by the camp guards of starving people, looking like walking skeletons, especially children, had a devastating effect on me.

But it was the pictures and films of women and children in chambers collapsing from the gas, bodies fed into the ovens of Buchenwald, Auschwitz, and Dachau. People being machine gunned and falling into long dugout trenches, the displays of a lampshade made from human skin, branding irons used on human beings, and tools used in experimental operation without anesthetic, left me with nightmares for years to come. I walked out of the exhibition distraught, crying, and ashamed to be German.

I had only two questions for my parents, "Why did they do that, and why did the people allow them to do this?"

Those were challenging questions for my parents. How do you explain to your child, in whom you instilled values, honor, and right from wrong, what it is that can make people turn into animals? Or why people turned a blind eye and deaf ears to the atrocious wrong doings. How do you explain profiteering, fear for your life, and fear for your family's safety? With this newfound knowledge, it was difficult for me to respect adults the same way as I had before. The questions always came to my mind when I looked at adults, *Were you one of those animals? Did you support these animals?* Coping with and freeing myself of these nightmares took many long years.

# Chapter 26

Law and order, imposed by the Allied Occupation Forces, gradually began to reunite German Families. The Red Cross organized a location grit to look for the whereabouts of missing loved ones. Refugees from the eastern provinces, fleeing from the advancing Russian troops who were raping women and committing other atrocities, were spread all over Germany. The country was apportioned off into four sectors—American, English, French, and the Soviet Union—each occupied and governed a part of Germany. Berlin, the capital of Germany, was also divided into four parts; however, all four sections were located within the Russian sector.

Refugees had a tough time locating their families. Some were never found and years later declared as dead. The same happened with military personnel that had been captured by the Russians. The western Allied Troops used German statistics and their own and released the names of German soldiers killed, wounded, or captured.

Slowly but surely life started to become normal again. The Nüremberg Trial was over and the captured Nazi leaders got their much-deserved punishments. However, while the western allies established a provincial government, agreeing on a joint uniformed governing of Germany, the Soviet Union created quite a rift. On June 24, 1948, the Russians blockaded Berlin and cut off all supplies to the city.

US Forces started Operation Airlift. They created an aerobridge to supply Berlin and its citizens with tons of food and essentials. After a year, supplying everything from food to coal, the Soviet Union ended their blockade on May 12, 1949. It was the beginning of the Cold War. As the Eastern Bloc Countries, and East Germany, became dominated and ruled by Moscow, the Kremlin pushed for a separate Soviet ruled communist German State, the DDR (Deutsche Democratische Republic). At the same time, the Western Allies created the Federal Republic of Germany on May 23, 1949, or West Germany as it was known.

In the interim, on June 19, 1948, the provincial government of West Germany declared the Reichsmark null and void and replaced it with the Deutsche Mark or D-Mark for short. Every penny or mark became worthless, and all bank accounts zeroed out. Each family could exchange 60-Reichsmark for 40-D-Mark per person. No extra funds were granted for small businesses.

Overnight, everything from food to clothing etc. became available at normal prizes. The problem was, no one had money to purchase anything. Stores were unable to fill their shelves. Creative thinking generated the answer. From the factory to the consumer, merchandise was manufactured, sold, and delivered on credit.

Dad spoke to his employees, and said, "I received only 40-D-Mark per head just like you. I have no money to pay your salaries. My customers have none either to pay me. They can only pay a little bit every week from their paychecks. Either I lay you all off, or you work, and I pay you as I can." All of them decided to continue to work and be paid when Dad could pay them. With arduous work and ingenuity, Germany rebuilt its infrastructure and economy.

Conrad Adenauer, the first Chancellor of the Federal Republic of Germany, and the Minister for economic development, Ludwig Erhard, created what was often called *the economic miracle*. From the ashes of death and destruction of the failed, *Thousand-Year-Reich*, rose a democratic, economically sound Germany.

Life in Schlebusch returned to normal with free speech, values, and religious practices. Old traditions, like the St. Gezelinus week and May Processions, were back. Opa Sheng and Uncle Heinrich's prediction had come true—*the reign of Hitler and his cohorts will not last forever. Evil like that is doomed to fail.*

Almost overnight we went from seeing an occasional car in town to a changed and mobile society. People turned from rebuilt cars and fixed up army vehicles to Volkswagens, Opals, Fords, Mercedes, BMWs, Fiats, DKWs, and Borgward. The once quiet streets filled with bikes, had become noisy motorways.

Dad bought a little Fiat and later a Volkswagen. The serene life in Schlebusch and Germany changed. Distances that use to take hours to cross were now done in minutes. But most of all, it changed family life as we knew it. The wonderful family get-togethers on Sundays disappeared and were replaced by drives into the countryside for coffee and cake at cafés.

Life was extremely formal in public places. Conversations were held in low voices and etiquette was observed from the sublime to the ridiculous. Simple country folks, intimidated by fine city restaurants and cafés, would avoid them. With this atmosphere in mind, you can appreciate the little story I am about to tell.

It was a nice sunny Sunday afternoon, a warm spring day. Dad, Mom, and I, took a drive towards Schloss Burg. A trip we had often made on bikes. Yours truly was stuck in the back on the rumble seat of the little Fiat. The delicate green of spring and the fruit trees in full bloom were a delightful sight. Driving along the country roads through forests and up the mountains looking down into the valley with a river snaking through meadows, made you feel alive.

By the time four o'clock came, Dad was ready for coffee and cake. Mom had taken a pound cake along, which she had baked. However, Dad, a coffee connaisseur, did not like coffee from a thermos bottle. He was very finicky when it came to coffee—it had to be fresh and brewed just right. When he spotted an idyllic café, he pulled into the parking lot. The café had indoor-outdoor seating and was fancy. Ladies in elegant dresses and stylish hats, accompanied by men in suits and ties were conversing in hushed voices. Those that were eating dinner, handled the food formally as prescribed by etiquette, with fork and knife. Others, having coffee and cake, were lifting their cups very daintily with their thumb and forefinger and pointed the little finger away.

The headwaiter, dressed in a black cutaway with the formal striped trousers and a gray double-breasted vest, showed us to a table. Mom and Dad ordered each a small pot of coffee holding two cups, and I had hot chocolate. Dad said to Mom, "Okay, let us have some of your cake."

"You cannot do that. You cannot bring your own cake into this fancy restaurant," replied Mom.

Being formal was not his forte, and intimidation was not a word in his vocabulary. Sitting with both hands on the table, a fork in his left hand and a knife in his right, smiling mischievously, he said, "Out with the cake. If I am spending my money here, then I also have the right to eat my own cake."

Mom was getting embarrassed and said in a hushed voice, "You cannot do that!"

Undeterred by all this, Dad knocked the fork and knife a couple of times on the table and said with a somewhat raised voice, "I don't care, out with the cake!"

Afraid that Dad would make a further scene; Mom, red-faced put the cake reluctantly on the table. With a grin, Dad cut the cake. I was ecstatic and with loud laughter enjoyed eating my piece of cake. I was always ready for a prank; but the pretentious fine people dressed to the hilt shook their heads in disgust. I am sure they called us the German version of hillbillies.

Though Dad and I had fun. The cake tasted great. But Mom had fire in her eyes. Kalte Hundeschnautze (Mom is not on speaking terms) was on the menu. We drove home with only the motor making any sounds.

# Chapter 27

My mother's cousin, Tanta Anna, daughter of Josef Rasquien, the Gendarme, was one of those self-conscious women that lived and died by the rules of etiquette. She adored the extravagance of the super fine cafés in the big cities. Not having any children of her own, she loved her brother's son, a little four-year-old boy. Her brother Josef was a down-to-earth farmer with no regard for fancy etiquette.

One day she took her little four-year-old nephew to Cologne. After buying lots of toys and showing him the big city, they were ready to have some refreshments. Tante Anna went to the finest café in the city and after sitting down, ordered hot chocolate and strawberry tart with whipped cream. Ladies dressed in the latest fashions, complete with hats and gloves, were conversing in hushed voices. Waitresses in black short dresses, white aprons and white-laced diadem-like hats, hurried quietly between tables serving coffee and cake on Rosenthal China. As Tante Anna was introducing her little nephew to the better things in life, the little boy suddenly said, "Tante Anna, pull on my finger." Thinking it was a game, she pulled on his finger. To Tante Anna's horror, little Josef passed wind so loud that it could be heard throughout the café.

With all eyes on her, embarrassed and red-faced as a tomato, she said, "But Josef, something like that is ill mannered. You don't do this."

To make matters worse, he answered, "Daddy does that all the time."

Under the disapproving looks of the patrons, she hightailed it out of there as quickly as she could. She never took little Josef to an extravagant establishment again. This episode became a comedy story told many times during family gatherings.

# Chapter 28

A year or two after the war, organizations banned during the Third Reich, resumed their activities. Schützenvereine flourished and youth groups, especially the Scouts, became very popular. The St. Sebastian brotherhood of protectors, a Catholic rifle club and successor of the minutemen, started their social and charitable activities again, and in the old tradition, held weeklong pageants with all the pomp and circumstance. The celebration revolved around electing a new king for a year. Clubs from surrounding towns, in old fashion green hunter's uniforms, white plumed hats, with some on horseback, joined the parade complete with brass bands.

Since weapons were banned for a couple of years after the war, the *King of the Schützen* was chosen by lottery. When weapons became legal again, the *King* was chosen in a shooting match. A wooden bird with a crown on its head, soaked for a year in all kinds of liquid to harden, was fastened on a high pole. In rotation, the members took turns shooting at the bird with a .22 caliber rifle. The shooting went on until the last little splinter of wood was gone. It had to be done according to set rules. Rifles were loaded by the Master-of-Arms to make sure everyone had the identical ammunition. Then, whoever shot down the last piece of wood was the king elect until he was crowned. Following the match, an elaborate coronation ceremony was performed by the parish pastor under the large trees of the forest around the St. Gezelinus chapel. The newly crowned king and queen marched in a parade to the Wald restaurant Kürten where the coronation ball was held. This large outdoor-indoor restaurant in the woods had a dance hall as well. It was the home of the St. Sebastianer. Festivities included eating, drinking, and dancing went on until the wee hours of the morning. Since the *King* had to entertain a court of six women and their husbands with food and wine, it was a rather expensive affair. Anyone who could not afford to do this, made sure not to shoot down the last piece of the wooden bird.

Encouraged by his friend Otto Marx, a big chief in the St. Sebastianer, Dad joined the club much to the chagrin of Opa Josef. Opa knew it was costly and meetings always ended up in a drinking affair. Dad said, "It is good for business." However, truth be known, he really liked it.

# Chapter 29

I was still an altar server and besides serving at mass, we went to weekly meetings. The saying, *boys will be boys,* was passed on from generation to generation. This was certainly true for us. Tasting the pastor's wine was fun and if the bottle showed it, well a little bit of water did not hurt the wine any; or so we thought. During a high mass, it was customary to use incense. One altar boy would handle the censer with the glowing charcoal inside, and one the little boat-like vessel with incense. During mass, the censer was carried in and out several times. Before the priest would use the censer to bless the altar or the faithful, he would put a spoonful of incense on the glowing coal. We figured, if we put a spoonful on the coal before bringing it out, we would save the priest the trouble. Making sure enough smoke would come from the censer; we heaped four spoons of incense on the coal. When we opened the censer for the priest to put the incense on the coal, the poor pastor got a strong dose of incense that ended in a coughing spell. I don't know why he insisted on doing it himself.

Altar boy's meetings were held in the evenings, which became for us the weekly mischief night. On the way home, doorbell ringing was a favored sport. We stuck wooden matches in the pushbutton bells for continuous ringing, but we had the biggest fun with an old pull bell. This Tudor-style house had an old-fashioned metal bell which was operated by pulling a chain.

One night, coming home from the meeting, we took an old burlap bag and attached it to the end of the sewer pipe that ran underneath the bridge in town. We knew sewer rats nested in this pipe. We banged on the pipeline until we caught one in the burlap sack. Having nothing better to do, we attached the burlap bag with the rat inside to the end of the doorbell. The rat went wild and swung back and forth inside the bag on the end of the chain. We watched from a distance the woman of the house answering the door. Her screams slightly aroused the neighbors.

Germany had three groups of scouts—the nondenominational scouts, the Lutheran scouts, and the St. George's Scouts, which were the catholic scouts. Religious youth groups and especially the scouts, were bringing values and principles back into the lives of the future young men and women in Germany.

I joined the Catholic Scouts; which was more challenging than the regular church groups. It was a great character builder. In our weekly meetings we played games and learned skills like understanding astronomy, how to construct things, living off the land, and exploring the wonders of nature. However, the most important lesson was the commitment to honor and principles. We lived and breathed according to Baden Powell's scout book.

One of our big trips was from Cologne to Konstanz am Bodensee. The Bodensee was a beautiful lake surrounded by the Swiss, German, Austrian, and Liechtenstein Alps. After an eight-hour train ride, we unloaded our bikes and backpacks and peddled to a beach on the lake. It was a beautiful warm summer's evening. The calm lake looked like a mirror surrounded by glowing snow-capped mountains at sunset. Overwhelmed by nature's beauty, we spread our blankets in the sand a few feet away from the water. Admiring for a while the sights and thanking the Lord for a wonderful day, we went to sleep.

The sound of crashing waves awakened us at dawn. During the night, a heavy wind had turned the mirror like lake into a wave crashing boiling pot. The beach was flooded and with it our blankets, possessions, clothes, and ourselves. We built a fire and dried everything as best as we could, packed up, mounted our bikes, and set course towards the *Black Forest*. The route took us through more of God's breathtaking nature. In the evening, we stopped and looked for a spot to pitch our tents. We found a meadow on the outskirts of a forest, a perfect place to spend the night. Tired from the long ride, we pitched our tents and went to sleep. In the morning, we cleaned up, had breakfast, and got ready to leave when a police officer appeared on a little put-put motorcycle. We said, "Good morning Officer," knowing we had done nothing wrong.

He answered with a very gruffly reply; "Did you not see the sign saying, 'Camping forbidden?'"

Since we had not seen the sign, we answered honestly, "No."

He replied arrogantly, "Yeah, right, that is 10-D-Mark fine for each of you."

None of our pleas changed this public bureaucrat's mind, we had to pay. He counted the five of us; turned around and pointed as he asked, "Does that defecating outfielder also belong to you?"

One of our explorers had gone for his morning constitutional. Despite our motioning for him to keep his head down, he lifted his head up to see what was going on. This turned our fine to 60-D-Marks instead of 50. Lesson learned, we continued our trip.

As we arrived at the outskirts of Bonn, approximately thirty miles from home, we decided to have a traditional midday dinner. We found a restaurant with a butcher shop. Those restaurants were known to serve hearty and plentiful meals. It was what sixteen-year-old boys needed. After sitting down, we ordered beer, some of us had schnitzel and others had bratwurst with sauerkraut.

While quenching our thirst, we listened to the news on the radio. When we heard our town mentioned, we got the shock of our lives. While we had been on our trip, a group of forty-five friends were coming home from a summer camp. An incoming train approaching the railroad crossing at full speed hit the bus. The gates were open. The train went through the crossing dragging the bus and the trailer several hundred feet along the tracks, leaving dead bodies in its wake. More than twenty boys were killed and others seriously hurt.

By now, we had lost our appetites. We paid up, leaving the food on the table and went home without stopping. Our parents, naturally very scared and upset, were happy to see us safely home. The next couple of weeks were heartbreaking for our town. In a somber procession, the many coffins were transferred to the cemetery. My friend Gerhard was one of the lucky ones that walked away unscathed. It took quite a while for the town to recover from the loss of so many promising young lives, but life continued as it always does.

# Chapter 30

In 1950, I had the privilege to be among a trainload of scouts going to Rome to celebrate the Holy Year. Included were six other scouts from our troop. Our first stop was Luzerne am Vierwaldstädter See in Switzerland. Luzern is an idyllic city on a lake surrounded by alpine mountains. After spending a day enjoying this picturesque valley, our train ride continued through the night to Genoa, Italy. On the way we passed a small lake illuminated by moonlight. The silver rays glistening on the water, with the shadowy mountains in the background, was awesome and so was the palm tree lined beach of Genoa. We spent a day of sunning on the beach and swimming in the waters of the Luganan Sea. That is, all except yours truly, the professional non-swimmer. It was a special sight for us land-locked flatlanders who were only used to the waters of a river.

The next stop was Assisi, the town of St. Francis. The quaint village, with its narrow cobblestone streets and alleys running up and down the hills, was truly unique. Since the trip was arranged on the cheap, boarding houses and restaurants were not of the highest quality. Being used to big hearty breakfasts with crusty rolls and lunchmeat, the one Italian roll with jelly did not fill our tummies. After a little bit of prodding, they brought out more rolls.

At dinnertime, we had soup. When the plates came, my friend Helmut, who was sitting next to me, had an additional piece of protein in his soup, a fly. We called the waiter over. Unable to speak Italian, and the waiter not knowing the German language, we tried to make him understand that there was a fly in the soup. Helmut made flying motions with his arms and hands pointing at his soup, but the waiter conveniently played dumb. He turned his palms up, raised his shoulders, and said, "no understand." Persistent as we were, we did not let him get away with this. We finally got him to look at the soup. Looking down he said, "ah..." He took his thumb and forefinger, fished the fly out of the soup, and pointed at the soup with his palms up, saying, "Okay." It was too funny; and with much ado, my friend did not eat the soup.

Overall, it was a memorable trip. It took us on to Pisa, Rome, Castelgandolfo, for an audience with Pope Pius the 12th and on to a stopover in Florence. From there, we boarded the train, which took us home.

# Chapter 31

In 1949, I was supposed to graduate from elementary school. However, the government added a ninth year to the elementary school terms to make up for the time lost during the air raids. Since my goal in life was to take over Dad's business, I needed to take my three years of apprenticeship in tailoring, make my journeymen's paper, take pattern making and industrial engineering for the apparel trade, business courses, and make my master's degree to own and operate the business. Those were the commerce rules at the time if you wanted to own and operate a business in Germany.

Dad did not want me to take my apprenticeship in his shop. He thought, nepotism would interfere with the education process, and therefore lined up a position for me with the number-one tailor shop in Leverkusen.

The problem was that the position was available in 1949, and if I had to finish the ninth year, the position would have been taken. With the agreement of my teacher, who thought I did not need the extra year, Dad conferred with the Chief Master Tailor, my boss to be. He had no objection to starting me off without going an extra year to school.

With that out of the way, I entered the working world. Three years was the prescribed time to complete my education. One day a week, we had to attend trade school, which I found very boring. They let me jump a grade, thus completing my journeymen's papers in only two years. While in trade school, I was offered a full scholarship to the university studying textile engineering. Since I was set on taking over dad's business, I turned it down.

As they used to say, *Lehrjahre sind keine Herrn Jahre*, meaning, as an apprentice you do as you are told. Besides learning things, you were also the slave of the master tailors who loved to play pranks on the apprentices.

Pressing was done with heavy, twenty-pound irons that were heated on a potbelly stove. The wooden-grip handles were taken off while the iron heated up on the stove and put back on when they were taken out. Exercising their authority, tailors would yell for the new apprentice to grab the iron and bring it to the stove in exchange for a hot one. For a fourteen-year-old, the 20-pound irons were heavy. I used to grab the iron on the run, expecting a heavy iron. The tailors, always ready for a prank, would take the handles out of the iron and put them on the top. Grabbing the handle of the iron on the run, your hand would fly up in the air without the weight of the iron. This was accompanied by loud laughter from the group of tailors.

You also had to pay your dues, which included cleaning the place after hours and delivering merchandise to customers before you could go home. However, after a couple of months you became part of the family.

It was also customary to pass spools of thread by throwing them across the room to whomever wanted them. One day, when I threw one of the heavier spools to a tailor, it hit my boss smack in the forehead. I got a dirty look and he, a bump on the forehead.

In my second year, I was elected to be the mentor of the new apprentice, a young girl. The front crease on pants used to be marked with a white thread pulled through the two layers and then the thread was cut between the plies. After telling her what to do, I turned back to my work. When she said, "Okay, I am done." I turned around in shock and with my mouth open, I noticed that she had split the front of the pants right down the middle along the crease line. I suppose, I did not make myself very clear.

Another embarrassing moment came when she wanted to know why one pant had the left front trimmed at the fly, and the other the right front. Fronts of pants in custom tailoring were trimmed on the side the man would carry his private parts. While my face got as red as a tomato, all the tailor's ears perked up. Grinning and waiting for my explanation. I never did explain it. I just said, "That is the way it is done."

After graduating, and completing the time left on my contract, I worked with my dad in his shop.

# Chapter 32

On the first floor of my grandparent's house, lived an elderly couple. After the death of her husband, the woman moved in with her daughter and left the apartment vacant. Since the business was in my Grandparent's house, and Dad worked from early morning until late in the night, it made sense to move back. This was not so easy. Germany had a huge housing shortage. All apartments were under government control. Palm greasing, or in this case, getting a suit made for nothing, convinced the bureaucrat at the housing authority that we needed the apartment. After fixing up the place, we moved from the three-room apartment on the Linienstrasse, to the first-floor apartment at my grandparents. They gave up one room on the second floor, which became my room. I felt like a King; I had my own room. Until then, I had slept in the living room on a sleeper couch. Being able to retreat to a room where I had privacy, felt wonderful.

Of course, like most old houses at that time, this one was a cold-water flat and had an outhouse. Bedrooms were always cold and without heat. However, stoves heated the kitchen, living room, workroom, and the store.

In the wintertime, Dad would get up at five in the morning to light the oven in the kitchen and the potbelly stove in the workroom. The living room was only used on holidays and other special occasions. It always took a while for the rooms to warm up, especially the workroom. Since the tailor shop was a one-floor addition to the house, the chimney did not have a good draft and until the air in the flue warmed up for fifteen minutes, the room filled up with smoke.

Winters were bitter cold. The water pipes would freeze. That is when my grandpa would defrost them with a blowtorch. Sometimes, the pipes or spigots would bust during the night and build an icicle from the faucet to the sink, especially in my parent's bedroom.

After Dad had the stoves going in the morning, he would make a small pot of strong coffee. He brewed it the old fashion way, by pouring boiling water on top of the coffee grinds with a pinch of salt for a hardier taste. Then dad would wake me, and after a shave and a cat-wash with cold water, the two of us would drink the pot of coffee; —the coffee being so strong that a spoon had no problem standing straight up without keeling over. To this day, I still love strong coffee.

Since I had always watched my parents and grandparents work hard and long hours, it was natural for me to do the same. Already, before I had started my apprenticeship, I had worked in my dad's shop after school. Besides getting a head start on learning the trade, I earned pocket money. My pay as an apprentice was 25-DM a month the first year, 35-DM a month the second year and 45-DM a month the third year. Considering that, a movie ticket was 5-DM, and a piece of cake and coffee 10-DM, the pay did not buy much.

As an apprentice, my working hours were Monday to Friday from 7:00 a.m. to 6:00 p.m. and Saturdays from 7:00 a.m. until 12:00 noon. I still worked for my Dad after coming home to earn extra money.

Leisure time with friends was drastically curtailed to a few hours per week, Saturday afternoons, and Sundays. We were a group of seven very close friends, we made our time count. Our prime interests were scouting, hiking, biking, the arts, going to concerts, listening to classical music, and to the theater. Attending plays rounded out our education. Discussions and debating sessions sharpened our wits.

# Chapter 33

In 1949, I was surprised by my parent's revelation that Mom was pregnant. My little brother Hans was born when I was fifteen years old. I thought he was the most beautiful baby I had ever seen. With the youngest of my cousins being already ten years old, this little bundle was Opa's pride and joy. Since Opa had retired, his time was spent chatting with Dad and his employees, carrying my little brother around, and working in the garden.

When the baby carriage was parked in the backyard, and Opa wanted to play with Hans, he would give the coach a swift kick, so he could pick the baby up saying, "Oh, he just woke up."

Oma still tended to the chickens and goats. I still did not like goat milk or the fried potatoes in buttermilk but on Fridays, I had apple pancakes at Oma's. Mom always cooked for my Dad's tastes, which were different from mine. Being a finicky eater, I would check what Oma had cooked and chose the lesser of the two evils.

My grandparents lived on the second floor. Since they did not have a refrigerator, Oma would keep a large ham hanging outside her window on two strings.

One day, Dad called, "Allo, (my nickname), quickly come and bring your air rifle." I quickly ran out with the gun asking, "what?"

"You want to test your shooting skills?" Dad asked.

"Yes," I replied.

He pointed at the ham and said, "Let's see whether we can shoot down grandma's ham."

That was right up my alley. Both of us were excellent marksmen and after a few tries, Dad managed to cut down one string and I the other and the ham came tumbling down. Opa was in on the prank as well and laughed when Oma was looking for the ham, shaking her head, saying, "how can this ham just disappear?" We let her wonder for a while and then Opa said nonchalantly, "Oh, this one?" As he held up the ham with the most innocent look he could manage.

Oma grabbed her ham and stormed off saying, "Oh, you men, will you ever grow up?" Opa and Dad were a lot of fun and always game for mischief.

# Chapter 34

It was at 11:30 P.M, on a Friday night, when I returned from the city. My friends and I had attended Tennessee William's play, *The Glass Menagerie*, with Rene Deltgen. My little brother was about two-years-old and had the measles. Suddenly, I heard mom and dad screaming, "No! No! Hans, no!" Running into their bedroom, I saw my brother having a convulsion.

The pediatrician lived about a mile down the street. This was the fastest mile I ever ran in my life. He came over and immediately called an ambulance to have Hans transported to the University Hospital in Cologne. He was comatose and diagnosed with a brain infection. Evidently, the poison from the measles had infected his brain. He ended up in intensive care and was on the critical list for a week.

Mom stayed the entire time in Cologne at the hospital. Not knowing whether he would live or die, or have brain damage if he lived, the whole family was distraught. Friends and family joined in prayer to guide the doctors in helping to heal my little brother.

When he came out of the coma, we could only see him through a crack in the door for fear he would get upset and want to go home. Hans had the best medical care available at the time, but for several weeks, the doctors did not know what the outcome would be.

Finally, after a long examination, the chief neurosurgeon approached Mom laughing and said, "I had the best conversation with your son. He called me stupid."

Mom was shocked that her little two-year-old had had the audacity to call the doctor stupid. However, the doctor assured her that this was the most wonderful word he had heard in weeks. During the examination, the doctor had bombarded Hans with questions, trying to assess his mental capacity. The little guy figured, if the doctor had to ask that many questions, he had to be stupid. That was the turning point; and thanks to the Lord, he had no after affects at all. It was a day of jubilation when the little two-year-old with blond curly hair came home.

Like most two-year-olds, he got into a lot of mischief. After returning from the hospital, Hans had gotten a little kitten that he loved as much as he did our dog Prince, a big German Shepherd. One day, we heard a kitten crying, but did not know from where the noise came. We traced it and found the kitten locked in a cardboard suitcase that Hans had been playing with earlier.

Prince was trained (Shepherd K9) and watched out for my little brother. When Hans played in front of the house and got too close to the curb, Prince would grab him by the seat of his pants and pull him back. That became a game. Hans would dash for the curb and the dog would pull him back. Giggling and laughing his throaty laugh, the little curly head would start the game all over again.

# Chapter 35

As my friends and I got into our late teens, the town began to shrink for us. By then, our interests turned to events in the big city and girls, but we were still very much into scouting. Two events during the year always held a special attraction for us. One of them was the day of the feast of St. John. That day all the church youth groups gathered in the evening for the big St John's Bonfire. Around a very large campfire, much like the ones on college campuses, the groups tried to outdo each other in song and dance. It was an evening of fun especially since the girls were present too. After several hours, when the fire had burned down to only glowing charcoal, the boys would try to impress the girls by courageously jumping over the fire. A few girls also had to show that they were as gutsy as the boys were and joined in. One year, a girl fell into the fire and was severely burned. After that, girls were no longer allowed to jump the fire; but the boys could continue to impress them.

New Year's Eve was the other special event for the older explorers that were elevated to the Knights of St. George. From all over the country, scouts would gather in the town of Altenberg. The organization of the catholic scouts of Germany were structured into Bund, Land, Gau, Stamm, Sippe, or Ritterrunde, in case of the Knights of St. George. Each Archdiocese had a contingent representing their Diocese at the New Year's Eve gathering.

After the 5:00 p.m. mass, we would mingle for a couple of hours to renew old friendships. At 10:00 pm, everybody would march off to a meadow surrounding a campfire. With song and readings, we would await the New Year. Midnight was greeted with the traditional Auld Lang Syne, which was followed by a Knight from each Archdiocese throwing a piece of wood into the fire declaring their loyalty to, *Valor, Honor, and Principles.*

As mentioned before, our interests had begun to change. Instead of hiking and biking on Sundays, we would walk through town hoping to get a glimpse of the girl we were sweet on. I had a crush on a girl a few years younger than I. Her father, afraid that if she dated he would be considered old, did not allow it. In fear of ruining my chances by approaching her the wrong way, I was too ill at ease to find the right words, even if her Dad would have allowed it.

Being friends with the girls in the church youth group was one thing, but conveying love was something altogether different. I still remember when my friend and I biked down a dirt road. I saw her on a bicycle ahead of us. My heart started to bump. As we came closer, she hit a stone with her bike and fell. This would have been the perfect moment to approach her, help her up, and inquire whether she was all right. But no, like a dummy, I stood there with my mouth open doing nothing while my friend helped her up. Well, I certainly was no ladies' man.

Dad must have thought so too; he insisted that I take lessons in ballroom dancing. Reluctantly, I attended the classes together with my friends, thinking that was the dumbest thing Dad had asked of me. Well, getting in close contact with girls, and learning how to swirl them around, started to become fun. After a formal graduation ball, we were ready to go to the dances.

But, I still could not get near my dream-girl. One of my friends lived next door to her and when she came by, all I could do was talk to her with *guggul* eyes but did not get enough courage up to ask her out. However, on the first of May I left the largest Birch Tree I could find in front of her door.

Gervers, the restaurant, in the village of Edelrath, had a hall that was used for dining and dancing. Every weekend they had a brass band playing; but occasions like Carnival, Mayday and Harvest fest, were big events. Mayday was a one-day celebration, Kirmes lasted three days, and Carnival lasted from Friday until Tuesday midnight with a big *Rose Ball Parade on Monday* in Cologne.

The city of Cologne was known for its wild celebration. Carnival in Cologne dated back to the Romans and was the oldest Mardi Gras gala, besides the Carnival in Venice. The people of Cologne, *The Cologne Crazies,* as they were known, were the most congenial people in Germany. On Rosen-Monday, the streets of Cologne became dance floors. Music was everywhere, and strangers danced with strangers, including the otherwise duty-minded police. A friend from Hamburg verbalized it properly. He said, "When people in Hamburg go into a restaurant, they look for an empty table. When people in Cologne go into a restaurant, they look for an occupied table with an empty seat, so they have company while they eat. In Hamburg people look for empty tables."

By now, my friends and I no longer frowned on dancing. We would attend the festivity every time we could. Together, with a group of girls, we enjoyed wine and danced until the wee hours of the morning. At midnight, Mrs. Gerver, the proprietor of the facility, took us into the kitchen and fed us cold pork chops and potato salad. She always said, "Boys, you cannot drink and dance all night without eating." It was a neighborhood family party. We would take the girls home and serenade them at their front doors. Singing was an important part of the German culture.

Many weekends we went to Cologne to the dancefloor at the fountain. It was a circular dance-floor in the open air, built around a fountain. We waltzed the night away to an all violin orchestra. At dusk, lanterns would illuminate the dance floor in colored floodlights. It was truly romantic.

141

# Chapter 36

Once a year, motorcycle and Formula-One Street races were held in Schlebusch. My friend had a 250 cm3 BMW and together, with the muffler removed for better sound, we would try to race with the practicing racers on the Autobahn. At that time, the Autobahn was still closed to traffic due to damaged bridges from the war.

For our Eagle Scout test, we had to take a first aid course, which was given by the Red Cross. They handled the ambulances and paramedic's service. On the end of the course, we were recruited into the organization. On our first job as paramedics, my friend and I were stationed in a curve during the motorcycle race. Nothing ever happened at that spot, so they said, until the day we drew the assignment. Two cycles collided in the curve and slammed into the spectators. Five people were down, and no one could get to us to help. We bandaged the injured as well as we could. A ten-year-old boy with severe head injuries died, but the others survived. After that, the races were discontinued.

\*\*\*\*

Dad's business flourished. Our workweek consisted of sixty-hour weeks. Before the holidays, when everyone wanted new clothes, the two of us worked seventy-two hours without a single break. Coffee and cigarettes kept us awake. However, I loved my profession. In 1950, at the age of sixteen, I attended the first National Custom Tailors Conference at the Bundeshaus in Bonn, the German Parliament Building. It was exciting to take the train into the city thirty miles away and to partake in this prestigious event.

I was in awe entering the famous hall where the Congress held their sessions. I felt all grown up dining in the distinguished restaurant, dressed in a brand-new suit that I had made. Watching the medal winners for the best product in the various categories walking down the runway, I dreamed of having this honor someday.

Before I joined Dad in his business, he tailored only men's clothing. Finding it more challenging and creative to tailor ladies coats and suits, I started to add ladies' attire to the production; using French magazines and Vienna fashion plates for ideas, it became successful.

# Chapter 37

For my twenty-first birthday, October 3, 1955, my parents planned a party for my friends and I. Mom cooked all kinds of interesting hors d´oeuvres and finger foods, and Dad bought a case of delicious white wine from his friend who had a vineyard on the Mosel. Celebrating with six of my closest friends and a few girls, we had a blast. My parents had every intention to let us have fun without them, but we eventually coaxed them into participating in the party. Dad was always ready for a good time. With singing, and lots of jokes, we polished off thirty bottles of wine. That party, and the thirty bottles of wine, is still a topic of conversation among my friends today.

However, that evening was also a bittersweet event. I knew that my parents contemplated immigrating to the United States. Ready-made clothes replaced custom tailoring. Something needed to be done.

One day in 1955, Mom and Dad sat me down in the living room and said, "We have something important to talk about."

"Gee, I said, another brother or sister?"

Dad laughed and said, "No, not this time."

I wondered, what could be so important that we needed to have a family pow wow?

Dad continued, "You know Allo; all three of us work very hard and spending many hours in the shop."

"I know, dad," I said, and thought, *are you telling me something new, I hardly see my friends any more.* Dad continued, "When we count all the hours that we work, our income is less than that of our employees. The custom tailoring business is going to the dogs. Very few people want to spend the money for costume tailored clothes anymore. They are turning to ready-made clothes. You are getting older, and some day you will have a family; but the business will not be able to support all of us. I have a cousin in America, 'Uncle Erich,' who was never known as a hard worker, but he is doing very well. Since the three of us are not afraid to work, I think we can make some money over there. For that reason, Mom and I have decided to immigrate to America. What do you think?"

I was stunned. All I could think of, *I must leave everything I love, my friends, and go to a country where I cannot even speak the language.*

Dad, seeing my anguish, said, "Well, this is not for sure. First, we must see whether Uncle Erich can get a sponsor and whether quotas are available for the USA. Otherwise, we will try Brazil or Canada."

Very quietly, I said, "Okay." That night I went to bed with a heavy heart and did not sleep a wink. After thinking it through and praying for guidance, I slowly came around. I figured if Mom and Dad, who are much older, could deal with that, so can I. Then I started to look at it as an adventure. From my friend's grandfather, who had lived in Brazil for several years, we had heard all kinds of adventure stories. I am sure very few were true, but by the next morning, when I got up, I was ready to take on the world.

Dad, knowing that I had overcome my anxiety said, "Nothing ventured, nothing gained. You come from a strong family, you are a Lohn."

To receive an Immigration Visa, in 1956, was not easy. First, an American citizen had to take fiscal responsibility for the immigrant for a period of five years. Second, you had to go on a waiting list, and if the quota for the year was full, you waited until the next year.

146

Mom and Dad wrote to Uncle Erich who promptly replied, "We would love to have you come over. Friends of ours, German's but American citizens, are willing to sponsor you. Start putting the application together for the American Consulate and we will process the papers for the sponsorship."

We filled out all the required papers, including yours truly signing a form to register for the draft within six months after arriving in the United States. Then the sweating began as we wondered if the United States Government would accept us? Would there be a problem because of my brother's bout with the brain infection? Does our line of work make us eligible, and how long will it take to get a Visa?

Those questions weighed heavily on our minds and put us in a state of uneasy limbo. Not sure of the outcome, we had told no one. Several months of anxious waiting had gone by when a large, official-looking envelope came in the mail stating that we were accepted. We had to appear at the American Consulate in Frankfurt for a physical, an oral interview, and the final signing of the papers.

Ready for the adventure, I jumped for joy over the news and could not wait to finally tell my friends. It had now become an adventure for me. Mom and Dad had mixed feelings—happy that all was going well, but the finality; going to an unknown country made them apprehensive. Now we needed to face the task of telling the news to friends and relatives. The responses were anywhere from, *how can you do this,* to, *I wish I could go with you.* My close friends were sad, and others called me *a traitor to your country.*

However, my old friend, Gerhard, was all excited for me and immediately said, "Boy, I would like to come too. Can you find me a sponsor?" We promised to find someone, and we did.

The trip to the American Consulate in Frankfurt went smoothly. Contrary to German government institutions, I thought this one was very relaxed and friendly, which made me comfortable. However, we found out this was not the case with most of the would-be immigrants. People were tense and nervous. After a day of physicals, interviews, and paper signing, we received our Immigration Visas.

Now came the time for preparation. Dad arranged with Holmes Lines for tickets on the vessel Italia, sailing on November 6, 1956 from Hamburg to New York.

"We will make the cruise into a vacation trip," said Dad. Therefore, my parents started to figure out what we would take, and what would be sold. A local carpenter made a wooden container, 6'X14'X4' for all the items we would take.

In the meantime, my friend Gerhard and I started collecting any reading material on America that we could find and specifically, Philadelphia where my aunt and uncle lived. American magazines, with pictures of wide highways, full of big fancy cars running through mountains and along the ocean, were exciting. Gerhard, who studied English in school, interpreted and taught me some words. At the British garrison in Cologne, the two of us attended English and American movies. With chewing gum in our mouths, we tried to imitate the Yankee Dialect as well as the walk and behavior of James Dean. We were ready to take on the adventures of the Wild West."

# Chapter 38

When the business and the furniture were sold, piece by piece, trepidation and regrets started to creep in to my parent's minds. I found out that Mom had ripped up a set of application papers once before they turned in the current ones.

Fear of the unknown and going to a strange land with no friends, got me down many times. However, the quest for adventure always would win out. I can imagine the turmoil my parents must have gone through—fighting off feelings of fear, anxiety, and loneliness at leaving behind all that was familiar to them. With Dad being forty-nine years of age, and Mom forty-two, their roots ran deep in Schlebusch with close friends and family that they had known their whole life. This was a very courageous undertaking for them, and all to gain a better life for their sons.

It had to have been equally traumatic for my grandparents, especially Opa who loved my little brother so much. Being a grandfather today, I can feel the anguish that they must have felt. They did not know when or whether they would see us ever again.

For my parents, doubt, regret, and the temptation to call it off, must have been a daily companion. However, they hid their feelings well—except for one day. After a get-together with his friends, Dad came home sloshed. He kept walking back and forth like a caged animal shaking his head and not listening to anyone. About twenty minutes later, he went out into the cold dark night and stood behind the shed staring in front of him. Not moving, not listening, and not responding to anyone begging him to come inside.

Mom and I were afraid that he might do himself harm, and Opa was already in bed asleep. "Go wake up Opa," Mom said. I went to get him.

Opa went outside, took dad in his arms and hugged him. Dad broke down crying. However, after a few minutes, Opa was able to put him to bed. The next morning, my Dad had a whale of a hangover, but he told us, "Do not worry. I am okay."

From that point on, he never looked back and never got into the dumps again. His only regret was that he had not immigrated twenty years earlier.

****

Goodbyes were said, tears were shed, and promises made to stay in touch at the many going-away parties. The belongings that we were taking, were packed into the big wooden crate, and picked up by the shipping company. We did not see them again until we arrived in New York. We were down to the wire with only our clothes, a bed, a sleeper couch, and few pieces of furniture that friends had bought and would pick up after our departure. It really hit home. Another week and we would leave all this behind, hopefully in search for bigger and better times.

On the day we left for Hamburg, choking with emotions and tears in our eyes, we hugged my grandparents for the last time, never to see Opa again. My friends, and my parent's friends, brought us to the train station in Cologne. The waiting time was past with jokes and laughter to overcome the parting sorrow. When the train pulled into the station, everybody helped to stow away the many suitcases, and with the last hugs and best wishes, we boarded the train. As the train pulled away from the station, we leaned out of the window, waving to our friends until they had faded in the distance. Dad sat down with tears in his eyes and said, "Off to a new beginning in the Promised Land." Off we went to the Land of Milk and Honey.

# Chapter 39

Arriving in Hamburg, everything was well organized. The cruise company took charge of our luggage at the train station and deposited them into our cabin. We boarded a small bus that took us to the harbor. It was still too early to embark, so we went into a restaurant across the pier. Looking out of the window, we were astonished at the size of the ship. It was the first time that I saw the ocean. I had only seen riverboats and barges before, but this ship was huge!

After a nice lunch, we moseyed down to the pier and boarded the ship. The Italia was a fancy cruise liner later used in the TV series *The Love Boat*. We were taken to our cabin, which was not the lowest price accommodation but certainly small and claustrophobic. However, it was above the water level. There was a porthole between the upper bunks. The friendly Italian crew was professional and made sure that our luggage was in the cabin. After making us familiar with the amenities, the steward informed us, that in forty-five minutes there would be a *Captain's Farewell Party* in the lounge on the main deck.

The cabin was equipped with a tiny bathroom and two narrow lower bunks, one on each wall. Above them were narrow foldaway bunks for my brother and myself. Space was so tight; you had to turn sideways to pass one another.

At the prescribed time, we went to the lounge for the farewell bash. The ship's large orchestra played soft romantic music. Buffets were set up with all kinds of elaborate hors d'oeuvres and waiters were serving wine and champagne. It was impressive. The party lasted about an hour. Then the ship's foghorn blasted three times. It was the sign for all visitors to leave the ship and return to port in preparation for the cast off.

Getting the visitors off the ship took a little while, but the service and music continued. By the time the ship was ready to leave, a storm had developed and the sea was very choppy. We were wondering whether we would get under way. At about 6:00 p.m., a loud whistle blew several times and so did the foghorn— it was time to cast off. While the orchestra played, *It's good-bye, yes, good-bye! Far away, I must go away I must go. Fare thee well, my dear, do not cry!* The ship pulled away from the pier.

With the assistance of two tugboats, the Italia turned into the wind and steered towards the open sea. The further out we went, the rougher the water and weather became. Huge swells rolled the ship, lifting it up and down with waves coming over the bow. Well, not to worry; we were inside and the captain, hopefully, knew what he was doing. After watching the angry sea for a while, we returned to our cabin to freshen up and get dressed for dinner.

Mom looked a little pale, but she did make it to supper. All the tables had boards that were flipped up to prevent the dishes from sliding off. Wine glasses were only filled halfway. If we did not want the wine to end up on our neighbor's plate, we needed to hold onto our glasses. However, I was in luck; a family with an attractive young girl was assigned to our table; wow to that.

After the captain toasted the passengers to a safe and enjoyable voyage, dinner was served. The meal was outstanding with appetizers, salad, soup, a choice of several entrees and fantastic desert.

The stewards kept filling the glasses with red wine, white wine, and champagne, whatever you wished to drink. It was wonderful, but Mom lasted only through the salad before she ran off. Dad went after her, and in a little while came back grinning his devilish smile saying, "I think Neptune got to Mom, she is lying down." From there on, Mom only moved from the bed to the lounge chair and back to bed. She stayed horizontal all the way to New York.

After we were finished with dinner, we went to the ballroom for wine and dancing. I very quickly joined up with a group of fourteen young guys and girls. We danced the night away. Heavy seas did not bother us, it just added to the fun. The young girl from our table was delightful to be with. Holding her close during the slow dances made my skin tingle.

When I climbed into the upper bunk in the wee hours of the morning, the bunk rocked back, forth, and sideways. The ceiling, being only one and a half foot away from my face, kept me awake for a while.

When I woke up the next morning, I bumped my head against the wall. *Boy, this bucket sure is rocking and rolling,* I thought. I looked through the porthole and saw only water; a moment later, I saw only sky. That is when I realized that heavy waves rolled the ship from starboard to portside and back.

While my parents and brother were still asleep, I quickly shaved, showered, got dressed, and went up to the forward lounge on the main deck. I was ready for day two out of five sailing days.

Some of my new friends from the night before were already there. Totally in awe, we watched the bow of the ship dip deep into the waves, reappear pointing upwards, and then climb the next swell with water washing over the front deck. What a sight it was to watch the fury of nature creating mountains and valleys on the ocean. The angry sea tossed the huge ship around as if it were a toy. Ropes were strung all along the deck from bow to stern and sailors in foul weather gear were holding on and pulled themselves forward.

We wanted to go outside and test our sea worthiness; the sea did not flood the first-class deck; it was several floors up. "There is no one on the upper deck, maybe we can sneak up there," said one of the fellows and off we went towards the first class.

A sailor, standing at parade rest, guarding the door said, "You cannot go in there."

We replied, "But there is no one on the first-class deck, can't we look outside?"

"Well," the sailor said, "the fine folks from first-class are not going to venture out on deck, they will be hiding out in their staterooms calling for room service. Okay, why not? However, take this door, it takes you right outside. Now, you people must be careful out there. You must hold onto the ropes—that wind is strong."

Up the steps and out on the deck we went. Boy, that sailor was not kidding. Holding on for dear life, we pulled ourselves along to the front where the wind pushed us against the wall of the bridge. There we were safe, and with the wind and spray of salt water whipping our faces, we sang old sailors songs and watched the ship rock and roll. Breakfast time was approaching, so we worked our way back into the bowels of the ship.

After changing into dry clothes, all of us, except Mom, went to the dining room. She turned green every time she lifted her head. My lady friend, looking all prettied up, was already at the table. Unlike Mom, the fury of the sea did not affect Dad's, my little brother's, the young lady's, or my appetite.

We ate a hearty breakfast, after which we, the young men, and women, congregated in the day lounge to get acquainted. We passed the time telling jokes, singing to the tunes of an accordion a fellow from Hamburg was playing, and with 'ahs and oohs,' watched the gigantic waves.

Snuggling up to the pretty girl, Marissa, and enjoying the company of my new friends was grand. I had not encountered this experience before. Lunchtime came, dinner went, and with *Wine Women and Song,* like Johann Strauss' waltz, the evening began. We drank the golden wine from Rhine and danced the night away until the music stopped.

Marissa, keeping always in close contact, looked at me with bedroom eyes. Wow, that girl was different; she gave me goose bumps. Looking deep into each other's eyes, in the middle of a wonderful waltz, the ship made a sudden move and the two of us fell over a table, cleaning off the glasses full of wine into the laps of the unsuspecting guests. I think the girl at home was sending me a message not to get too carried away. We were embarrassed and apologized but continued to dance. After the music stopped, I brought Marissa to her cabin, said good night and went to our cabin. The swaying of the ship put me to sleep in seconds.

It was morning of day three, the weather had not changed, and the ship was still being tossed around like a toy in the heavy seas. I went into my usual routine of cleaning up and going to breakfast. The day went by as the day before, with a first-class deck adventure, singing and having fun with Marissa. Here and there, I stole a kiss from her.

After lunch, suddenly, the ship slowed down. The captain came on the intercom system and announced that one of the engines had broken down. That they were trying to fix it, but there might be a possibility of a delay in our arrival. However, he assured us that we did not need to worry and it would not affect the safety of the ship. We had no problem with a few extra days at sea and jubilantly clapped our hands.

That evening was *Captains Night*. Everyone got dressed up in evening attire for dinner. Dad was dressed in his tuxedo, Mom in a pretty evening dress, Hans looked cute with a little bow tie, and yours truly in his maroon velvet tuxedo. Marissa wore a black velvet dress and sat next to me.

Yes, this time Mom was able to attend dinner. She had gotten some Dramamine from the ship's dispensary. That night we had the honor of-El Capitano-sitting at our table. After the customary toast, a lavish dinner was served. For dessert, the lights dimmed, and the stewards marched in carrying Baked Alaska complete with lit candles. It certainly was romantic. Moreover, when Marissa looked at me and stroked my leg, it did not escape my parent's eyes. Dad grinned his wicked smile, and Mom gave me the evil eye that said, *be careful, son.*

The Captain's Ball followed the dinner. It was a wonderful evening with entertainment and dancing. Mom and Dad were sitting at a table with friends they had made during the three days at sea. Among them was a gentleman from New England, who got bored in first-class and preferred our kind of fun, and a Catholic Priest who always said at midnight, "Hurray, I have another hour before I must stop eating and drinking!" Passing through the different time zones gave us an extra hour every night.

The evening ended, and as usual, I accompanied Marissa to her cabin, gave her a shy good night kiss in front of her parents and went to bed.

Days four, five, and six went by like the others; except we were two days delayed and would not get into New York until day seven. Since we were having an enjoyable time, it was not difficult to swallow. Marissa had not changed either. In fact, she was really coming on to me. Taking my hand, she led me down to her cabin. With her parents and brother upstairs in the lounge, we went inside, and she started to kiss me very passionately. A tingling feeling crawled up my spine and I thought, *oh, boy, is this going to be the weak hour of fifty-five minutes?* This thought put me into a bind, as I was not in love with her. Those feelings still belonged to my hometown sweetheart, however, passion was riding high, and I was struggling with my sense of loyalty, commitment to honor, and saving sex for marriage. Temptations were about to win when I heard the key unlocking the door. Her parents entered and embarrassed, we went up to the lounge. Our honor was saved by the bell, or if you prefer, by the key in the door.

The excitement of soon seeing the shores of the United States of America grew by the minute. After the last dance in the night of day six, we packed and got our luggage ready to put outside in the wee hours of the morning. For most of the night, I was awake waiting for dawn to arrive. At 6:00 a.m. we got up, showered, dressed, and went upstairs. The wind had calmed down and the sea was quiet. People were arriving on deck hoping to get a glimpse of the Statue of Liberty. With the sun trying to break through the fog, my friends and I were waiting for the big moment. As the sky cleared, there she was; the Lady Liberty, the most beautiful lady, and the gateway to the land of opportunity—what a sight it was with the skyline of New York in the background.

Excited, we went to have our final breakfast on board. After that, the ship docked in the New York Harbor. It took a couple of hours before freight and luggage were unloaded and we could disembark. First-class passengers went ashore first, then returning passengers, and last were the emigrants. Wishing each other well, with last good byes and a kiss, we left the ship.

# Chapter 40

Getting in line at Immigration was the first stop. After handing over our papers, which were checked and stamped, we received a temporary green card, and officially entered the US of A. After we exited the Immigration hall, we entered the customs area. Belongings were lined up alphabetically by last names. We went to the letter "L" and found our crate and luggage. Before a custom official could clear the contents of the crate and luggage, we had to get a longshoreman and pay him $50.00 to open the crate and after inspection seal it again, for shipping to its destination. The custom officer took a quick look and stamped the papers. My friend, Gerhard, who worked for a custom brokerage and freight forwarding company in Cologne, had arranged for our belongings to be moved on to Philadelphia.

All set, we grabbed a porter and with our luggage moved on to the waiting room where Uncle Erich greeted us with a big "Hello!" and a hug. In the parking area, we saw for the first time his big black Cadillac. It was a used car, but it was still very impressive. We stowed away our luggage and drove off to Philadelphia. My parents exchanged all the latest news with my uncle while I was in awe over the big buildings and fancy cars.

Fifteen minutes went by, when my uncle informed us that he was lost. He went to ask someone and said, "Okay." However, not all was all right. After twenty-minutes of driving around in circles, we were still in New York trying to find the Lincoln Tunnel. Well, he had a nice car, but I became a little skeptical about his driving ability. We stopped again and Dad said, "Go out and help Uncle Erich; you are good with directions."

"Okay," I said and joined my uncle. I did not understand much if anything of the conversation, but it dawned on me, maybe neither did my uncle. Together we were able to get the police officer to draw us a map. Finally, we were able to find the tunnel and the New Jersey Turnpike.

Moving along towards Philadelphia, the big highway with the many cars and trucks was imposing. However, what really caught my eye were all those huge billboards, which certainly were different. A couple of hours later, we exited the turnpike and got onto the Roosevelt Boulevard in Philadelphia. Wow, it was an enormous road! Driving along the Boulevard, taking in the sights of the unaccustomed architecture of the city, where we were about to make our home. We finally arrived in the Germantown section where my uncle lived.

My aunt and uncle, with their eleven-year-old daughter, had an apartment in a two-story Brownstone home on 22$^{nd}$ Street. Aunt Anni, and Cousin Monika, greeted us with heartfelt sincerity and then they gave us the cook's tour; we were impressed. They had two bedrooms, a nice living-dining room, a kitchen, and bathroom with hot and cold running water—that was a luxury. We used to take a bath in the basement laundry room and heated up the water in a kettle.

In the living room they had a beautiful German Gründig cabinet radio with a record player and a lit-up bar. However, most impressive was the big TV. No one in our town had a television set in those days. This was indeed the land of opportunity. It was Sunday, my uncle turned on the German language news. The commentator at that moment said, "The inventory of pigs in Germany has been drastically reduced."

Breaking out in laughter Dad said, "Yes, a shipload just came into the US."

Before we left Germany, my parents exchanged their money into dollars and traveler's checks. Around, at the traditional coffee and cake hour, ad gave my cousin $5.00 and said, "would you go and get some pastries?" He was thinking of German cake like the French pastries.

My aunt said, "They do not have German cake here, but she can get donuts."

"Okay," Dad said, and off went my cousin to get donuts, while my aunt put on the coffee pot.

After a couple of minutes, Monika came in with a box of donuts she could hardly carry. In 1956, for $5.00 you could buy enough donuts to feed an army for a week. We could not believe our eyes.

My aunt said, "I thought you gave her one dollar." We ate donuts for a week.

Then my aunt asked, "Would you like to take a stroll through the neighborhood?"

"We'd love to," we answered, and out we went for a stroll.

Walking through the streets of Germantown, Mom said, "How come all the streets and people have the same name here, One Way and Letter?"

My uncle and aunt broke into laughter and explained what *one way* and *letter* meant.

In the evening, a friend of Uncle Erich came to visit. He was a German that had immigrated many years ago. He was an insurance salesperson.

Wine was served, and the party began. He was a nice person, but we had a difficult time understanding him. Besides, having a heavy *Schwäbisch* accent, he mixed so many English words into the conversation that it was no longer recognizable as German. However, he knew many business people and said he would find us all a job, and he would sponsor my friend Gerhard to immigrate.

163

Uncle Erich had already secured a temporary job for me at a German costume tailor on Fifth Street. With wine and jokes, my first day in the USA ended. We planned to explore the city the next day and go apartment hunting after my uncle and aunt came home from work.

# Chapter 41

It was our first Monday morning in Philadelphia. My aunt and uncle had gone to work and Monika to school. Dad said, "Allo, take us into the city, you speak English." My English vocabulary did not exceed much beyond the words: bread, meat, coffee, and cigarettes.

Since all three of us smoked, our cigarette of choice became Chesterfield, because that word was familiar to us. A fly-front men's topcoat in Germany was called a Chesterfield.

This reminds me of a joke—An Italian had taught his newly emigrated brother to say, *Apple pie and ice cream*, so he could get something to eat while he was at work. After three weeks, eating apple pie, and ice cream for lunch, he asked his brother to teach him how to ask for another dish. His brother said, "That is easy. Ask for steak."

"Okay," the new emigrant said very proudly to the waitress at lunchtime, the new word his brother had taught him, "Steak."

The waitress looked at him and said, "How would you like it cooked?"

The new emigrant looked bewildered, but after a few seconds replied, "Apple pie and ice cream."

That is about how I felt when Dad asked me to take them downtown. Lucky for me, my Aunt had written down, *Round trip to Reading Terminal, 3 adults and one child.*

When we went to the train station, I stopped at the ticket window. I had remembered Reading Terminal but was too proud to use the note my aunt had written down. It made me feel like a child. Addressing the ticket agent, I said, "Reading Terminal" and held up 3 1/2 fingers.

Puzzled, the agent looked at me dumbfounded and said, "What?"

Blushing, I took out my piece of paper and gave it to him. He looked at the piece of paper and laughed saying, "Okay."

Excited to explore downtown Philadelphia, I paid and boarded the train. We loved the city with all its stores, city hall with William Penn on top, and Independence Hall that we had heard so much about.

The prices were unbelievable. You could get a pair of shoes for $5.00, a shirt for $2.50 and so forth. When we got hungry, we walked into Horn & Hardard, an automated restaurant. There you could buy food without being able to speak the language. All you had to do was put the coins into the machine and open the door of your choice. The food looked great, the taste was something altogether different, but it filled our stomach. After all the walking, we were tired. We took the next train home without getting lost.

When my aunt came home from work, she took us to see an apartment that was for rent on 22$^{nd}$ Street, a block down the street from their place. It was a first-floor apartment with one bedroom, living-dining room combination, and a kitchen with room for a table and chairs. A very friendly Irish couple, Jimmy and Kate, owned the two-story row house. We rented the apartment and went back to my aunts where we ate and watched Gun Smoke without understanding a single word.

# Chapter 42

The next Saturday, Erich and Anni took us to the Olney section in Philadelphia, which was predominantly German. We were introduced to a German deli, signed up in the German speaking church, opened a bank account, and went to Becker's furniture store that was owned by Ed Becker, who became our long-time friend. We needed furniture and were happy to find fair prices for quality merchandise.

The next day at church, we met our benefactors who had sponsored us. They invited my uncle, aunt, and us for dinner at their house. It was a wonderful dinner. They were a generous family who owned a dry-cleaning store. He was a member of the Colping's Verein, a German Catholic club that ran inexpensive hotels for young men, like the YMCA. However, this one was mostly a social club for Immigrants. Dad, a green immigrant, only a few days in the country was already recruited into a club.

Within a week, the crate with the stuff from home arrived and Ed delivered our new furniture. Now we were all set and had our own apartment. I started to work at the German tailor, but it was not what I had envisioned. Expecting the same fine quality work, I was used to, this was only mediocre, ready-wear clothes made to measure, and mostly constructed by machine. I was used to the old pedal sewing machines and not the electric motor driven ones. Every time I touched the drive plate, the machine ran away on me. I did more ripping than sewing, but after a week, I had learned how to master the beast.

Mr. Hans W, the friend of my uncle, came by and asked, "How is it going?"

"All right," I said, but I think he knew I was not very enthusiastic about the job.

He said, "I want to take you on Saturday to a factory that makes army uniforms. I know the owner and he need help."

Dad and I started at the factory a couple of weeks later. Of course, without understanding the language, we were doing menial jobs like basting lapels on army greens. With all my knowledge of the trade, this was as boring as it could get. I thought, *if I must do this all my life, I will die*, but dared not to complain, because we had an income.

A German tailor we got to know through church, said to me, "You are still young; the best thing you can do is get out of the apparel industry, start at a machine shop, and learn to operate a lathe machine. You cannot make money in this industry."

I was at a low point—not knowing the language, no friends, and doing a job not even worthy of a first-year apprentice. It really had me depressed. There had to be a way I could use my talents, but first I needed to learn English. Someone told me that one could learn the language by watching and listening to the action on TV. Reading my cousin's comic books helped. The text was supplemented with drawings.

It was a painful time. Hans went to the Catholic School with Monika and repeated the first grade to catch up with the language, which he did very quickly. Neither my parents nor I complained. We did not let each other know how we really felt. Day after day, we went and basted lapel points.

Again, Mr. Hans W came to the rescue. He had found two expensive Italian tailor shops downtown and each of them needed help. On a Saturday, he took us to the shops. We were both hired. The shops were on Walnut Street, separated by a block. Hurrah! Finally, we were back into the fine tailoring that we knew.

# Chapter 43

We gave the factory owner a week's notice. He understood that the work we were doing in his factory was not for us. That evening we were all invited to celebrate the good news at Mr. Hans W's home. He was a great cook and had prepared a delicious meal. After eating, we convened in his finished basement, which was beautifully furnished with a bar. Over the shelves, with the many bottles of liquor and wine, was a sign and a clock. The sign said, "I never drink before 6:00 p.m." However, the clock was stuck permanently at six. The mood was up and everybody had a good time drinking, singing, and feeling no pain.

When we started our new jobs, I told Dad in the trolley car going to work, "When you leave the shop tonight, make a left turn and I will be waiting for you in front of the store." I did not want him to get lost.

At 5:00 P.M, I went outside and waited. Fifteen minutes had gone by and Dad had not shown up yet. Another fifteen minutes, and he still had not shown up. Well, I figured he must have been working overtime. This being before cell phones, I passed the time by walking up and down the street looking at store windows. Then, an hour later, there was still no Dad. Therefore, I walked over to the tailor shop where he was working and waited in front of the door. I figured he would come out soon.

Someone came out, but it was not my dad. He locked the door. *Oh, boy,* I thought, *where is dad?* In my broken English I asked the man, "Is my dad still inside?"

He answered; "He left a long time ago."

169

What to do now, was the $60,000 question. Searching for him in a city of 1.5 million people, would be like looking for a needle in a haystack. Worried half to death, I went home. Mom asked, "Where is dad?"

I replied, "I do not know."

"What do you mean you do not know?" Asked mom.

"Dad did not show up! The boss from the tailor shop said, that he had left at five o'clock."

Mom was visibly shaken and started to cry, so we went over to my uncle's and told them what happened. "Oh, my god!" They said. "How can we find him in a city of millions? The police will not look for him until he is at least a couple of days missing."

They called Mr. Hans W, who came over right away. It was dark, hours had gone by, and all of us were worried that harm had come to him. Suddenly, the doorbell rang, and there stood Dad in front of the door laughing.

Mom's worry turned to anger and lacing into him she, said, "Where have you been? Where were you? We were all worried sick."

Dad, very nonchalantly said, "If you calm down, I will tell you," and so he did. "When I came out of the shop, I turned left, as you had told me. However, I left through the back door and could not find you. After a while, I was totally lost. I tried to ask people and pointed at my ticket, but one sent me one-way, and another sent me in a different direction. A couple of hours went by; and I was still running around in circles getting more and more lost. Out of my wits of what to do, I approached another, but older man. Trying to explain that I was lost, he very politely listened with a grin. Helplessly looking at him, I expected another dead end. Then the man said in my Cologne dialect, "Where are you from, you dumb snuck."

At that point, we all had to laugh. The man had taken Dad to the trolley and physically put him in the streetcar, so he would not get lost again. Dad remembered the trolley stop where he needed to get out. It was right behind a store with mirrors. Then the anxiety returned. He worried that if they redecorated the window and took the mirrors out; he would not know where to get out, because all the brownstones looked alike to him.

I am sure every immigrant has his or her own story to tell. Getting along without the language skills in a strange country has its anxieties but also its humorous side.

# Chapter 44

Through a German group, Mom found a job working as a seamstress at Van Horn's, the largest maker of theatrical costumes on the East Coast. Mr. Van Horn, an elderly Dutch gentleman, who spent little time at the business, owned the company. Mr. Weidler, a German-American, and a friend of Mr. Hans W, was the general manager, and Mr. Valentino, an elderly Italian gentleman, ran the manufacturing division. Mom worked for Matilde, also a German-American, who ran the ladies department.

Mom loved her job. Every night she came home all excited telling us how creative the work was. She was making costumes for different Broadway shows. She described the dazzling dresses she was working on for the Orange Bowl, and the amazing string band outfits with the big plumed headpieces the men's department were making. Knowing how I enjoyed the creativity of the trade, she said, "Allo, you would love to work there!"

After a couple of weeks, hearing how much she enjoyed her work, she came home one night all excited. The general manager, Mr. Weidler, had spoken to her. In the conversation, Mom had mentioned that both dad and I were tailors. Mr. Weidler had said, he would like to speak to me. The company was looking for someone that could take over Mr. Valentino's job. He wanted to retire. Mr. Weidler told her that so far, no one that applied for the position had the creative talent to replace Mr. Valentino. Naturally, I was thrilled and told Mom to arrange an appointment for an interview.

Nervous, I went to see Mr. Weidler armed with pictures of items I had made like ballroom dresses, uniforms, and costumes for two dance groups etc. He took me into his office and conversed with me in German, which helped to put me at ease. At least I did not have to conduct my interview by using sign language!

He was a very distinguished looking gentleman with white hair wearing gold-rimmed eyeglasses. After the usual small talk, he explained to me the company's different operations and structure. Then he asked me, "Would you like to work here?"

Enthusiastically I replied, "Yes!"

I showed him the pictures of the garments I made before. After he studied them, he said, "Very nice," and smiled. --So far so good. Then he said, "However, it will depend on Mr. Valentino who runs the department. If he likes you, you can start in the New Year."

With that, he excused himself and went out of the office. After a while, he came back with an elderly gentleman and introduced him as Mr. Valentino. We all sat down and then with Mr. Weidler as the interpreter, Mr. Valentino questioned me about what I had done and how I had learned my trade. Mr. Weidler showed him the pictures of my garments and his face lit up. Patting me on the shoulder he said, "That is nice. I like you to come and work for me."

When Mr. Weidler translated that to me, I was ready to jump for joy and said, "Yes, when do you want me to start?"

"Right away," he said. Mr. Valentino, an Italian immigrant with a heavy accent, knew I would learn the language quickly; and he knew how the trade was taught in the old country.

For whatever reason, Mr. Valentino took a liking to me. He became my most enthusiastic mentor. With him as mentor and Mr. Weidler as my biggest supporter and confidant, I began my career in America. Not in my wildest dreams had I imagined

174

anything like that. I capitalized on my knowledge and talent. To the contrary of the discouraging news from the tailor friend in the German community, I had a chance to become the head of the manufacturing division.

Mr. Valentino took me on a tour and explained the different departments. There was the men's department, the ladies department, a hat department, a wig department, and an accessories department. All kinds of elaborate costumes from around the world and through the ages, were being made there. As well as some wild fantasy costumes that some designer had dreamed up like dragons, bears etc.

The accessory department made anything that could not be bought—from jewelry, headdresses for string bands, weapons, armors, and uppers for shoes and boots. He showed me the warehouse full of three million rental costumes.

I was totally at awe and with a friendly pat on the back, and a smile, Mr. Valentino said, "See you Monday!"

With that, my career got its start in the land of milk and honey. Thrilled and overjoyed, I felt like hop skipping all the way home and went to the trolley stop. Then it hit me, and I thought, *Can I really do this kind of work? I do not know anything about the history of garments through the ages and across the globe. What if they ask me to make a pattern for some of these Elizabethan costumes? What am I doing? Am I getting in over my head?*

Suddenly, my joy was replaced by fear and anxiety. When I got home and told my parent's I had the job, Mom and Dad were ecstatic. However, when I mentioned my apprehensions and fears, Dad, like always, calmed me down and boosted my confidence. Immediately I hit the books and started to study the history of costumes through the ages.

# Chapter 45

Our first Christmas in the USA was fast approaching. In Germany, we had heard stories about how no one celebrated Christmas like in Germany. They said that in America, they did not even have Christmas trees. Contrary to that belief, in America it seemed to us that people were trying to outdo each other with who had the nicest tree and decorations. The houses were decorated with lights creating a spectacular show, thus, making liars out of the storytellers back home in Germany.

We all went to the midnight mass at the German church with aunt, uncle, and cousin on Christmas Eve. We thanked the good Lord for all the blessings He had bestowed upon us; and all was well. We had a nice apartment. We had an income; I had a job that was challenging and creative.

When I started working with Mr. Valentino, my fears soon subsided when I realized that Mr. Valentino would teach me and was very patient with my lack of language skills. When I brought the wrong fabric, like sateen instead of satin because sateen was a term we used in Germany but not satin, he would just laugh and show me the difference.

We celebrated New Year's Eve at Mr. Hans W's house with German songs and plenty of wine. On New Year's Day, I watched with excitement the Orange Bowl Parade with costumes made by Van Horn. Van Horn's also made the costumes for the Ferko string band who won first prize for costumes that year.

Every weekend I looked forward to Monday, awaiting a new and exciting challenge. Still studying hard, my English was improving.

One day I heard from my friend Gerhard that his paperwork for the Immigration Visa was progressing, that made me glad. Hopefully, I would soon see my best friend in the USA.

Weekends were very difficult for me. I was used to lots of friends and familiar surroundings. In Philadelphia, walking the streets alone was extremely lonely. The downtown area was a busy place with lots of stores, restaurants, movies, and theaters. Yet, being amidst a crowd of people can be the most lonely and depressing place, if you have no one with whom you can talk and share your likes or dislikes. I would go to the movies in the Germantown section. There was a cute girl at the ticket counter, but I could not converse with her. I always had the feeling that when she saw me she thought, *here comes the friendly dummy again.* After the movie, I would do some more window-shopping and watch people rushing by, not noticing that I was even there. It always made me feel lost. Walking among millions of people that did not notice you, and whose language you could not speak, is the loneliest place on earth.

I began to hate the weekends and could not wait for Monday. One time, a son of my uncle's friend, and another young fellow picked me up and took me to the Cannstätter, which was a German club. Boy was I happy to make some contact with other young guys who spoke German—but that was short-lived. When we got to the club, we teamed up with three girls who only spoke English. They all jabbered away and had fun while I had to sit there not understanding more than a word here and there. After a while, I was totally ignored and felt that some of their fun was at my expense—the dumb outsider, the fifth wheel on the cart.

That was the day I slipped into a real depression and all I thought off, was, *when is my friend Gerhard coming?*

My parents and I went with my uncle and aunt to the various German clubs. They enjoyed clubbing and I had hoped to contact some young people my age. Well, there were no young people at the clubs; all of them were my parent's age or older. What made matters worse, by midnight they were all sloshed and cried in their beer being homesick. I needed that like a hole in the head. Oh, how I hated Sundays! However—then came Monday and I immersed myself in my enjoyable work!

# Chapter 46

Our company had rented out costumes for a big gala affair for the opening of the Four Seasons Hotel in Philadelphia. The affair was fashioned like a *Mardi Gras* event. The president of a railroad company was the *Prince*, and a wealthy debutant the *Princess*. About twenty people in all were to be dressed in costumes. However, since the guests were from all over the country, they were unable to try the garments on beforehand. Therefore, a tailor was requested to be at the hotel so that when the guests arrived, they were to be fitted and alterations were made if needed.

I was asked to go and happily agreed, I would make some extra money. The pay for that Saturday afternoon was to be sixty dollars, which was as much as I made in a whole week. Besides the money, I was eager to rub shoulders with important people. They were extremely nice and treated me as if I were part of the guest, and not like a little tailor that was too dumb to speak the language. The guests were happy with my work and complimented me to no end. It made me happy. I regretted not to have a better command of the English language, especially since there was no shortage of young girls.

After my work was finished, I was invited to the ballroom where a cocktail party was in full swing. "Help yourself to food and drink, the moderator of the affair told me, and when you are ready to leave, let me know."

When I had enjoyed my fill of the exquisite hors d'oeuvre, and the delicious champagne, I went to the man in charge.

"Okay," he said, "Let me make out a check. You did a superb job."

Not knowing anything about American finances, I replied, "I prefer cash."

"Oh, I am short on cash. You need to come back tomorrow and pick it up," he answered.

"No problem," I said. "I will be coming into town tomorrow anyway." I took the trolley home and was proud of my accomplishment.

Sunday afternoon, I went to the Four Seasons Hotel to collect my money. I approached the front desk and asked for the man that owed me 60 dollars. They informed me that he had checked out.

"Did he leave anything for me?" I asked.

"Let me see," said the desk clerk and went to check. He came back and said, "Sorry, but there is nothing here in your name."

"But he owes me money for the job I did here yesterday," I replied.

"Sorry, there is nothing I can do. You must take this up with the gentleman himself."

With a long face and disappointment, I headed back home. My euphoric bubble had burst. As usual, Dad was the calming mentor and said, "I am sure Mr. Weidler can do something about it."

Monday morning, Mr. Weidler came to see me and said, "The people at the Four Seasons Hotel left me a message. They thanked me for sending you and said you did a wonderful job. They said, you almost remade a whole dress in a truly short time."

"Yes, I did, but they did not pay me." I explained to him what had happened.

He told me that it would have been all right to take his check. "I am sure there is a misunderstanding. He must have left the money there with someone. I will call the hotel."

After a while he came back and angrily said, "That cheap cheat left without leaving your money with the hotel; but do not worry, I know where to get a hold of him. I will get you your money."

Four weeks later, a check arrived with an apology that it had slipped his mind, maybe yes, maybe no. However, the check that I could have had the same night did clear. I was one experience richer.

# Chapter 47

The time had come for me to register for the draft, and so, on July 31, 1957, I went to the Local Board No 145 on Broad Street and did my duty. With the help of the clerk, I filled out my papers. I was not too eager to serve in the military as the war years in Germany were still too vivid in my memory, but I did what all young men had to do.

Four weeks later, I got a notice for my physical. Which was the same day when my friend Gerhard's letter arrived, telling me he had his Visa to emigrate and had booked his voyage. It was a good day—bad day scenario because there was no question in my mind that I would be classified 5-A. However, Gerhard's coming overshadowed the bad news.

Sure enough, with a knock on my back and a knock on my chest, accompanied by the usual frills of military physicals, I was classified 5-A—fit for military duty. Of course, I was told it did not mean I would get drafted. I remember thinking; *yes sure, I was not going to be that lucky.*

****

During all this time, Dad had seen two row houses that were empty on a nice street next to St. Henry's Catholic Church. Dad, eager to buy a house asked a realtor whether they were for sale. The realtor was the brother of our sponsor. "No," he replied, "They belong to the church. They have used them as a kindergarten. The houses have no kitchens but a bunch of toilettes. In addition, there are doorways on the first and second floor connecting the two houses. You really do not want them."

However, Dad was not easily discouraged. He really liked the location. The following Sunday he went to see Pastor Koenig after mass. "I'd like to buy the two properties. How much do you want for them?" Dad asked.

The pastor, who spoke German, said, "They are not for sale." My Dad asked, "But they are empty. Are you going to use them?"

"Well, I have no plans for them now," admitted Father Koenig.

"Then, why don't you give it some thought?" said Dad. Since the pastor spoke fluent German, Dad was able to communicate and negotiate quite comfortably.

"Okay," said the pastor, "I will give it some thought."

Persistent as Dad was, he went back the next Sunday and offered Father Koenig $10,000 for the two homes. To make a long story short, after a long hour, Father Koenig agreed to sell the property to my Dad for the $10,000. The realtor was floored, but my Dad had closed the deal; we were now neighbors of St. Henry' on one side, and our dear friend, Ed Becker and his parents, on the other.

Then the real work began. Working day and night, we refurbished the one house as quickly as we could, so we could live in it.

Dad had found out that a salvage company was selling off kitchen sinks, cabinets, gas stoves, bathtubs, and anything useable from the homes that were being torn down to build a highway. Upon checking it out, he found that quite a few items were in decent shape. Always the negotiator, he was ready to bargain. However, unable to speak English, he went to the demolition supervisor and used sign language to explain that he wanted to buy some appliances and cabinets.

The supervisor laughed, amused over this foreigner that pulled out a dollar bill, waved it in front of him, and said, "Me buy this," and "Me buy that," pointing at himself and then at the items. The supervisor got such a kick out of my Dad; he ended up almost giving the items to him.

Thanks to Dad's keen negotiating skills, we now had enough cabinets and appliances to remodel both homes. We turned the corner house into two apartments and the other one we lived in. It had three bedrooms, a living-dining room combo, a kitchen, and an enclosed porch. It was also on a nice quiet street, and close to stores and transportation. My brother could walk to school and the neighbors became good friends.

The Becker's were of German descent and spoke fluent German, which was nice for Mom and Dad. Both, Mr., and Mrs. Becker were hard of hearing. In addition, their son, Ed, had a problem remembering to take his house key. One night, coming home late without a key, he could not get into his house. Ed rang my parent's doorbell, apologized, and then asked whether he could go through their bedroom, climb out of the window and onto the roof of the porch. Dad, having been there many times in his young days, laughed and said, "Okay, come." Ed climbed out of my parent's bedroom window onto the roof over the porch and through his parent's window into their bedroom, all without Mr. and Mrs. Becker being any the wiser. This became his standard approach when he forgot his keys. Every time he did this, my parents just laughed it off.

# Chapter 48

The day finally came when my friend Gerhard was to arrive in New York. Mr. Hans W graciously offered to drive me to the city and pick up the young man he knew nothing about, but on faith had sponsored him. Not knowing the exact time of his disembarkation, we drove early in the morning to the city. When we arrived at the pier, all the parking lots in front were taken. Mr. Hans W, a man of the world pulled into a *Do not park* space in front of the door. He got out and said, "Come, let's see what time he will get off the ship." Then he walked over to a police officer with a ten-dollar bill in his hand, shook hands in greeting, and asked, "Would you watch my car for a minute? I just want to find out how long the wait is."

"Sure, go ahead," said the police officer.

We went in and found out it would be at least three hours. He said, "All right, let us go and have some breakfast."

When we came out, a different police officer was in front of the door. Seeing us he yelled, "Get this piece of crap out of the no parking zone!"

"But I took care of this with your friend," explained Mr. Hans W.

"I don't care. If you don't hurry, I will give you a ticket," replied the cop.

It turned out these cops had a regular racket going. One cop would collect, and then exchange places with the other cop. Then the new cop would chase you out, so they could collect again from another unsuspecting driver.

After a leisurely breakfast, we went back to the pier and waited for Gerhard to come through customs. Finally, he came out and with a big 'Hello,' I had a friend again.

Gerhard was fluent in both German and English. In addition, being a custom broker and freight forwarder, had arranged for his belongings to be shipped directly to my parent's home. After loading his luggage into the car, we went home.

That evening, we celebrated with friends and family, thus beginning a tradition between Dad and Gerhard. Dad introduced Gerhard to his friend *Julius Wile French Brandy*, which gave both a whale of a headache the next day. Since my Dad was also a long-time friend of Gerhard's father, he consequently became part of our family.

Happy to have a friend again, I told Mr. Weidler about him and his profession. Mr. Weidler, whose name was also Gerhard said, "Bring your friend in when he comes. I can help him with a job. I know the owner of the custom brokerage house that does our imports."

So, I took Gerhard with me to work and Mr. Weidler called the custom broker to arrange an interview for Gerhard. Within a week, Gerhard was working there.

At home, we called Gerhard, Gert for short. When Mr. Weidler heard me say, "Gert," he said, "don't tell anyone your name is Gert. Tell them it is Gerhard because they are going to butcher your name and all you are going to hear is a gurgling sound." Therefore, Gerhard it was from then on just as mine was changed from Allo to Al.

All was perfect now. I had a fantastic job, and a friend again with whom I could explore the new world. My English had improved and I was now able to hold a conversation. A couple of weeks later, Gerhard's company sent him to their New York office. There he stayed at the Colping Society, which, as I mentioned before, had hotels like the YMCA. Now we could explore New York on the weekends. Together we went to Radio City. What an impressive place that was. It had to be the biggest theater, the biggest stage, and the biggest film screen in the world. You even could smoke in there. Leaning back in the plush chairs and having a cigarette, we enjoyed watching the beautiful Rockettes with their long legs dance. Moreover, after that, we watched the newest movie on the big screen. Life was good, life was fun, but the possible induction into the Army, loomed over my head.

# Chapter 49

At the same time Gerhard arrived, I received an 8x11 envelope with the, *Uncle Sam Wants You* letter from the government. It stated, *Report at the Local Board 145 on a certain date and time to be inducted into the army. From there you will be transported to Fort Jackson, SC, for basic training. Failure to appear will be grounds for deportation.*

Well, I had expected this untimely news, but wondered why it had to come when everything was going my way. When I told my boss, he said, "Oh, no, this is our busiest time of the year and I need you here. Let me see what Mr. Weidler can do. Maybe he can get a deferral."

The company sent an official letter requesting a deferment. It was granted; they postponed my enlistment until February 20, 1958. Mr. Valentino said to me, "Ask your dad if he would like to come and work for me."

"I know he would love to work here," I promptly said.

"Then bring him in as soon as possible."

A couple of days later, all three of us were enjoying our work at Van Horn's.

\*\*\*\*

With the day of reckoning moving closer, I tried to enjoy my free time as much as I could. Gerhard had registered for the draft as well, and he, too, was classified 5-A. Six months after my induction, he was drafted.

At lunchtime, on my last day of work, Mr. Valentino cleared off a fifteen-foot cutting table and covered it with a patriotic tablecloth and flowers. A caterer came in and set up a full Italian buffet with Chianti and Pinot Grigio. There were hors d'oeuvres from shrimp to Oysters Rockefeller, from calamari to antipasti, and dishes ranging from veal scaloppini to lasagna and more.

Wow, Mr. Valentino gave me a wonderful, big farewell party! At noon, everyone in the company joined in, and wished me well and a safe return. The party lasted for two hours. My boss gave a speech and was all choked up with tears in his eyes. Afterwards he hugged me, looked into my eyes, and said, "God bless you and keep you safe. Do not stay a day longer than you must because I want you back as soon as possible. I will only stay here until you get back, and then the job is yours." Wiping the tears from his eyes he said, "Stay in touch, and write. Now go home and enjoy the last free hours that you have."

I said my good-byes, thanked everyone for the well-wishing and went home.

****

As ordered, on February 20, 1958 I said good-bye to my friend, my parents, and my little brother. Mom was crying; remembering Dad leaving for the army, and now it was her precious son. At least there was no war. Korea was now quiet, but the Cold War was flourishing, and you never knew what lay ahead.

Dad, unsuccessful at hiding his emotions, said, "May God bless you and keep you safe. Take care, keep your butt down, and do not volunteer for anything." With hugs and kisses all around, I took a last look and then left and took the trolley to the induction center.

Always the tailor, I was dressed in my best suit and tie, a double-breasted wool overcoat and, unbelievably, a hat and leather gloves. When I arrived at the induction center, there was a group of thirty young fellows who gave me strange looks. My dress up did not fit the occasion, as they were all dressed very casually.

Going over to the desk, I checked in. The sergeant frowned, shook his head, and said, "Wait with the others."

I went over and introduced myself. They were a nice bunch of guys, and we all had one thing in common, we really did not want to be there. I found out that one of the fellows, by the name of John, lived on Fifth Street, only a couple of blocks from my parents. Being quasi neighbors, we became friends very quickly.

Another one of the fellows asked, "Hey, Al, why did you dress like that? Did nobody tell you that we must roll our cloths into a small bundle and ship them home when we get there?"

"I am a tailor, I always dress like this," I said. That created a good laugh, but they did not hold it against me.

After a short physical checkup, we were sent into a hall where a lieutenant gave us a speech and an explanation as to what was to happen. I did not have a clue what he had said. I was able to hold a conversation by asking many questions, but understanding a heavy accented speech was a little much. My buddy, John, explained, "We must take the oath of allegiance.

With that the lieutenant called, "Lohn, front and center." I walked up in front of the officer and he said, "Okay Lohn, we are going to take the Oath of allegiance. Do you understand what that means?"

"Yes," I said.

"Good. Now, since you are not an American citizen, you do not have to take the oath. Are you willing to take it?"

"Yes," I said again.

"Then you are taking this at your own free will?"

Again, I said, "Yes."

"Okay, sign here and go back with the others." I signed and returned to the group.

"Attention, fellows!" The officer bellowed, we all stood. "Raise your right hand and repeat after me..." and with that we swore our Oath of Allegiance to the United States of America. Then the lieutenant said, "Congratulations, gentlemen, you are in the army now. Then he turned to the sergeant and said, "Carry on, Sergeant."

The noncom saluted, and the guy with the bars on his shoulders left. *Gee,* I thought *they are very civilized. He called us Gentlemen,* hold that thought.

"I am Sergeant Felix and you are mine for the next couple of hours," he yelled. "You are GIs now and that means *Government Issue*. You are nobody. You are a piece of shit owned by the army. When I say jump, you say, 'How high, sir.' Is that understood?"

"Yes," we mumbled.

With that he roared, "I can't hear you! That is **YES...SIR!**"

"Yes...sir!" we hollered.

Back came, "I cannot hear you babies!"

Again, we hollered, only louder, "**YES...SIR!**"

This game went on for a while, and I thought, the dumb schmuck! Is he hard of hearing?

That was the last time we were addressed respectfully. "Okay, girls, line up and get your box lunches, he bellowed. We must give you food but not time to eat. Hustle, hustle, move, move, or you can just look at it and leave it."

We hustled, got our lunch, gulped it down, and then, waited. We learned our first lesson in the army, *hurry up and wait.* This was the way of life in the service. After waiting a couple of hours, we were hurried into army busses and driven to the train station with the usual, "Hustle, hustle! Move! Move!"

When we got there, we marched into a railroad car parked on an offside track. Sergeant Felix looked at the group and said to

196

a tall fellow, "You, what is your name?" The young fellow told him his name and while writing it down the sergeant said, "You are elected to take care of the group's papers. Do not lose them or you will be spending the beginning of your military career in the stockade. Understood?"

"Yes, sir," he said, and with that, he became the leader of the misfits.

We were issued boxed dinners and several cases of soda. "Good luck, P... s, sleep tight," Felix said, jumped into the jeep, and left.

There we were, sitting in a railroad car, all to ourselves, sitting on an abandoned track and waited, and waited, and waited some more. After several hours of waiting, a locomotive moved us to another track where our car was coupled to a train. Finally, we were off to Fort Jackson, SC.

After eating our box rations, we spent the time telling jokes and getting acquainted. One of the fellows had managed to smuggle a bottle of bourbon on the train, which helped us to go to sleep. When we woke up in the morning, we noticed that we were parked on a deserted sidetrack again. Upon looking out of the windows, we saw the most awful, desolate countryside, I had ever seen. There was not a single soul in sight.

# Chapter 50

After an hour went by, a small locomotive came, and twenty minutes later we arrived at the train station in Columbia, SC. This time, we saw an army bus from the windows, and mean-looking guys in uniforms with stripes on their sleeves, spit-shined boots, smokey-the-bear hats, pulled down low onto their foreheads and sticks under their arms. My friend told me, they were called swagger sticks.

Then the yelling started again, and I thought, *Boy, they must all be hard of hearing.*

"Off the train, Hubba, Hubba, fall out and line-up," yelled the one with the most stripes. "Who of you babies has the papers?" The tall fellow with the papers handed them over. "When I call your name, you will take your ass and get on the bus!" Bellowed the one with the most stripes.

On the bus, in a loud voice with a heavy southern accent, a sergeant informed us of the itinerary for the day. No matter how hard I tried, I could not understand this guy. But when my friend tried to interpret, trouble came his way. On arrival, we noticed that there were more busses coming in, and with the usual fanfare we were hurried off.

Our reception committee consisted of a sergeant with six stripes, (three on top, and three on the bottom) and four sergeants with four stripes, (three on top, and one on the bottom). The sergeant with the four stripes on the top, and four on the bottom, gave a speech. "Welcome to Fort Jackson. Through these gates passed the best infantrymen in the world. You too will be top grunts by the time we are finished with you. I am your first sergeant, and these four gentlemen are your platoon drill sergeants. For the next eight weeks, they will be **GOD** to you; and you will address them as **SIR!** You will do as you are told, and say 'Yes, sir,' and speak only when spoken to. If you have a question, you will ask by saying, 'Permission to speak, sir.' Now, the sergeants will call out your names and when you hear yours, form four lines in front of the lord and master that called your name. This will be the platoon you will eat with, sleep with, train with, and suffer with for the next eight weeks. Do you understand?"

Again, we went through the, I don't hear you, circus. Then the names were called; John and I ended up in the same platoon, but in different squads. Among the guys lined up in formation, I must have looked like a clown in my suit, tie, coat, hat, and gloves. Naturally, this did not escape the platoon sergeant. He walked over with his smokey hat down to his eyebrows; he put his nose a half-inch away from mine, and bellowed as loud as he could, "What are you, a clown? Where did you think you were going...to see the queen? Don't you know we have done away with kings and queens? Answer me!"

I thought, *Well, dummy, if you give me a chance I will.* With that, I tried to explain and said, "I am a tai..."

However, that was all I could get out before he interrupted and yelled, "I did not ask you for a commentary! That is, 'Yes, sir,' or 'No, sir.'"

"Yes sir," I said.

"Give me ten," he replied. Looking helplessly around I thought, *Ten what?* This made some guys snicker. That did not sit well with the sergeant, so he yelled at all of them, "You, you and you, give me ten too." In addition, to me he yelled, "Get down on your belly and push yourself up with your hands dummy!"

I got down and barely made three push-ups with him standing over me saying very softly, "Oh baby, I will have fun with you."

After that episode, we were marched off to the mess hall for breakfast. However, before we were allowed in, we had to do pull-ups on the bar. I, wearing my tie, jacket, coat, hat, and gloves must have been a sight.

The next stop was at the quartermaster's supply depot. There, we were given a duffle bag, underwear, boots, socks, gloves, fatigues, field jacket, and a fatigue hat. Then we were marched off to an area where we were told to undress, take a shower, and change into our army clothes.

Now, I looked the same as the rest of the guys. No longer did I have to worry about standing out and being ridiculed by the sergeant. Then, just as my buddy had said, they made us roll our personal belongings into a small bundle and mail it home. Mine was not so small, what I was wearing needed a bigger box. With a grumble under his beard, the supply sergeant found a bigger box.

Haircuts were next on the agenda, or, shall I say, if that is what you want to call it. Wow, now we looked like convicts with clean-shaven heads and went to the mess hall for lunch. We did the usual pull-ups again.

My mother's food was not much to write about, but the army's food really took the cake. *Where did they find these cooks? Whatever they slopped on my tray was not even identifiable.*

Back to the supply depot we went. I wished they had let us get rid of the stupid duffle bag. Lugging that thing around was not fun, and it got worse. After issuing us an advance of a couple of dollars, called, *the flying twenty*, which we had to trade in for toiletries, we marched to a building where they gave us our field gear, rifle, gasmask etc. With the rifle over one shoulder, the duffle bag over the other, and holding the footlocker full of heavy field gear in front of us, we marched off to our quarters about a mile away.

Weighted down, stumbling around with that stupid wooden box, and the loudmouth sergeant yelling in my ear, "What's the matter, hotshot? Can't the baby carry the little box?" It became the longest mile I had ever walked. Oh man, would I have loved to drop that darn box full of stuff on his toes.

We arrived at our quarters called, *Tent City*. Four men were assigned to each tent, and each tent was with narrow bunks, a locker with each bunk, a potbelly stove, and now our footlockers. Then we were shown how to properly arrange the locker, and how to make up a tidy bunk with hospital corners, so that a dime could bounce off it like on a trampoline. February in South Carolina is not Florida and it was cold in those tents. However, we were given only ten minutes to straighten out our new home. Two of my roommates were cousins from Pittsburgh. We hit it off and became instant friends.

A whistle blew, and the sergeant yelled, "Let's go, let's goes! Hubba, Hubba, fall out!" Assembled outside, he hollered some more, "While you are in training, you will not walk...you will always double-time unless I say otherwise. Do you understand?"

After the usual, *yes sir!* and the, *cannot hear you* circus, we were double-timed to a large auditorium and instructed to be seated by company and platoon. Our battalion of new recruits was ready for the orientation. The Sergeant Major yelled, "Atten---tion!"

By now we knew enough to know that this was the command where we had to jump up like a jack-in-the-box. Down the center aisle marched a group of men led by a bold, short person with lots of ribbons on his chest. I assumed they were all officers. I still could not identify them by their rank insignia. But since we had to address them all as *sir*, it did not make any difference to me. When they all walked with bellies sucked in and chests pushed out, I thought they looked like strutting peacocks.

When they marched onto the stage, they grouped themselves so that the short guy was in the middle and the rest about one-step behind and on each side of him.

"Be seated," ordered the bold guy in a stern voice. He continued, "I am your battalion commander for the duration of your eight weeks of basic training. My name is Major Mueller. That is M-u-e-l-l-e-r, pronounced Muller...like M-you..."

Then he had us repeat his name a couple times in unison like first graders. I guessed he thought either we were all stupid, or he was afraid of being overlooked. He continued, "Men, I will turn you into proud and hardened soldiers..." When he had finished his rah-rah speech, he introduced his staff.

Our company commander (of company A) was a dark-haired, tall, slim, and refined looking first lieutenant. When he spoke, he was much more polished, and it gave me hope that maybe the officer's corps did not consist of only morons.

Next, the company commander introduced his executive officer, a short skinny second lieutenant. The lieutenant looked as if he had muscles of iron and ate new recruits for breakfast.

After the major had finished introducing his entire staff, he turned the podium over to the base chaplain and left with his entourage. The chaplain, in a more normal speaking voice, gave us a talk on how we should conduct ourselves and reminded us to stay in touch with our families. He also told us that if we had any personal problems, to be sure and come to see him, that he was always available.

By then it was dinnertime and we all took off double-timing it to the mess hall again where we were greeted by the usual pull-ups and unidentifiable chow that not even the army called food. After finishing our meal, we went back to our tent and lit the stove. Our tent turned into a smokehouse. It took us a half hour to clear out the smoke and soot.

Seeing my discouraged demeanor, my friends explained that once we were out of boot camp, life would be much different. We would have regular assignments, the sergeants would be civilized when talking to us, and a lot of the current nonsense would disappear. To myself I thought, *from your mouth to God's ears.*

At four o'clock in the morning, the stupid whistle that would haunt us throughout boot camp blew. Right behind it, the sergeant began yelling in his vernacular language. "Rise and shine! Hubba move it! You got thirty minutes to shit, shave, shower, and straighten up your place!" Scurrying around like frightened mice, we started our second day at Fort Jackson.

Again, that darn whistle blew and when the sergeant yelled, "Fall out!" We all scrambled into formation. I soon found out what a *roll call* and a *police call* was. Roll call was shouting as loud as you could, *here...* when your name was called. Police call was to pick up cigarette butts and trash from half the garrison. To me, these were strange names to be given to such activities.

That morning we had *Eggs to Order* and *S.O.S.* for breakfast. To order meant any way they came, while S.O.S. was chipped beef on toast, or as the army called it, *Shit on the Shingle.*

As I liked my eggs sunny side up, I was fortunate since the cooks were always in a hurry that was the way they usually were made. I had to be the only one in my outfit that liked S.O.S. Another thing I liked was the coffee. They must have boiled it for hours and thus was strong enough for me.

To my surprise, the officers and sergeants waited until the troops had their food before they got in line. Suddenly, my low opinion of them went up a notch.

When we had finished eating, we double-timed it over to the base hospital where a corpsman shouted, "Strip down to your T-Shirts and form a single line!" Then we had to pass through a gauntlet of four medics, two on each side, which jabbed us with needles. Just as we would turn our heads to the right to face the guy that had just jabbed us, another jabbed a needle into our left arm. A couple of the recruits fainted. We received four shots in all, with the compliments of the army and the pleasure of the medical corps.

By the time we had to double-time it over to the parade ground, my arms had really begun to ache. On a platform stood the executive officer, dressed in a T-shirt, and not his uniform shirt. We all were ordered to spread out across the field in formation and then to strip down to our T-shirts. Next, we were introduced to the *daily dozen*. After the pushups, sit-ups, squat jumps, and other exercises like running and yelling for a half hour, I thought my arms were going to fall off. Those sons-of-bitches were deliberately trying to make us miserable, whenever and wherever they could. Yes, they got us to curse too.

That morning, after exercising it was back to the supply depot where we were fitted for our dress uniforms. Since this was my field of expertise, I tried to tell the sergeant in charge that my topcoat was too tight, and my uniform jacket did not fit right. Boy, was that a mistake! He called me more names then there were words in the dictionary. Then, he followed that up by ordering me to do another set of push-ups.

After our fingerprints and mug shots had been taken for our ID cards, we went into another room where we were told to get into our dress uniform—minus the pants because the pants had to be hemmed to the proper lengths. The pants we got a few days later. There, standing like good soldiers next to a flag, despite being pants-less, they photographed us from the waist up. We all received a 5x7 picture to send home with the compliments of the United States Armed Forces.

Next, we were herded into a classroom where tests were given to evaluate our IQ, and if you spoke a second language, you were given an interpreter's test. A captain came over to me and very politely asked whether I wanted an interpreter. I responded,

"No Sir," because I wanted to make it on my own like the rest of the gang.

"Very well, he said. If you change your mind let me know."

"Yes Sir," I replied.

Most of us thought the psychology test was a joke, and the skill test was easy. To me, the IQ test was a mystery because I did not understand the questions; but even so, I scored 124. Naturally, I passed the German language test with an A.

When the tests were completed, we were informed of our scores at the final interview. The captain said to me, "Okay, you did very well, especially on your language test."

"Thank you, Sir," I replied.

He continued, "With these scores, you will most likely go to the language school in California to teach German after basic training. The army is looking for good language teachers. Would you like that?"

"Yes Sir, I said."

Later, when I told that to my buddies, they said, "Wow, you're going to have it made! You will live the life of Reilly!"

# Chapter 51

In the days and weeks to come, the army turned us into physically fit soldiers. My chest expanded from 38 to 40 inches, and my waist retracted from 34 to 29 inches. We certainly were getting into good physical shape. Those weeks of hard training turned us into a combat-trained, spit and polished marching unit. During weapons training, I was able to get my expert marksman badge for all single-action weapons.

We were getting used to the military life and with that, our existence became a little more civilized. The sergeants became less like gods and more approachable. Griping at every opportunity was the norm, and complaints from those who had volunteered were told, *"We do not want to hear it! You asked for this."*

Two fellas were so determined to get out of the army, that they played a game that would get them discharged. One Italian fellow, who had no problem telling jokes when we were alone, played dumb in front of the sergeants and officers. He acted as if he did not understand a word they said, and just shrugged his shoulders. They gave him every dirty detail from the latrines to the grease pit, but he was steadfast in his game of not understanding English, he got an *Unfit for military duty* discharge.

Another guy deliberately wet his bunk every night. To embarrass him they made him hang his wet bed sheets outside and woke him up several times during the night. It was to no avail; he still managed to wet his bunk. He also got an *Unfit for military duty* discharge.

****

Our first payday came. After saluting properly, stating my name and serial number, the company executive officer handed me my monthly pay, minus the twenty dollars advance. I could not help but notice he had a gun lying next to all the money.

After seeing nothing but tent city, and the training areas for weeks on end, we were finally permitted to go to the PX and a movie on Sunday night. To me it felt as if we were being let out of a maximum penitentiary and moved into a minimum-security prison.

In our fifth week, we were taken on busses to a Saturday night dance at a Baptist Church in town. Before we left for the affair, we got a lecture on how to behave. Dressed in our *Class a Green Uniforms*, and spit-shined shoes, we arrived at the church hall. A long table was placed along the wall with delicious finger foods, fruit punch, and lots of soda; but the beer was missing.

With more chaperons than young ladies, the prim and proper dressed girls were sitting on chairs along the opposite wall. After we were introduced as members of Company A from the First Training Battalion, a local band began to play, and the party began. It was hard to determine whether we liked the girls or the food better. Most of us took the girls over to the food after the first dance and conversed with them between eating. In my case, I should say, I tried to converse.

Chaperons circled through the crowed, bombarding us repetitiously with questions such as, *"Are you enjoying yourself? -- Where are you from? --Is this your first time down south?"* It kept us from having any serious conversation with the girls. Since every door and even the hallway by the restrooms was guarded by MPs, there was no chance of privacy or intimacy. We had come from the confinement of the base to the confinement of a church hall.

Sometimes I wondered if they used us to train the young girls for their debutante's ball—but at least it was a change of scenery.

After an evening of dancing, tasty food and having to say, *yes, ma'am,* or *No, ma'am,* which seemed like every turn, we thanked them for their southern hospitality and were bussed back to the base.

The following weekend we were able to get our first pass to leave the base and to venture out on our own. However, that again depended upon how well we could recite the *General Orders,* and how well we fared on our tests that week. The general orders were the rules that governed guard duty. Since I could not understand a lot of the words and phraseology, I had a tough time memorizing them.

On Friday evening, my friend from Pittsburgh tried to help me memorize and remember enough so that I could get a pass on the following day. After staying up half the night studying, it enabled me to get by.

The next morning, we had another prerequisite after breakfast. We had to pass *Inspection.* Fortunately, for us, we passed after a few nervous moments. Then, when we were waiting in line to pick up our passes, I watched the guys in front of me. Everyone saluted, reported, and then was asked to recite one, sometimes two of the general orders. If the recruit did not know it, hesitated, or the sergeant did not like the way he recited it, especially if it was delivered in collegiate English, the sergeant would find an excuse to send the trooper back to the end of the line.

The closer it came to my turn, the more nervous I became. I knew I couldn't remember enough of the general orders. I was positive that I would wind back at the end of the line. My friend was in front of me. The sergeant tried to trip him up. He asked my friend for three different general orders before he gave him his pass

It was my turn next. By now I was so tense that I even had trouble getting the words out when I reported. The sergeant looked up at me, and said, "Oh, you, here." He handed me my pass without asking anything. Then he said, "Have a good time. Go."

I could not believe that after a sleepless night, and jittery nerves, I was just handed a pass without a problem. I was blurry-eyed and felt more like going to sleep than into town.

Nevertheless, five of us jumped on a bus and went into Columbia, SC and walked the streets. However, there really wasn't much to do besides going to a restaurant to eat and getting drunk. Since two in our group were under age, we didn't go to any bars. Instead, we bought a case of beer, a bottle of Seagram's Seven, a couple of bottles of soda, and rented a single room in a seedy motel. To save money, all of us piled into this single room, got drunk, and created a ruckus. I do not know why they didn't throw us out. Nevertheless, we made it through the weekend with a whale of a hangover without getting picked up by the MPs.

In the last weeks of basic training, we had several exercises to complete. Since we were physically fit, the obstacle course was not much of a problem. However, stories circulated about live hand-grenade exercises. The most prevalent story was about recruits that had dropped grenades after pulling the pin. According to the stories, the sergeants had to scoop them up and chucked them over the cement wall before they exploded. That made some of the eighteen-year-olds a little nervous.

That aspect did not faze me much since I had fished with grenades when I was 12 years old. However, the live-firing exercise was a different story. On a fifty-yard wide field, a simulated approach to an enemy fortification was set up with barbwire barriers, pits with dynamite to simulate exploding artillery shells, a trench on one end and a platform with machine guns on the other. The exercise consisted of crawling from the trench to the platform, through and under barbwire with live bullets flying overhead, and dynamite going off all around you.

This was a day and a nighttime drill. During the day it wasn't so scary; but in the night it looked real. The dynamite exploding in the pits, flares going off in the sky, and the tracers from the machine guns flying overhead, brought back the nightmares from the war. When the order came to move out, I froze for a couple of seconds, took a deep breath, pulled myself together mentally, slid over the edge of the trench like everyone else, and started to crawl under the barbwire towards the platform. With fireworks all around and above, I hugged the ground with only one thing in mind, to get there and make it through the exercise.

# Chapter 52

Eight weeks of boot camp were finally completed. We were ready to graduate. Suddenly, the sergeants became regular guys and said, "Don't sir me. I am not an officer." What a change that was. On the day of our graduation, dressed in our army greens, bloused pants, spit-shined boots, polished helmets, and rifle, we marched to the large parade ground. Lined up in formation at parade rest, with flags and regimental banners, the army band played while we awaited the base commander, visitors, and high-ranking brass to fill the grandstand.

After a congratulatory speech from the general, pronouncing us full-fledged soldiers, he gave the order, *Pass in review*. With the band playing Stars and Stripes Forever, we proudly paraded past the viewing stand with pulled in stomachs and puffed out chests just like the rest of the peacocks.

We were off for the remainder of the day. The next day we received our orders for our next assignment. Knowing that we had fourteen days leave coming, plus travel time to the assigned destination, we all made travel arrangements to get on a plain or train for home. The following day after breakfast, the sergeant called off name after name along with the assignments. Most of my friends, including my roommates, and my friend John, were assigned to Fort Leonard Wood, MO for combat-engineer training.

I was anxiously awaiting my orders to sunny California, or so I thought. My name was called, and so was the assignment; Combat Engineers Fort Leonard Wood MO. The word *engineers* sounded impressive. Except, I had found out that it meant a weak mind and a strong back. Well, so much for my wonderful assignment in the sun and beaches. I picked up my records, traveling orders, and duffle bag; said my, "Good-byes" and "See you in Leonard Wood" and took a taxi, together with John to the airport and a plane to Philadelphia.

****

It was great to be welcomed home by family and friends. Dad told me that they wanted to see me at work in uniform. So, I obliged and visited Van Horns. I received a hearty welcome from Mr. Valentino and Mr. Weidler and the rest of my colleagues. Since everyone complimented me on how good I looked in uniform, I did not wear civvies during my two weeks furlough. The uniform had other advantages. At the movies, on busses and trains we got discounts. Sometimes, in restaurants waitresses would give us a piece of cake and coffee for free. Those were the days when soldiers were held in high regard and patriotism was alive and well.

My fourteen-day leave went by very quickly. John and I met at the airport where we said good-bye to our parents and flew to St. Louis. We checked in at the base and were processed into an engineer training company. My roommates from Pittsburgh and a lot of the guys from boot camp, ended up with John and I in the same outfit.

We spent the next eight weeks in classrooms and on field exercises where we learned how to build bridges, roads, and buildings handling all kinds of tools. We were also taught how to lay and clear minefields, and how to handle explosives. The weather was hot and humid. However, this time it was a learning experience without the shenanigans and harassment of boot camp.

On weekends, if we did not have guard duty, we could go to St. Louis. That first Sunday, seven of us crowded into a Chevy convertible owned by one of the guys. We all headed into town. Just before we got to St. Louis, we were pulled over by a police officer who informed us that it was against the law to have more than five people in the car. He did not heed our pleas, instead he made two of us get out. Standing by the side of the road, I said, "What are we going to do now?"

John said, "We wait until the cop leaves. The guys will come back and pick us up." As he had said, our friends drove a couple of times around the block until the cop was gone. We jumped back into the car. But this time we put the top up on the convertible so that the police could not see that there were more than five of us in the car.

When we got into St Louis, we learned about discrimination. All of us were from Pennsylvania, New Jersey, and New York and were not familiar with segregated restaurants. When we went into a diner on Main Street, we sat down and studied the menu. The waitress brought water and then pointed at one of our friends and said, "I can't serve him."

Confused we asked, "Why not?"

"Because he is Indian," was the reply.

In unison we said, "If you don't serve our friend, you don't serve us." We stood up and walked out. Outraged, we tried a few other places and received the same treatment. After that, we went into a super market, bought a picnic basket, and filled it with food, beer, sweets, and went to the park ignoring the local bigots. We ended up having a wonderful time.

\*\*\*\*

Before I had left for basic training, we had made costumes for the St. Louis Outdoor Theater in the Park. Mr. Weidler

215

contacted the director of the theater and told him that I was in Fort Leonard Wood. He in turn left two free tickets at the box office for a friend and I to see the musical Showboat with Andy Devine. My friend from Pittsburgh and I went to the theater where I identified myself at the box office. A young lady at the ticket counter asked us to wait a minute and made a phone call. Shortly thereafter, a gentleman came out and greeted us saying he was the director. He showed us around and explained that the first ten rows of the theater had ice water running under the seats and air-conditioners blowing chilly air over the rows. It was a magnificent outdoor theater. He then gave us two tickets for the best seats in the house and told us to enjoy the show. We enjoyed the splendid performance with Andy Devine as the captain. They put on a spectacular show with a black slave singing Old Man River. His deep, resonating voice was fantastic. I guess the fine people of St. Louis did not object to a black performer, as the restaurants did.

# Chapter 53

After the graduation, we were all assigned to units for the rest of the two years. Most of my friends got split up and were sent all over the globe. Several of us got assigned to Germany, including yours truly.

John had to finish his training with another company, because he broke his foot during an exercise in the fifth week. We had to say good-bye to each other not knowing where he was going to be sent.

After a week of leave, plus travel days, I reported for processing at Fort Dix in New Jersey. This was the base where troops were processed for deployment to Europe. During the two weeks of waiting for deployment, there was not much to do. Since we were not part of a regular unit, we learned how to make ourselves scarce. Because, we discovered that those who didn't, were grabbed for work details that were mostly undesirable jobs.

One day, my friends and I were goofing off away from our barracks and the office, when I heard my name being called over the loudspeaker. I hightailed it down to the orderly room where the sergeant told me, "The Captain wants to see you."

Uh oh. It was not good when you got summoned. I knocked on the door and a voice said, "Come in."

Inside were two captains, one seated behind the desk, and the other sat in front. After I saluted, and reported; the captain behind the desk said, "Stand at ease soldier. Get into your dress uniform. This is Captain Jones, he will take you home for the weekend."

"Yes sir. Thank you, sir," I said and went off to get dressed in a hurry.

Naturally my friends came running and wanted to know what was going on. They figured that it surely could not be good. I explained that Captain Jones was the husband of my mom's boss and was giving me a lift home for the weekend.

"Some guys have all the luck," was the goodhearted comment from the gang.

It was indeed a lucky break for me. But I was also uneasy on two accounts. The first being that I had never met Captain Jones before, and the second that I was not sure how to react after having been drilled for weeks in military courtesies. However, the captain quickly set my mind at ease. He said, "Until we get back to the base on Monday, you can forget that I am a captain." After that was settled, we had a pleasant conversation. He gave me some good pointers for my upcoming overseas duty.

****

It had been a great weekend. I was able to spend time with my family, and upon my return to Ft. Dix, I found out that my luck was still holding. I was shipped overseas by MATS, (Military Air Transport Service) which was a lot better than by boat. Being shipped out on a ship, was no fun. Guys that came back from overseas by ship, told of seasickness and polishing brass from morning to night.

We were served coffee and sandwiches on the plane by a sergeant no less. When we landed in Reykjavik, for refueling, we were taken to the Air Force Mess Hall for dinner. Wow, what a difference a real cook can make using the same ingredients as our grease monkeys in the Army. Their meal tasted like restaurant food while the army's chow was just that, *chow*.

After a long flight on a four-engine prop plane, we arrived at the Rhine Main Airbase in Frankfurt at nine o'clock in the morning. At the U. S. Forces desk, our papers were checked and we were split up according to our destination. Then we boarded a bus and were on our way to the assigned garrisons. Mine was the 237th Engineer Battalion at the Wharton Barracks located in Heilbronn Germany.

I checked in and was assigned to a room. I was pleasantly surprised at the great accommodations. The barracks were two-story brick and stucco buildings with floors of highly polished hardwood. Another surprise was that we were only four guys to a room. I met my roommates, my new squad leader, a staff sergeant, and the assistant platoon leader who was a master sergeant.

I noticed the difference in the camaraderie between my new roommates. They joked around with the sergeants and kidded them about their Polish heritage. They were all dressed in combat gear with field packs, helmets, rifles, and gasmasks lying in front of their bunks. It looked like they were ready to go on maneuvers.

However, I had another surprise coming. The sergeant said, "Lohn, go downstairs and pick up your combat gear and change into it. Then ready your field pack and leave the rest of your clothes in your duffle bag. We are standing by to ship out to Lebanon to support the 24th Airborne Division that has been deployed on the beach over there."

That is when it hit me, this was no playtime, *another* war was raising its ugly head.

When I came back upstairs, I met the platoon leader, a second lieutenant. After saluting, he shook my hand and welcomed me aboard. My friend sure had been right when he told me that once we were assigned to a regular unit, the nonsense of boot camp would become history.

\*\*\*\*

We sweat it out for a couple of weeks, however, the crisis in Lebanon blew over, and the 24th Airborne Division was pulled out and we stood down.

The days were spent maintaining equipment, explosive ordinances, the grounds, and buildings. Painting took up a lot of our time.

Our battalion was always combat-ready; weapons and equipment were always in top shape. The nice part was, we did not have to pull *KP,* meaning Kitchen Police. It was a fancy name for scrubbing pots and pans. The garrison had an agreement with the City of Heilbronn to hire German civilians to do the job for which we gladly paid them four dollars a month. When we went on field exercises, the permanent KPs also went and that made it very convenient for us.

Besides the back gate, the Amex office, and other areas on the post, we pulled guard duty out in the woods at the Battalion Ammunition Dump. The facility was located in the boondocks miles away from civilization. Trailers and trucks, parked in the AMMO Dump, were filled with ammunition, explosives, mines, and grenades. Our vehicles, heavy equipment, and carriers were parked in the garrison. All of it was ready to be moved at a moment's notice in case hostilities broke out. During the night, only two guards were on the grounds of the ammo dump making the rounds. We were each given a single clip with five bullets instead of the usual six. We were also ordered not to load our rifles and to keep the clip in our pockets. Considering the sensitive material stored in the compound, and only two guys to guard the pitch-dark area, it made no sense. Against orders, we fully loaded our rifles. We were glad when our shift was over without an incident. It always gave me an eerie feeling seeing things in the dark that were not there, and hearing sounds that gave me goose bumps that crawled up my spine.

When we were not maintaining equipment, we would be out on field exercises. Some were executed locally while others were conducted in training areas like Vielseck and Hohenfels. My Dad trained Hohenfels as a German soldier and years later, I was being trained as an American GI in the same place. Not only was it ironic, but also it showed that times really do change.

My new band of brothers and I formed a close friendship. The sergeants were great guys and part of the gang. Our platoon leader, a second lieutenant, was a civil engineer and ROTC officer. He was putting in his mandatory three years and was just as eager as the rest of us to get out and back to civilian life. We nicknamed our company commander, Captain Nagasaki, as he was a little strange.

# Chapter 54

The battalion commander, a lieutenant colonel, was fanatically determined for our battalion to be first in everything. Thus, we held First Place in the bridge building competition of all the NATO units. Our actual time for a class-sixty floating bridge across the Danube River, was one hour and forty-four minutes. The stopwatch began to count when the first truck hit the river's edge and stopped when the first tank rolled across the bridge. A footbridge across the same river, next to the class-sixty bridge, we built in five minutes and forty-five seconds. To celebrate the accomplishment, all officers were thrown into the river, including the lieutenant colonel.

Quite often we took country roads to the training areas in Bavaria. The small quaint towns, with narrow streets turning at right angles and sharp curves, were very difficult to negotiate with our large trucks. Especially hard to maneuver were the *low boys* that carried the heavy earth-moving equipment. They could cause the convoy to become backed up for quite some time.

One time, our squad truck was stopped in front of a bakery that displayed delicious pastries in the window. Kids always gathered around us when we moved through the towns. Since I spoke the language, my friends asked me to have them get us some pastries. Unfortunately, we had no small change, so we gave them a twenty-dollar bill for only ten DMs worth of pastries. We didn't worry about it because the kids always brought back the change. While we were waiting, the convoy moved up a short way and a different truck was now in front of the bakery. The guys behind us had watched our negotiations with the children, and when the kids came out with the pastries, those wise guys on the truck behind us let them believe it was their money. Much to our dismay and protest, the kids not being able to tell who had given them the money, the pastries went to our friends behind us. Not only did we have to watch them laughing and enjoying our pastries with exaggerated oohs and ahs, they told the kids to keep our change. The sergeant behind us laughed and hollered, "Thank You!" It ended up that we not only got our pastries, but also lost our money.

Not all the exercises went smoothly. At one of our local skirmishes, our company was split up. Three platoons were together on the opposite side of the forest with the commanding officer, Captain Nagasaki, and the executive officer. Our platoon, with our platoon leader, Lieutenant O'Hern, was a couple of miles on the other end of the forest. We were working with artillery simulators that were filled with black powder. Military dynamite can burn without exploding unless it is fixed with a detonating cap. Black gunpowder explodes if it meets fire. The ones given o us for the exercise were and did not work. Our platoon leader ordered us to dig a deep hole and bury them. Which was the proper solution to dispose of the artillery simulators.

Unfortunately, Captain Nagasaki was not that smart. No sooner had we finished burring the artillery simulators when we heard an explosion. The CO had ordered the other platoons to pile up the simulators into a heap douse them with gasoline. Then he lit the pile with a cigarette lighter. Naturally, the black powder in the cardboard tubes exploded and severely burned the CO and the XO. Both ended up in the hospital for quite a while. That is how he inherited the name Captain Nagasaki.

For an officer, commanding an engineering company that was supposed to be trained to handle explosives, he was not just dumb, he was plain stupid.

A captain, who was a great leader, and a down-to-earth guy, whom we all liked and respected, replaced the old CO. After being released from the hospital, the former CO became the *Intelligence Officer* of our battalion. This was incomprehensible to me; how could a dumb schnook like him become an intelligence officer?

The new Company Commander heard that I had a demolition MOS and a secondary translator's MOS. Since his driver was rotating back to the states, he needed a new driver. I was ordered to report to the orderly room. The First Sergeant asked me, "Lohn, do you have a driver's license?" "No Serge," I replied.

"Okay. You need to get one. But first, you have to see the CO."

"Yes, Sergeant," I said.

"Go right in, he is expecting you," replied the First Sergeant.

When I went in and reported to the captain, he said, "At ease. Sit down," so I did. He continued, "I understand you were born here and speak fluent German?"

"Yes sir" I answered. "I immigrated into the US two years ago."

"Great, then you know your way around here. I want you to become my driver. Do you have a driver's license?"

"No, I don't, but I would love to become your driver."

"No problem," he informed me. "The First Sergeant can arrange driving lessons for you. I will see you back here after you get your license. I assume you know all the German road signs."

"Yes Sir."

"Great, get your license. It will be good to have a driver that knows the language. Go see the First Sergeant and tell him that I said to arrange for a driving lesson."

I went back to the orderly room and saw the First Sergeant. Before I could tell him what the CO had said, he said, "I know, I know, go to the motor pool and report to the sergeant in charge; good luck."

After completing a crash course in driving, I became the CO's driver. In the beginning, I gave him a few tense moments. One time, when we were heading for Hohenfels, he had me pull away from the column. I had trouble controlling the vehicle on the snow-covered road. We went sliding all over the place. The captain said calmly, "Pull over, I'd like to drive for a while." I pulled over, we exchanged seats, he put on some music, and then he drove until we came close to the training area. However, he never let me know that he had a problem with my driving.

# Chapter 55

About a month after I had arrived in Heilbronn, John walked into the garrison. He had been assigned to the same company and the same platoon. On that night and many thereafter, we went celebrating. During my deployment in Germany, one US dollar yielded 4.20 DM, which was a great exchange rate. For 4.00 Dollars you could buy a whole magnum of good champagne. That night, John and I got sloshed and had to sneak into the gate after curfew. Fortunately for us, guys from our own battalion guarded that gate.

Word had gotten around that, *Lohn is a good interpreter.* After that, everyone wanted me to go shopping with them. The prices were always better if you spoke German.

Besides my primary MOS, which was demolition, I had an interpreter's MOS. That got me the job going with the Battalion Investigating Officer on their investigations. That had advantages and disadvantages. The advantage was that it was easy duty. The disadvantage was that when one of our guys had an accident during a fieldtrip, I had to stay behind to talk to the police.

Our platoon leader, who was by then a first lieutenant, approached me and said, "Lohn, would you come to my room and interpret a letter for me?"

"Yes sir" I replied.

"Okay, come see me after work."

When I saw him after dinner, he gave me a letter to translate and added, "When we are away from the troops, I am just another buddy to you. None of this 'Yes sir and No sir; all right?"

That was great; a first lieutenant became a friend. When I began to read the letter, I realized it was from his German girlfriend. I thought to myself, *Now, this is going to be interesting. I could not help making a few wisecracks.*

To which he replied, "No wisecracks or I'll get you for that!"

The translating of his letters soon became a regular routine. It increased our friendship.

Every Saturday we had an inspection. After that we were free to go into town. On one of these mornings, we were impatient to get out of the garrison. We could not wait to get the inspection over with. Lieutenant O'Hern had weekend duty and was stuck at the garrison. When he grabbed my rifle, he started in on me. "When did you clean this rifle last, Soldier? This rifle is filthy; the bore is full of garbage, and the chamber is full of timber. You will thoroughly clean it and see me after formation in my office."

I went to his office without cleaning my rifle. I knew he was just pulling my chain because my rifle was clean. When I walked into his room, I said, "C'mon…timber? Couldn't you think of anything better? That sounded like those clowns in boot camp."

"Well, I'm stuck here for the weekend. I can make you clean that rifle all day long unless you are willing to translate this letter without any wisecracks."

"Okay, is that what this is about?"

He responded, "Don't be a wise ass and interpret the letter."

I translated the letter, and then turned to hit the road saying over my shoulder, "Have fun."

Laughing, he warned me, "Careful now." However, he never had me translate any outgoing.

\*\*\*\*

Our battalion was given the project to build a road and a permanent bridge crossing a valley at the Hohenfels' training area. The German civilian post engineers had been sitting on the job for three years and had not come up with a plan. Our lieutenant, a brilliant civil engineer, was given the job to design the bridge. He designed it in fourteen days. We went out to Hohenfels and completed the project in four weeks; a permanent concrete bridge and a road leading to and away from the bridge. This was another diamond for the colonel's crown. Lieutenant O'Hern received all kinds of offers to make the army his career, which he turned down because he knew that no matter what they offered, he could do better on the outside.

****

In a drive to create a better relationship between the army and the German townspeople, fairs were held in the garrisons with bands, dancing, and food buffets. Soccer teams were formed to play in the Seventh Army tournament and against the German clubs.

As I mentioned earlier, the colonel had to be first in everything. Therefore, he hired an English soccer pro to coach our team. I joined the team with five others who had played some soccer before. The rest of the team joined because it was easy duty. They had never kicked a soccer ball before. We were a sorry looking group. Since the colonel insisted that we train every day from eight in the morning until five in the afternoon, our coach was able to teach us a fair amount of ball handling and strategy.

However, we were no match for the German teams and their superior techniques. However, after several weeks of running from morning to night, we were physically fit. With that kind of stamina, we were able keep up a murderous fast pace throughout the game. Playing two halves of forty-five minutes was just a warm-up for us.

At every game, the battalion commander brought the whole outfit to the stadium to cheer us on. He and his staff were the loudest fans of all. Because of the German's long-time soccer experience, we were always the underdog. Usually within the first ten minutes of a game, the German teams would outmaneuver us every inch of the way. However, due to our superior physical fitness, we would take over after that and ran them to death. Much to the colonel's delight, we won game after game and ended up winning the 940th Army Group Championship.

The colonel honored us in front of the entire battalion and rewarded us with a couple of days. To celebrate, we rented the banquette hall at the stadium, a caterer, and a band for the following weekend. The stadium had a bar in the hall which came in handy.

# Chapter 56

Dressed in my full-dress uniform, complete with spit-shined shoes, a good conduct ribbon and an expert sharpshooter badge on my chest, polished brass on my lapel, new Private First-Class stripes on my sleeves, and the red engineer cord around my shoulder, I walked through the gate ready to celebrate at the stadium. Outside of the gate waited a team-mate. He was also a German immigrant. I said to him, "Are you on your way down to the stadium?"

"Well" … he said, momentarily hesitating. "I want to pick up this girl and bring her with me as my date."

"Okay, so what is stopping you?" I asked.

Embarrassed, he scratched his head, and said, "I stood her up last weekend. Why don't you come with me?"

Laughing, I told him, "I guess you have a bit of a problem. But I am not going to wash your dirty laundry for you. You will have to do that yourself."

He kept insisting, saying, "They are nice people. Why don't you do me a favor? Besides, she has a girlfriend, and you have no date. Maybe she can get her to go with you."

I said, "Wait a minute. What kind of girls are they? What does she look like? I have never gone on a blind date before."

He replied, "First, they are nice girls. And second, her girlfriend is pretty…"

After going on and on, he talked me into going with him. When we got there, the people were indeed very pleasant. His date agreed to ask her girlfriend to double date. While she was getting ready, we had an enjoyable conversation with her parents over a glass of wine. I explained how I got to the US and what it was like to live there as an immigrant.

However, it bothered me that my friend's date was not that good looking. I assumed he would be dating the better looking of the two. Which made me wonder what this girlfriend of hers would look like. Also, I remembered that he had mentioned she was young, still sixteen, but he assured me that she did not look like sixteen and would be seventeen in three months. Still, it made me uneasy.

Therefore, with mixed feelings on my part, we went over to a butcher shop where my blind date both lived and worked. We waited outside while Rosemarie, my friend's date, went inside. When she came out, she said, "Her friend Heide would soon join us." and went back inside.

I was getting cold feet and tried to figure out how I could get out of this situation. However, before I could figure it out, the door opened and both girls came out. *Wow!* My mouth dropped open, and I became tongue-tied. My blind date was gorgeous. I fell instantly in love. I pulled myself together as we were introduced, and then escorted her down to the stadium like a perfect gentleman.

Being in love and walking along the Neckar River in the early evening light, weeping willows sweeping gracefully along the riverbanks, was extremely romantic. My friend had been correct in that Heide was very mature and did not act or talk like a sixteen-year-old. We had a stimulating conversation and I was in heaven. She only drank one glass of wine and I behaved by taking it easy nursing a couple of beers.

It was obvious that my friends were envying me as Heide and I waltzed and danced the evening away. I did not want the evening to end but, end it did. I escorted her home. Eager to secure a date for the following weekend, I asked her whether she would go out with me on the upcoming weekend. Well, in my experience I had heard both *Yes* and *No,* but I was not prepared for this girl's answer. She said, "I do not know."

No matter what I said, I was unable to sway her. Her answer remained, "I do not know."

By the time I got back to the garrison, I was furious. If the club had been open, I would have tied-one-on. Instead, I went to bed.

Lying there, I thought to myself, *she could not even say yes or no. What kind of answer is 'I don't know?' I am never going to see that dumb broad again.*

# Chapter 57

During the following week, I could not get her out of my mind. When Saturday came, I went into town and walked up and down the street trying to muster up enough courage for what I planned to do. My main fear was outright rejection, or that I would get a vague, or evasive answer from her again.

After walking around for a couple of hours, I finally gathered enough courage to walk up to the door where she worked. My civilian clothes had not caught up with me. That's why I was dressed in my uniform. With my heart racing and my stomach tied in knots, I rang the doorbell. When a little boy opened the door, I asked, "Is Heide in?"

He answered, "Yes." Looking at me curiously. The boy turned and hollered, "Heide, it's for you!"

When she came to the door, she almost fainted when she saw me standing there dressed in my uniform. German girls dating GIs, was frowned upon. My unexpected arrival threw her for a loop. Just to get rid of me, she said, "Go to my girlfriend's house. I will meet you there."

With a lump in my throat, and my heart still pounding, I happily went over to Rosemarie's house. Again, her father was hospitable and brought out the wine. He was interested in hearing all about the USA. But my mind was on my newfound love who was still working.

Heide took her sweet old time. For a while I thought she wasn't going to show up. But then she finally arrived. We had a lovely evening and ended up at the Café Reinecke, which became our café of choice. We became regulars patronizing the establishment. I was dying for something to eat—like dinner or at least coffee and cake. However, Heide refused to order anything other than coffee. I felt if she would not eat anything, neither could I. Later, I found out that she had been just as hungry as I. But did not wanted to order, because she was afraid if she did, she would feel obligated to me. With that, a romance started that still gives me goose bumps when I think about it. That week we met every night and always ended up at Reinecke's. Our regular meeting point was a large clock that stood on an island at the main crossroads of town. Afterwards, I always ended up running back to the garrison to return before taps. Every minute became precious.

Full of excitement, each evening I would get dressed, go into town, and wait by the clock for Heide. My friends commented, *this must be the real thing. We don't see you anymore.* It sure was. The excitement turned into bliss during the minutes I waited.

Much to my despair, after that first week, we were separated for a couple of days. Since we had won our soccer tournament, we had to go to Frankfurt and play for the 7th Army title. On Saturday night I said good-bye to Heide. Sunday morning our team was trucked to the train station.

A young second lieutenant, from the headquarters company accompanied us. He laid out the rules; "If we are alone, I am one of the guys. If there are other officers around, I am the lieutenant." He was a great guy.

On the way to the train station, I saw Heide with Rosemarie walking to church. My heart leaped when I saw her and eagerly waved while my friends mocked me.

As usual, the army's rule #1, *Hurry Up and Wait,* was in full force. We were at the train station way too early and had to sit around for at least an hour. During that time, I wished Heide would come to the station to see me off. I kept looking through the window, hoping. Then, suddenly, there she was. She had not expected to see me. She was caught off guard. Forgetting her formality, she let her guard down and to the applause of my friends, leaped into my arms. This delighted me as her reaction confirmed that my love was not one-sided.

An old gentleman, walking with a cane, smiled as he walked by. He remembered his youth. I think I floated inside the train all the way to Frankfurt.

Since playing on the soccer team was easy duty, normally I would have loved for the tournament to go on forever. But now, I couldn't wait to get back to the garrison.

The next day, when the games started, we realized that these teams were of a different caliber than the ones we had played previously. They were just as fit as we were. What made it even worse, all the players had been soccer players before. They were very physical and played as if they were on ice with a puck. We lost our first game one to two. And on top of it, in the second half I got kicked right behind my anklebone, rendering me incapable of running. My ankle swelled up like a balloon leaving me to spend the night with my foot soaking in Epson Salts and Evergreen. In the morning I wrapped my ankle tightly with an ace bandage and was ready to play again. Shortly into the first half, I got kicked in the same spot once more. That took me out of the game for good. Our three to nothing loss ended the tournament for us. At noon on the following Wednesday, we were back at the garrison in Heilbronn.

# Chapter 58

My courtship with Heide continued. We were very much in love. Every night we met at the clock, go for walks, and if it rained we spent hours at the Café Reinecke talking and drinking coffee. Soon we were regulars in there. Some of the older folks would give us a smile thinking, *Young lovers, how cute.* While others gave us dirty looks, thinking, *disgusting young girl running around with an American GI.*

Heide took the bus one Sunday to see her parents in the neighboring town of Weinsberg. She was to come back at four o'clock in the afternoon. I was to meet her at the bus station in Heilbronn. But when the bus came, she was not on it. I waited another agonizing hour for the next bus, but Heide was not on that one either. Very distraught, I assumed that her parents must have stopped her from seeing me. Since my world seemed to be ending, I walked into a bar and within a half-hour I consumed eight Cognacs with Coke,

Royally sloshed, feeling sorry for myself, I managed to get back to the garrison and went to bed. About fifteen minutes later, the orderly came up to my room and said, "Hey, Lohn, there's a girl at the gate looking for you."

I was instantly sober. I quickly dressed and hurried down to the gate. I had it all wrong. Heide had missed the bus and then had begged her father to bring her back to town on his motorcycle. Prodded and encouraged by her friend, Heide had finally mustered enough courage to come up to the gate and ask for me. We had a wonderful evening. It was amazing how fast my depression changed into a state of exultation.

# Chapter 59

Our battalion had been given the assignment to build new barracks at the NCO Academy in Bad Töls Bavaria. The project was expected to take about three weeks to complete. Despite the enchanting town and the beauty of the surrounding area, I was unable to truly appreciate nature's splendor because my heart and soul were back in Heilbronn with the girl I loved so much.

As I mentioned earlier, the men in the Lohn clan do not waste time when it comes to the love of their lives. Being no different, I knew I wanted to marry Heide despite having known her for only six weeks. The question I kept asking myself was, *what is the best approach?* I worried that if I asked her she might say, *I don't know.* Therefore, I proposed to her in writing, it would not put her on the spot. Gathering my thoughts, I wrote a letter that included the magic question, *will you marry me?*

The next day, Saturday afternoon, my friend and I went into Bad Töls to buy a gift. I found a pair of earrings with little hearts worked into the filigree. They were pretty and I was anxious to give them to her. However, every mail call was another disappointment. A week went by and there was no answer to my letter. That was not a good sign and I began to think I rushed her too much. Day after day I waited, but there was no mail for me. In desperation I wrote Rosemarie and asked her why Heide did not answer my letters. There was no response from either one.

Then two days before we were to return to Heilbronn, there was a letter at mail call for me. Positive that the answer would be negative, I took the letter and sat with a heavy heart on my bunk.

I was afraid to open it. Finally, I mustered up enough courage and tore it opened. To my surprise, the letter had only one word in it, *Yes*. In shock, I jumped up and jubilantly danced and shouted, "She said yes…She said yes!"

\*\*\*\*

When I returned to the garrison, a package with my civvies had arrived. That was fantastic; as I no longer had to wear my uniform into town. I did not have to worry to attract unwanted attention from the townspeople.

At lunchtime, I took my clothes to the dry cleaner, so they could be pressed while I ate. That night I planned a surprise for my sweetheart. I would show up in civilian clothes and give her the earrings. Ecstatic, I went to our clock and waited for Heide. I saw her coming, and being overly excited, I took her in my arms, hugged, kissed her, and showed her the earrings. But I could tell something was wrong. Her response was lukewarm at best. This was not what I had expected. Unlike the excitement she had showed when I gave her one of the 4x6 photos of me, she now showed little enthusiasm for the earrings.

I started to worry, I wondered whether she had gotten cold feet and wanted to call everything off. We walked quietly for a while. I just did not know what to do or say. Hesitantly, I asked, "When do you want to get engaged?"

The answer she gave, was, "I don't know."

Back to the famous answer. However, at least she had not said the whole thing is off. I continued and said, 'My parents got engaged on Christmas Eve, how about Christmas?

"Maybe," was the answer.

I then asked, "What did your parents say? Is it Okay with them?"

"Yes," she said.

"Don't you think I should meet your parents?"

"Maybe," she replied again.

Things did not go as I had expected. The rest of the evening went by in a very subdued tone and ended by her excusing herself. She said, "I am tired, I want to go home early." I escorted her home and unsure of what her answer might be, I asked, "Are we meeting tomorrow?"

"Yes," she said. I went back to the garrison with mixed feelings.

The next night, not knowing what to expect, I went into town with apprehension instead of being all excited with anticipation. When I saw her approaching, my heart started to pound double-time. A game we used to play as kids came to my mind, she loves me, she loves me not—

When Heide walked up to me and gave me a hug saying, "I love you." All my doubts were forgotten. We strolled happily through the streets as we discussed and planned for our future. We agreed to visit her parents the following weekend and decided to get engaged on Christmas.

She was not wearing the earrings that I had given her, nor would she for some time, but I did not ask why.

I'd like to put some of this into proper perspective. Our first date was at the end of September. I wrote the famous letter the second week in November. And it was now the end of November. We were getting engaged on Christmas and planned to get married in June. On October 3, 1958 I had my twenty-fourth birthday. Heide would be seventeen on the second of December.

As I said before, the Lohn guys are determined suitors that move things along. Although, I did not beat my grandfather's record of six weeks, I did beat my Dad's courting time of ten months and held the record of having the youngest bride. As my dad always used to say, "Son, if you drink wine, make sure it is aged, but when you pick a bride, make sure she is young."

243

Here I wish to clear up and explain some of the mysteries you might not be able to figure out. Not all the answers were forthcoming before Heide and I got married. But here they are.

• The *I do not know* answer on our first date: Heide explained that she was tired and did not want to have any regrets the next day on a decision she might make.

• As to the delay in answering my letter: Heide explained that every time she tried to write, she did not like the way it sounded and kept ripping up the letters.

• Her strange behavior on our date, when I came back from Bad Töls: Heide explained, *I was not prepared to see you in civvies. You had looked so sharp in your uniform but in your custom-made clothes you looked so different from all the other guys. So, I was just taken aback.* (So much for my expensive clothes)

• Not wearing the earrings: I did not realize that she did not have pierced ears.

• One incident I did not find out about until after we were married and were in the US. I had a photo taken of me by a local photographer in Germany to send home to my parents for Christmas, and of course one for Heide. Though I had paid for them, I was out on a field exercise when they were ready to be picked up. I asked Heide to pick them up for me, which she happily did. What I did not know for some time was that the cheat had also charged her for the pictures when she went to pick them up for me. She had wondered why I did not say anything about the money but was too shy to mention it to me.

As has been said, *Communication is life's blood to a relationship.* We certainly rectified that.

\*\*\*\*

At two o'clock, on Saturday afternoon, I waited at the bus stop for Heide. This was the day I was supposed to meet her parents who lived in a refugee camp in Weinsberg, a quaint small town about ten miles from Heilbronn. Mountains covered with vineyards surrounded the village. It was a lovely area with an old castle overlooking the town. The Weibertreu, as the castle was called, has an interesting history. During the Staufen–Welfen War in the year 1140 AD, the Weinsberg castle, belonging to Welf VI Herzog of Spaleto, was besieged by the Staufen under King Konrad III. The townspeople had taken refuge in the castle. After the deciding battle that took place on December 21, 1140, King Konrad gave permission for the women to leave the castle unchallenged with anything they were able to carry. The women carried their men on their backs out of the castle without objection from the King. Henceforth, the castle was called *Women's Devotion.*

In the meantime, as I waited for my devoted love, the bus came, but Heide was nowhere in sight. I thought that I might have misunderstood her. So, I took the bus to Weinsberg. The refugee camp was outside of the town and was off limits to US military personnel. This was for security reasons, but also to keep anyone from taking advantage of the refugee girls. Since I was in civilian clothes and spoke fluent German, I figured no one would be the wiser.

# Chapter 60

I made my way down the road to the gate and asked for the home of the Riechen family. The barrack that they lived in had a hallway with rooms on each side. Heide's parents, along with two younger children, lived in a single room. Nervous and wondering whether they would like me or not, I knocked on the door. Her father opened it and said, "You must be Ali, come in."

Now I had three nicknames. My friends in Germany and my family called me, Allo. At work and in the army, I was Al. Now, at Heide's family, I was Ali, because my lovely bride had decided that *Allo* sounded too much like *Hallo*. Also, my lovely, smart, little cookie, chickened out on introducing me to her parents, and waltzed in about three hours later.

Anyway, her mother, fourteen-year-old sister, Hannelore, and five-year-old baby sister, Karin, greeted me warmly. Immediately I had a good feeling. These were warm, friendly folks and easy to like. Their one-room apt. was clean and homey despite it being the kitchen, living room, and bedroom all in one. A curtain separated double military bunks, and the room was furnished with a table, chairs, and a single bunk that served during the day as a sofa.

After we sat down, Heide's mom brought out cookies and her dad, beer, and schnapps. We passed the time by getting acquainted. The beer and the schnapps did its job and we bonded very quickly. I knew right there and then, they would be wonderful parents-in-law.

It was three hours later when Heide walked in. After a hello and a hug, her mom asked her, "Where have you been?"

Heide had some lame excuse about having had problems with her hair. But we all knew the truth was that she did not want to be around when we were getting acquainted.

Her dad grinned and saw right through her excuse. He turned to her, patted me on the back, and said, "He is all right." I had passed the drinking test. Her father figured, after enough beer and schnapps, you could not help but to show your true colors. From then on, I was her parent's favorite and could do no wrong. My relationship with my parents-in-law could not have been any closer. Now I had a second set of parents, not in-laws.

In the evening I got acquainted with her mom's great culinary skills. She made a delicious meal of fleischknödelsuppe (meat dumplings in a broth), which became one of my favorite meals.

What a wonderful day it was when I met Heide's parents. From then on, we would meet during the week in town, but on the weekends, we would go to visit her parents. Just like my beloved Oma had done, Heide's mom cooked meals to my taste. The following weeks we made plans for Christmas and I got to know a little more of the Riechen family history.

I found out that Heide had been born in Damerow, a small farmer's village in Mecklenburg and so had her father. There were five girls in her family and Heide was the third child. The small town, with a one-room schoolhouse and no stores, sits on the Jabeler See. It is a lake that connects to the Mürritz, and is part of the Mecklenburger See Platte, Germany's largest area of fresh water lakes. The village is located sixty kilometers south of Warnemünde on the Baltic Sea and eighty kilometers north of Berlin. Surrounded by forests, fields, and water, and only one way in and one way out, this town was once an idyllic farm and fishing village. But now it had become a favorite vacation spot for campers and boaters, for the *Communist Bosses*.

Heide's mother had been born in Schwandorf, Bavaria. It is a small charming city in the mountains. She was also one of five children. She had two brothers and two sisters. Heide's maternal grandmother had died from pneumonia one year after giving birth to her youngest son. Heide's mom was six-years old at the time.

Several years later, Heide's grandfather remarried. At the age of twenty, Heide's mom followed her girlfriend to the Baltic Sea and got a job at a hotel in Sweenemünde. From there she ended up working for the game warden in Jabel, a neighboring town of Damerow.

She and her dad met at a dance and within a year, got married. The young couple moved in with Heide's grandmother. Oma Riechen had been widowed at an early age and raised her children, two boys and three girls, as a single mother tending the fields. They lived in one of the four homes in a row-house block. It was a cold-water-flat with a manual water pump outside, and an outhouse. In the kitchen was a wood burning stove, and a kacheloven (A tiled floor to ceiling wood or coal fired oven) in the living and the bedrooms

Being from the city, Heide's mom had a challenging time adjusting to farm life. She turned the house into a spotless, polished, homey surrounding. When Oma Riechen walked in with muddy shoes from the field, or stable, onto the freshly waxed and polished floor, it was hard for her to accept.

Much to Heide's dad's disappointment, daughter after daughter was born but no son. Other than the town's young men were drafted into the army, the war did not touch the small village. However, many did not make it home. Heide's uncle, her dad's brother, was a POW in Russia. He did not come home. The only information the family received from him was a letter promising he would be home soon. That was in 1948. Later they learned from another POW, that had returned after several years, that a prisoner of war, fitting Heide's uncle description, had escaped the POW camp twice. However, after his failed first escape, he tried it again. But this time he did not return. He was presumed dead or sent to Siberia.

Her father had only been in the army for a short while. He had been sent back to work in an airplane factory where a propeller fell on his foot and cut off several toes. After a lengthy hospital stay, he was released and declared unfit for military duty. He spent the rest of the war in Damerow, where the farmers elected him as their mayor. His duties consisted of handling food stamps and small local matters. It was a part time job. He continued working in the airplane factory.

The war was nearing its end. Refugees, fleeing from the Russian Army, were flooding the area. They told horror stories of plundering by the Soviet Troops, and of drunken soldiers' gang-raping women of all ages, leaving them to bleed to death. Shooting people for target practice was another favored sport of the Russians. As the Allied troops advanced, more people fled west. The fear of what could happen to them, and their children, was so intense that Heide's parents had taken the four little girls down to the lake, contemplating drowning themselves and their children. Only the pleading of the children stopped the distraught parents from doing so.

It was a scary time. Fear became a constant companion for years to come. A troop of Cossacks on horses came charging into town, trying to circle the lake on the northern side. However, since Damerow was a peninsula, the dirt road dead-ended at the forest that was surrounded by water.

When the Russian's searched the town, they confiscated what food they could find. Two farmers, who had mistreated Polish forced laborers, were shot to death on the spot. Soldiers came after my father-in-law, because he was the mayor. The same

Polish workers spoke up in his favor and so he was saved. They did arrest some other people and took them away. But, as I understand the story, there was no widespread plundering or raping in their small village. The young women in town were in hiding.

During the reign of Hitler and his cohorts, the small town tucked away in the farmlands of Mecklenburg, was spared from political oppression. Not so, during the communist era. The hard times for Damerow began at the end of WWII. The province, once known as the bread basket of Germany, soon became neglected farmland.

Anyone who owned livestock, or had fields to grow grain or potatoes, were assigned quotas to deliver X number of eggs per chicken, X liter of milk per cow, X amount of potatoes or grain per square meter and so forth. Harvests, with low crop yields, left little for the farmers who were not entitled to food rations. The same was true when animals got sick and died—the quota of meat still had to be delivered. Stores had little merchandise to sell, and the city people, who had no livestock or land, had a challenging time putting food on the table.

Heide's parents had leased a parcel of land that her father farmed for their own use. They raised a cow, two or three pigs, and chickens. Based on the number of animals, they had to deliver a set quota of milk, eggs, meat etc. to the communist government. They had to live on what was left over. Besides, the animals on the leased property, Heide's father had two horses and he subsidized his income by transporting logs for the forestry service.

Eventually, they could not produce enough from the land and livestock to satisfy the government's demands, and still have enough left over to feed their family. Thus, they relinquished the rented land. It turned out it was better to live on food rations, little as they were, than gambling on the leftovers the government would allow them to keep.

Sometimes Heide's father and some friends would go boar hunting with their dogs and a knife mounted on the end of a six-foot stick. Since weapons and hunting were forbidden, it had to be done secretively and before sunrise. The meat helped supplement the food supply to feed the family.

Naturally, spies were everywhere and always ready to report any anti-government sentiments, or any irregularities not permissible according to the rules of the communist regime, such as hunting, or even listening to the western radio station Reo. Many of the new rulers in the communist regime, were ex-Nazis and governed like the thugs they had been, and just as ruthless. For many it was living life only a step away from arrest.

In the 1950s, the Soviet model of state-owned farming and manufacturing was adopted. And by the mid to late 60s, ninety percent of the farms and businesses were consolidated into what was known as collective farms and Volkseigene Betriebe (state-owned businesses). Everything was confiscated and those who resisted, were arrested. Farms became government run cooperatives. Since they were run without incentives, they became nonproductive.

Life became increasingly difficult. When in 1961 the wall was built, East Germany was sealed off from the rest of Europe. This lasted throughout the reign of the DDR until the wall came down in 1989. When the economy in the DDR hit rock bottom, Gorbachev became the General Secretary of Russia and pursued *Glasnost* and *Perestroika*. Even Honecker, the East German President at the time, realized that the *Economic Model* did not work.

Finally, farmers could work small parcels of land for themselves as an incentive to boost agricultural production. This made life a little more tolerable until 1989 when the wall fell, East Germany regained their freedom at last.

Heide speaks fondly of her life in the little farm town playing with friends and siblings in the woods, barns, and the lake; the whole town was their playground. But her most precious memories were about her loving grandmother. Much like my Oma, hers would tell stories of fairytales, read out of books, calm them when they got scared, and helped them with their homework and chores. She had an outstanding knowledge of mushrooms and wild berries and would take her grandchildren into the forest to gather them. She taught them which ones were edible, and which ones were not. Oma Riechen knew her birds and taught the children the bird's names and how to recognize them.

Oma Riechen was a short, hardworking lady that wore her hair pulled up into a bun and an apron to protect her dress. At the crack of dawn, she would get up to feed the animals. She was a wonderful grandmother who, despite her arduous work, was never too tired to fuss with her grandchildren.

The countryside, with its fields, meadows, forests, and lake, provided the perfect setting in which to raise children. During the harsh winter months, the lake would freeze, thus providing the children a shortcut to the school, in the neighboring town of Jabel. The normal way by land was about 3.5 kilometer. Going across the frozen lake, cut the distance to less than half. In the summertime, the state provided a ferryboat for the school children. The ferryboat was a rowboat propelled by a local man who brought the children across, providing they were there at the prearranged time.

Chores like homework, tending the cows, chickens, pigs, and helping in the fields, were the agenda after school, but there was always some time to play. Special fun was playing from dusk to dark or during the wintertime, sledding, ice-skating, and sitting around the tiled stove with Oma Riechen telling stories while only the flickering fire lit the room.

By 1955, Heide's family had grown to include five children, ages nineteen, sixteen, fourteen, eleven, and two years respectively. Struggling to support his family, Heide's father saw no way to survive long term.

After her Mother returned from a visit to her sister in Bavaria she started to work on Heide's dad to flee to the west, they decided to leave East Germany. This was a dangerous undertaking but still possible since the wall wasn't built yet. Sixteen-year-old Christa had already gone to visit a friend in Westphalia, West Germany. The oldest sister, Renate, had followed nine-months later. Very quietly, their parents sold their belongings to friends and got train tickets to visit friends in Eberswalde, a town outside of Berlin, but still in the DDR. For fear of accidentally leaking the information to the wrong people, the two younger children were told that they were going to visit friends.

Heide remembers being excited to go to the west—*the land of milk and honey*. She had heard so many thrilling stories of all the things one could buy such as bananas, oranges, chocolate, and genuine leather shoes. Since she was an avid reader and books without communist propaganda were impossible to come by, she managed to borrow some good old books, without communist propaganda, from a neighbor who was a city girl.

To get to Eberswalde, the train had to pass through Berlin. There was one stop were one side of the tracks was East Berlin, and the other West Berlin. They planned to exit the train on the wrong side and run for their lives, seeking asylum in West Berlin. During the night, prior to leaving, they took boxes with some of their belongings to Heide's aunt. She was to send them to the west when they were settled in. To avoid suspicion, they only packed a small suitcase, but dressed in several layers of clothes, and stuffed a down featherbed into the baby's stroller.

They knew that saying goodbye would break Oma Riechen's heart. They all knew that they would never see each other again. Early in the morning, without saying a word, Oma Riechen went into the fields. Thus, they did not get to say goodbye, which pained Heide for years to come. I do not think her grandmother could have been able to bare the pain of a formal parting.

The children were excited. But Hannelore and Heide pretended they were going to the city to see a movie. However, Heide's Dad, with a last look at what had been his home for 47 years, boarded the train with a heavy heart.

# Chapter 61

Since one of Heide's uncles worked in Berlin, he accompanied them until the last train change. Knowing the area well, he informed them where they had to go and what they had to do. Scary as it had been already, when her uncle left, and they were all by themselves, it became ungodly frightful. Especially when a man that sat across from them, told them he knew what they were doing. He asked if they wanted his help with the escape. They had already witnessed people being taken off the train. Not knowing whether he was an informer, or the Stasi, (Secrete State police in the DDR) they assured him they were visiting friends in Eberswalde.

When he left them, they expected to be escorted off the train. They feared that the man would report them. I cannot imagine the panic and fear that Heide's parents felt every time the police came to check their papers. I remember my mother-in-law telling about a young border guard who checked their papers. He had looked at their small suitcase and then at them. They were sure that fear and guilt were written all over their faces, but he said nothing. By the intense look he had given them, they were sure he had suspected they were not going to Eberswalde.

Shortly thereafter, an older, very uncompromising looking officer, came to their compartment door to check their papers. But for some reason, the young officer interceded and said, "I have already checked their papers. Everything is in order."

They must have been sweating blood during the entire trip. The next day, they got to the stop in Berlin where the east and west met at the train tracks. Exiting the train on the West Berlin side, they ran to safety of the West Berlin Authorities. They had made it out of the Soviet Occupied Germany into the free western sector of Berlin. There, they were given a bowl of watery soup by the Red Cross and were directed to a refugee camp in Tempelhof.

It was a long walk from the train to the refugee camp. On the way, Heide's dad afforded himself a real quality beer that he had not tasted in years. The camp was an old four or five story military garrison with a turn-style checkpoint where their IDs were inspected. People were housed four and five families to a room. There was no privacy.

All too soon, they found out that even West Berlin was not a safe place as they had believed it to be. Individuals were being abducted and dragged back to East Germany. Heide tells about a scary incident when she and her eleven-year-old sister took a stroll outside the camp. They were followed by a stranger in a black leather trench coat (The uniform of the Stasi, the Secrete East German Police). Retreating quickly back into the camp, they no longer ventured outside.

Money and belongings had to be watched every minute or they would disappear. Heide's parents spent much of their time at the authorities while Heide and Hannelore took care of Karin, the baby and watched their belongings. Being awarded political asylum in Berlin, was next to impossible. However, after a string of red tape, they were finally issued temporary refugee papers. Since Heide's parents still had some money left, a friend recommended to request to be flown out of Berlin and into a refugee camp inside West Germany.

Four weeks after their arrival in West Berlin, the family was finally put on a plane to another camp in Lüneburg. More bureaucracy and red tape followed. Finding an apartment in West Germany, in an area with opportunities for jobs and housing, was extremely difficult. Housing was the key issue. Due to the destruction from the war, apartments that were not destroyed were scarce and the building of new apartments was a slow process. The camp's accommodations in Lüneburg were a left-over POW camp with barracks that had long halls housing multiple families separated with blankets used as curtains. The camp's doctor, a woman, took advantage of the kids by having them clean and wash dishes and paraphernalia without paying them or giving them a piece of candy.

While in there, the Lutheran Church had a program for children to vacation with families in other cities and towns. Heide was sent to a town near Bremen and stayed for a couple of weeks with a minister's family. Homesick for her hometown, her parents, and her loving Oma, her stay was plagued with tears. At times, she even entertained the idea of hitchhiking back to her family.

Several months later they received three offers from towns that would accept them. One was in Bavaria where Heide's aunt lived. Another was in Westphalia where relatives, Christa, and Renate lived. The third was in Weinsberg in the province of Württemberg. The chances to get housing were best in Weinsberg. They chose to go there. The refugee camp was also an old converted POW camp. Heide and I believe that this was a divine intervention.

In the beginning, they lived with three other families and their three children in one room until they were awarded one whole room to themselves. Heide's father got work at the city's gas company and became eligible to be on the waiting list for an apartment in Heilbronn.

Her mom worked in the camp's hospital and later at a publishing company doing piecework. In her spare time, she cleaned the office in the camp.

I believe that God planned this to bring Heide and me together. If destiny would not have moved Heide to Heilbronn and stationed me there, the chances of us meeting would have been zero. We have often said, "God played a chess game and we were the pawns."

# Chapter 62

Christmas was approaching. I bought the gold wedding bands, several bottles of whiskey in the commissary, and a gold cross for my sweetheart. For this festive occasion, Heide's sister Christa, with her fiancé, Friedel, and Renate who had joined Christa in Westphalia, came to visit. During a three-day pass, I stayed with Friedel, Christa's fiancé, in a neighbor's room who had an extra bed.

After the family's traditional Christmas-eve dinner of wieners, potato salad, and cold-cuts, we exchanged gifts. Heide gave me a beautiful engraved silver cigarette case and I gave her the gold cross. The big moment had finally come. On the Christmas tree hung two little red hearts with our initials and the rings on a golden ribbon. Love was in the air; we exchanged the rings and celebrated. Heide's mom had baked all kinds of delicious cookies and sweets and we had beer, wine, and whisky to flush it all down.

We had a fun evening. But Friedel developed a whopping toothache. He was a beer drinker and rarely drank any hard liquor. Heide's dad and I, enjoyed *curing* his toothache with good old American whisky. It worked, after a while he felt no pain. However, he had traded his toothache in for a whale of a headache the next morning.

Following a tasty midday dinner of pork roast and potato dumplings on Christmas day, we were ready for a stroll through the vineyards, up to the famous Weibertreu. Before we left, I briefly experienced what it was like in a house full of five girls and a mom. It must have taken us an hour to get out of the camp. Every time we were ready to leave, one of the girls would find a spot on her skirt that needed cleaning, the other did not like her hair and needed to fix it, another one did not like her shoes with her outfit and needed time to decide whether she should change her shoes or dress. But the real kicker came when Heide's mom, who was pressing something, called Christa over because she had detected a wrinkle on the back of her pants. Not thinking, she took the steam iron and pressed the wrinkle out of Christa's pants while she wore them. With a yell and a scream, Christa nearly jumped through the door. That got us going, it became one of those, *remember when* stories that families have and like to remember at family gatherings.

# Chapter 63

I found out that getting married while in the army, was not so easy. First, I had to get permission from the army to marry a foreigner, even though I was not yet an American citizen. It took five years to be eligible for citizenship. The first step was to fill out an application, which the company commander had to approve—that was the easy part. The Captain said, "Any time you need help with your paper work, let me know."

The procedure consisted of a background check on Heide, a physical check up, and an interview with the chaplain. A military wedding on the base would have been wonderful, but since Heide and her family did not speak any English, we decided to get married in a German Catholic church. Now we needed to conform to the German laws. This meant that we had to get married first by the justice of the peace and then, in the church. German law does not recognize a church wedding.

To live off base, we had to find an apartment, which had to be approved by the company commander. It also had to be within twenty minutes, walking time, of the garrison.

After the wedding, I had to apply for Heide's visa, which meant more red tape and bureaucracy. We muddled through the papers for the army, but the German's were the ones that gave us a hard time. Heide did not have a proper birth certificate and getting one from East Germany was impossible. Therefore, we needed witnesses to swear that she was the daughter of her parents. The *Birth Statement* she had, was good enough for the American authorities but not for the German paper shufflers.

After some help from Gerhard's father, who was the justice of the peace in Schlebusch, we finally got it all straightened out.

We planned to get married at Peter and Paul, the Catholic Church in town, and went for the Pre Cana-instruction. The pastor, though a pleasant person, had a bad habit of fingering his nose with his hanky wrapped around his finger. It did not enhance his lecture. I am positive the Army Chaplain would have done a much better job.

We looked around and finally found an apartment that was reasonably priced. It was a pleasantly furnished, cold-water flat with one attic room and a tiny galley kitchen big enough for a small table and a hotplate on which to cook. We thought it was fantastic—our very own apartment! Getting it approved by the CO was no problem. His exact words were, "If you cannot find an apartment, who can?" With that, he signed off on it. Unfortunately, the apartment was not vacant until three weeks after our wedding. Therefore, we decided to visit my hometown for our honeymoon. The wedding was set for June 6, 1959.

# Chapter 64

In April 1959, the cold war started to heat up. The Russians threatened to move into West Berlin. The fear of an actual war breaking out, became real. Our battalion was on constant alert. We were ready for combat. It was a well-known fact that the main battle line was drawn in France and that Germany was to be the *bleed and retreat* space. Still terrified from my first-hand experience in WWII, I was distraught and worried for Heide and her family's safety. I tried to get her to become part of the dependence evacuation group but she refused to leave Germany without me.

Those were dark days and it overshadowed our love and the excitement for our upcoming wedding. The Soviets set an ultimatum for the Americans to leave Berlin by the fifteenth of May. On the thirteenth of May, our battalion moved out of the garrison in full combat gear. Our trucks and trailers were loaded with ammunition, explosives, mines etc. We moved into a strategic area, in case the Russians held true to their word. Our orders were to slow down the advancing Russians by blowing up every bridge and tunnel in their way. After a couple of nerve-racking weeks, the Russians stood down. It became a mere saber-rattling event.

\*\*\*\*

My Mom had sent white lace for Heide's dress and my Stresemann Suit (a black double-breasted jacket, striped pants, and a silver-gray vest) to wear for the wedding. I rented a top hat and bought white gloves to complete my attire.

I knew Heide was going to the fittings for her dress. Since that was my field of expertise, I wanted to attend. I was told that to see the bride in her dress before the wedding was bad luck. Well, I have never been a superstitious person, but it made no sense to rattle someone else's cage.

The wedding was going to be small. My parents could not afford to come, my grandmother had died a couple of months earlier, and the rest of my family and friends were seven hundred miles away. That only left my army friend, John, and my friend Gerhard, who had been drafted and stationed in Nürnberg, to be there by my side.

From Heide's side there would be her immediate family, her girlfriend, Rosemarie, and her parents, plus two friends of Heide's parents. In all, about fourteen people would be at our reception. Gerhard was to be my best man and Heide's friend Rosemarie, the maid of honor. A friend of the family was going to do the cooking and Heide's mom would do the baking beforehand.

As luck would have it, Heide's parents had gotten an apartment in Heilbronn two months before our wedding. That was going to be our *banquet hall* for the reception.

Gerhard came into town the night before the wedding and stayed at a small hotel around the corner from my in-laws to be.

John rented a tuxedo for the occasion and on Saturday morning, June 6, 1959, the two of us got dressed up and with the best wishes of my friends, sergeants, and officers, we went to Heide's parent's apartment. John, Gerhard, and Friedel, who was now Christa's husband, Heide's dad, and I, had to wait in the kitchen while her girlfriend and Heide's mom and sisters, were busy helping her get dressed in the bedroom. The hairdresser was supposed to come and arrange the veil but arrived extremely late.

While we were waiting, we guys had a shot or two to calm our nerves. Heide's father said, "Now you can call me by my first name."

"How about Mom and Dad?" I replied.

"I like that," he said, and with that, we toasted again.

When the hairdresser was finally done and Heide came out in her wedding gown and veil, I thought she was the most beautiful girl in the world. I was totally at awe. City hall was close by so with my top hat and white gloves in one hand and my stunning bride on my other arm, we walked to City Hall. It was a hot, sunny morning. By the time we arrived at the Justice of the Peace office to get married, we were late. We were passed over and had to wait while another couple got married. Luck was with us, as we had time to spare between the civil and the church ceremony. You see, I had already learned the first lesson of a married man. If you want to be on time, move the hand on the clock a half hour ahead.

After the civil ceremony we walked a block from City Hall over to the church. Since Heide was not yet eighteen, her dad had to sign the consent forms in both the church and at city hall. Our wedding ceremony was a simple one. We walked together up the aisle with the organ playing and a lady singing Ave Maria. Following prayers, songs, and a homily, we exchanged our vows, slipped the rings on each other's finger, and were then pronounced *Husband and Wife*. At first, I could not believe that we were really married. Then we took some pictures and marched ecstatically off to Heide's parent's apartment to celebrate. With lots of gourmet food, wine, and song, we had an enjoyable afternoon.

John, representing the guys in my platoon, made quite a production as he presented us with a silver-plated teapot and cups paid for by the men in my platoon.

Since we could not get into our apartment, we had rented a room in the same hotel where Gerhard stayed. When evening arrived, we flew the coop and went to the hotel while our guests were still going strong.

John had planned to go to Stuttgart after the reception. But he never made it out of the armchair after we departed. The next morning, we all congregated at Mama Riechen's for breakfast. When we arrived, John, still in his tuxedo, was just waking up with a whale of a headache...ha, ha, ha. He had a tough time focusing, trying to figure out where he was.

After a nice leisurely day, strolling along the riverbank of the Neckar, we enjoyed a few beers. Heide and I prepared for our trip and honeymoon.

I had a thirty-day leave from the army, However, I did not have the money for us to go on an exotic trip. We had accepted my Aunt Martha's invitation to stay in her home. Aunt Martha was my mother's cousin and lived in Schlebusch, my hometown. We took a small suitcase, said good-bye to Heide's family, and boarded the train to Schlebusch.

# Chapter 65

When we arrived at my aunt's home, that warm and wonderful woman made us feel most welcome. She turned over her own bedroom to us and told us to come and go as we wished.

Naturally, we had to make the rounds through town visiting with family and friends. All were eager to know about us, and to learn about my parents, and America. My Aunt Gretchen, also one of my mom's cousins, gave us a set of silver flatware for six setting.

I was happy seeing old friends and family and showing off my new bride. However, as the day wore on, Heide became quieter and quieter and that night she cried. My love was hurting and I did not know why. Young and dumb, I had not realized that with all the friends and relatives rehashing old times, she had felt like a third wheel on a cart. That was not exactly what a young married bride expected on her honeymoon. Well, we talked it out and then we continued our honeymoon. We spent a couple of days sight-seeing in both Cologne and Altenberg.

All too soon it was time to go back to Heilbronn. We said our goodbyes, thanked everyone, and took the train home. We were eager to set up housekeeping in our first apartment.

****

The next two weeks we were busy setting up house. Having our very own place was fantastic. We went shopping at the PX, both in Heilbronn and Kornwestheim. Kornwestheim was the

Group's Headquarters. The PX was much larger and had a greater selection of merchandise. The dollar had a great exchange rate of 4.20 DM. Being thrifty, we compared prices between the German stores and the PX. We bought where the prices were lower, or when items could not be gotten at the PX or commissary. Every new blanket, bed sheet or dish we bought became a treasure and was cherished with joy.

Heide knew how much I enjoyed her mother's cooking, so she had to show me her cooking skills. She had planned to make her mom's goulash that she knew I loved. I was not allowed to peek into the kitchen until she was finished and had set the table. We sat down at the table to eat our very first dinner, in our own apartment. She had set the table with flowers, a bowl of noodles, salad, and the scrumptious Paprika Goulash.

After saying grace, I started to eat. Oh, it tasted great, only one minor problem, the meat was a bit tough. To be honest, it took all the pressure per square inch of my teeth to chew the morsels of goulash. Heide kept looking at me saying, "It's awful, isn't it?" However, I kept insisting that it was great. Full of love for my pretty bride, I kept chewing my goulash.

That was the first and last time that Heide cooked a flawed meal. She was, and still is, a gourmet chef. Collecting cookbooks of international cuisines became a hobby of hers. Not only did she cook delicious meals, she was also very frugal and knew how to shop to make the money go further. One of our money-saving dinners was pan-fried bauchfleisch (A piece of lean bacon) with salad and noodles, or potato soup. Not only did we both love it, but it also was cheap.

On the weekends, we were always invited to Heide's parents for dinner. Weekend dinners were served at noontime. Being young lovers, and much to her mom's chagrin, we were always late and had to eat warmed up leftovers. She would scold us for being late by saying; "The food needs to be eaten when it is hot, not when it is cold!"

My furlough was up. I had to be at the base at eight o'clock in the morning for work call. If you were married and lived off post, you did not need to attend reveille. Right after work call, the sergeant said, "Hey, Lohn, welcome back. Now get to the barber and get yourself a decent haircut. You look like Elvis."

Heide had asked me to get a fashionable box cut, which the sergeant thought was not a military haircut. He continued, "And while you're at it, go to the PX and buy some birds for your sleeve, you're out of uniform!"

While I had been on my honeymoon, my promotion to Specialist Fourth Class had come through. The birds were the rank insignia for a Spec 4.

That was great news. It meant an increase in pay for the other stripe, plus housing allowance since I was living off post, and extra pay for my spouse. My total pay allowed us to live comfortably and enabled us to buy German china and stemware that was reasonably priced and of excellent quality.

Life in the army, as a married man, was okay with the exception of the training exercises and maneuvers. That always meant a temporary separation, which was painful for us newlyweds. The worst was the surprise muster alerts. Usually they were called at two or three o'clock in the morning. I had twenty minutes to get into the garrison in full battle gear. Our battalion had to clear the post in forty-five minutes and regroup in the forest to await further orders. We never knew where we were going or for how long. Sometimes, the alert was called off after only a couple of hours. While at other times, we would get orders to move out to a training area and were gone for a couple of days. Regular workdays were from eight in the morning until five in the afternoon, unless you had guard duty.

****

We filed the necessary papers for Heide's visa, which was only a formality. However, it was still a lot of red tape. I don't know why they could not use the papers we had already filed for the approval to get married but that would have been too simple. Heide had to go through the normal routine of interviews, a physical, and the screening at the American Consulate in Frankfurt.

# Chapter 66

In our free time, we walked along the river, or through the beautiful vineyards up in the mountains, to a restaurant called Wartberg. Looking down into the valley on a fall day was a breathtaking sight. The sun made the colors of the grapevines along the mountainside come alive. Thick, healthy, dark blue grapes weighed down the vines, asking to be harvested. It was a carefree life, which we fully enjoyed.

It was three months into our marriage when I came home from work and Heide surprised me with the news, "We are pregnant!" Our happiness was complete.

****

Time moved on and soon it was Christmas again. This was to be our first Christmas as a married couple and the second one since we had met. The presents revolved around our expected baby. The tiny clothes were admired repeatedly. Feeling the baby, as it did summersaults in Heide's tummy and the mystery of whether it would be a boy or girl, kept our excitement growing.

However, the good tidings and expectancy were overshadowed by the knowledge that we would soon be leaving for the US. I had become very fond of Heide's family and hated to say goodbye. It must have been hard for Heide's mom and dad to see her leave, not knowing when they would see her again and not being present at the baby's birth.

The end of January 1960 was my time to rotate back to the US for my discharge. We decided to ship our household goods to the states ahead of time. Belongings of returning servicemembers were duty free and sent via the military, directly to your home. We decided to book a flight for Heide in February, so she would arrive in New York after I had been released from the army. The date we chose was just before the airlines would ban her from flying due to her pregnancy.

New Year 1960 arrived. The days in January were numbered and went by quickly. All too soon it was time for me to leave. It was a difficult farewell. After saying teary goodbyes to Heide's family, she went with me to the train station and waited until I boarded the train for Frankfurt. I was distraught having to leave her behind and worried about her well-being flying to the US. I experienced a conflict of emotions —happy to be getting out of the army and yet there was the sadness of parting from the people that I had learned to love. Some last minute hugs, kisses, and tears, and the train pulled out of the station.

Heide moved back in with her parents until she left for the USA.

# Chapter 67

The Army flew us via MATS from Frankfurt to the McGuire Air Force Base. Upon arrival, I was temporarily assigned to a holding company at Fort Dix for processing. After a thorough physical and mental examination, pay and paper processing, I was honorably discharged from the army on February 6, 1960.

When I arrived at my parent's home, I found that they had prepared an apartment for us in their corner house. As I walked through it, I found they had furnished the kitchen, dining room, and bedroom. All our houseware, china, and stemware that we had shipped home, had been lovingly placed in the cabinets. It was a neat little apartment with room for a crib. I was so pleased and couldn't wait for Heide to see it.

The next day, I went with Dad to work, where they welcomed me back with open arms. It was good to be back and in control of my future. Despite having an enjoyable time in Germany, and finding the love of my life, military life was not for me. Now I waited anxiously for Heide's arrival.

The morning of February 22, 1960, I got ready to pick up my sweetheart at the JFK Airport. I was both excited and nervous. Excited for the obvious reasons, yet nervous because I wanted her to love this country as I did. I was worried how she would adjust to her new home.

When I returned home, I had realized that the row houses could look monotonous compared to the quaint villages of Germany. Therefore, I tried to prepare her in advance. I did not want Heide to have any false images of what she would find.

A friend of my parents took Mom and me to the airport. Armed with a bouquet of roses, I waited anxiously in the waiting area. After what seemed to be hours of waiting, she finally came through the doors of the custom processing facility. It was so good to hold her in my arms. The flight had been very rough on her and being seven months pregnant, had not helped. She had gotten sick on the flight.

I introduced her to Mom and our friend, Rudy. Then we sat down in the cafeteria to have something light to eat and drink to settle down her stomach.

On the drive back from the airport, I kept apologizing for the lack of quaintness along the way. She kept telling me not to worry, she did not see anything negative. But it was not until we came into our own apartment that she was happy.

Other than missing her family, Heide felt at home very quickly. When my final paycheck from the army arrived, we went downtown to a department store. We bought an upholstered couch and chairs, a living room lamp, a radio-record player, and a carpet. Being able to get all of that, we felt like royalty. To establish credit, we borrowed some money from the church's credit union and later we opened a revolving loan account at the bank. The next thing we bought was a TV set from our friend, Ed Becker and we got two lamp tables, a wall clock, a small moveable bar, and a teddy bear for our baby, with Green Stamps.

\*\*\*\*

My work was challenging. I enjoyed working on the costumes of Broadway shows. The reproduction of historical uniforms for the different military branches, as well as reproduction of historical attire for the Smithsonian Institute were both challenging and exciting. After eight weeks back at work, Mr. Valentino retired. As I was promised, at the age of twenty-six, I

276

was put in charge of the manufacturing department. Now, I had a title but not the money. Now that I was the boss, I no longer got overtime pay. However, being still in the army reserve, gave us a little bit of extra money. Whenever possible, I did work at home after hours, for which I got extra pay.

Money was tight; we made every penny count. Since the baby was going to be born before my health insurance would go into effect, we had to save money for the doctor and the hospital. As a present, our sponsor had given us a crib for the baby. We had already bought a coach and stroller in Germany, as well as clothes and the old-fashioned cloth diapers. Disposable diapers were too expensive.

We were now ready for the big event and were excitedly waiting for the baby to arrive.

# Chapter 68

Late in the evening, on May 15, 1960, Heide started to go into labor. Like any first-time father, I was a nervous wreck. When we thought it was time, I borrowed our friend Ed's car, and drove to the hospital. It was about forty-five minutes away. This panicky dad to be, yours truly, thought he would not make it to the hospital on time, but we did. After filling out the paperwork, they took Heide and wheeled her away.

In those days, they did not let fathers into the delivery room. Not yet nineteen and unable to understand or speak English, my poor wife did not know what was going on. All I heard was her calling out, "Please come with me. Don't leave me alone."

An hour later they brought her into a labor room where at least I could stay with her and explain what the doctor had said. Soon, the contractions started to slow down and then completely stopped. I asked the doctor, "What now?"

"We wait," he said.

Since I am not a patient person, waiting was not my strength. Also, being new at my job and its responsibilities, I worried whether I had left proper instructions for my people and so forth. I was coming unglued while waiting for our child to be born and the worrying about work. The doctor said, we had hours before anything would happen and by today's standards, I did the unspeakable—I left my wife at the hospital and went to work to make sure everything was all right.

When I got to work I found everything was fine but now I started to panic because I was not at the hospital. Frightened, jumpy, and nervous, I jumped back into the car and high-tailed it back to the hospital. As I flew through the maternity ward doors I saw Heide walking around smiling. The doctor explained that she was dilating slowly and that once she was far enough along, they would give her something to induce labor. I thought, *just like the army, hurry up and wait.* Seeing Heide so chipper made me calm down.

Finally, after twenty-four hours, it was time. With a last kiss from me, they wheeled her into the delivery room. This time she was calm and prepared. Following another thirty minutes of nerve-wracking waiting, at last I got the happy news. The doctor announced, "Congratulations, you have a healthy boy. Mom and baby are doing fine and in a little while you can see her."

Wow! I was floating on cloud nine. Before they settled Heide in her room, the nurse came and asked me, "Would you like to see your son?"

"Yes, I cannot wait."

She took me to the nursery where for the first time, I saw that little miracle, our first-born son. I had never seen a newborn baby. No one had prepared me for what they looked like. I was shocked. I was expecting this beautiful little baby, looking like a six-week-old. But there was this little bundle with dark hair growing into his forehead resembling a little monkey more than what I had envisioned my son would look like.

The nurse must have seen my face because she laughed and said, "You have never seen a newborn baby, have you?"

"No, I have not."

"He is a beautiful little boy. Just wait a couple of weeks and you will see it too."

When I went into Heide's room, she was glowing. I don't think I had ever seen her look so stunning. "Did you see him?" she asked.

I nodded and said, "Yes."

"Isn't he beautiful?" I could not tell her what I really thought, so I answered, "He is gorgeous."

We were happy, we were a real family now. The nurse was correct. A couple of weeks later, he really was a beautiful baby.

When I went home, I was all excited. I had told my parents we have a little boy by the name of Peter. Boy did I have it all wrong! Heide had gone back and forth with names so often that I was totally confused. I knew she had no name picked for a girl, but I was positive she had settled on Peter. Well, it was not Peter; it was Henry.

At least the damage was not as big as what happened to my boss's father in Germany. There you had to go to the city hall and register your newborn baby. Between the hospital and city hall, were quite a few taverns. By the time he arrived there, he was so full of golden wine, he registered a girl instead of a boy. He had a bit of a problem fixing the registration of his girl named Arthur.

# Chapter 69

When Heide came home with our little boy, Henry, we could not stop admiring this little miracle. Our happiness was complete.

Of course, I had kept Heide's parents up to date and when Henry was born, I called them right away. They were happy. However, not being able to be there when he was born, or for the christening, I am sure they shed a few tears.

My dad was in his glory at the christening. Encouraged by the golden juice of the grape, Dad was making speeches and led everyone in song at the celebration. However, if the baby cried, everything stopped. He would pick up the baby and carry him around until he would go to sleep—as he did with all our children. He was a good grandpa. But I do not think my mom was quite ready to be a grandma, nor did she ever become a full-fletched nana.

Life as a young family, was both wonderful as well as tough. Money was tight, and we turned every penny over a few times before we spent it. When we were out and became thirsty, rather than spend money on such luxury as soda, we would return home to quench our thirst. Being in the same boat as our friends, we did not feel as if we were missing anything. We did not have a car, we had to rely on public transportation. On weekends, we would drive with my parents to places like Long Wood Garden or French Creek etc. We also did a lot of walking then.

# Chapter 70

I worked many long hours and enjoyed my work, both at the company as well as at home, to make extra money. As the new department head and under my direction, we had finished the first order of historical uniforms for the Marine Corps. A military historian, Colonel Mc Gruder, came to inspect the uniforms before we could ship them.

Since it had been only a few months since I had been discharged from active duty, I was still under the spell of military courtesy. A Marine Corps Colonel was someone to respect and fear. I was terrified on the day he was to arrive. Mr. Weidler brought him back into the workroom to inspect the uniforms. He was a tall, dark-haired man that evoked respect. He was dressed in civilian clothes and was very friendly. It helped to stop me from shaking. My dad used to call him the *pipe man* because of the fancy carved shell briar pipe he used to carry in his breast pocket.

It was a sweltering day. The factory had only fans and no air-conditioner. After saying hello and shaking my hand, he took off his coat and placed it on my worktable. Then we went to the back where I had laid out the uniforms of thirteen periods from the inception to the modern days of the Marine Corps. He took out his tape measure, and a little ruler and checked everything to the sixteenths of an inch. I watched him nervously. When I saw a little smile on his face, I figured that this was a good sign.

When he was done, he turned to me and said, "You did an excellent job. These uniforms are the best Van Horn's has ever made." I saw Mr. Weidler's proud smile; he was my strongest supporter.

We went back to my work area and from a distance I saw that Heide had come in to visit with the baby. I thought, *Great! I can show off my lovely wife and my handsome baby boy.* When I got closer, I thought I was going to die from embarrassment. My lovely young bride had placed the baby on top of Colonel Mc Gruder's jacket. Here was a Full Bird Colonel whose inspection I had just survived and my wife was using his jacket for a changing pad!

The Colonel and Mr. Weidler burst out laughing upon seeing this young mom, not yet old enough to buy beer, trying to change her baby's diaper on top of Colonel Mc Gruder's suit jacket. I found out that colonels can be human too. I survived my first mission under fire.

**** 

The job was challenging. I worked on projects like the Louis Tussauds Wax Works in Atlantic City, the Holiday on Ice show, Broadway shows in summer theaters, and the Broadway show Hello Dolly with Carol Channing.

One day I was called into the front office. When I got close to the office, I heard loud laughter. Upon entering, I saw this gray penguin running all over the place. The client and Mr. Weidler were laughing. The job was for the new aquarium that was about to open in Camden. They wanted tuxedos for the orchestra made from materials that would absorb little or no water, and dry fast because they would be sitting in a pond.

That challenge was not so hard. But then came the kicker. He wanted a tailcoat, bathrobe, and a top hat for the penguin. Now that, was what I called a challenge. To measure and make clothes for a penguin would be a bit of a problem. However, despite his noisy objections, I measured the little critter as best I could and managed to make the garments. When dressed, the little guy looked cute in the outfits.

But, that was not the end of it. They had me come to the aquarium and measure the porpoises. They wanted phosphoric plastic tail-like outfits that strapped onto their bodies and would glow from the floodlights when they jumped out of the water.

Since I cannot swim, going into the water in swim trunks was out of the question. Finally, the trainers coaxed the dolphins to the edge of the tank, and after getting thoroughly soaked, I did manage to measure each one of them.

The job came with plenty of excitement and stress but little money. My ulcer grew faster than my salary. I was tired of getting a raise only whenever I asked for it.

# Chapter 71

It became apparent to us that the young and old should not live under one roof. We had little privacy because my mother thought that my first responsibility was to her. Every evening she would come straight into our apartment and talk all night about work. My young wife got a little upset and so did I. After an argument with her, we moved out and rented an apartment fifteen minute away.

It was time to get a car. We found an old, bed type Nash parked in the street with a for sale sign on it. The car looked good and for 175 dollars, the price was right.

We felt like millionaires; we had our first car. Heide polished the car and tried to rub out any rust spot on the chrome. Still remembering my active service days, I cleaned the motor just short of steam cleaning. I had learned from a friend in the reserves, who had steam-cleaned his car, that it leaked like a sieve afterwards. Dirt had sealed the leaks.

Our wonderful car that we were so proud of, ran well for about six months and then died. Since we were now used to having our own transportation, we needed to get a new car. With the unpleasant experience of a second-hand car, we started to shop among the new ones. On the floor of an Oldsmobile dealer we found a blue Polara 500. It was heavily discounted to the price of $2,800, and it was a good-looking car. We felt that we had moved up another notch.

When we bought the car, I had counted on another raise, which was not forthcoming. That presented a problem. Now we were in a financial bind. Heide and I talked it over and decided to go for broke. I went to my boss and said, I have been offered a job with more pay. I love my work here but unless you can match the money, I have no choice but to leave. I have a family to support. It paid off, and suddenly, the money became available.

****

One evening Dad came over and told us that there was a nice house in the neighborhood for sale. He said, "The price on the house is $11,500, which you can probably get down to $10,500. The mortgage is going to be less than what you are now paying for rent." Then Dad offered to give us the down payment, which was $1,000.

He had become a real expert in the real estate market and had bought another house that he had turned into two more apartments and was making 9% on the bank's money.

We looked at the house. It was a Philadelphia row-house with three bedrooms, a living-dining room combo, and a kitchen. It was perfect for us and we loved it. Excited, we took Dad's offer.

After Heide had a miscarriage, which scared the living daylights out of us, we did not know what to expect but now she was pregnant with our second child and we knew that we needed more room.

While looking at the house, Dad and I made plans to build a workroom in the basement like he had. Together we went to the realtor and haggled down the price to $10,500. Our mortgage was $84 a month including the tax and insurance. Which was less than the rent we were paying at the time.

Again, a step forward. Now we were homeowners as well.

****

It was time for our new baby to be born. We went back to the same hospital with one big difference, now, Heide spoke English and we knew what to expect. We did not care whether it was a boy or girl as long the baby was healthy. After six hours of labor, instead of twenty-four hours, our little girl was born on July 20, 1962. She was so beautiful, because this time I was prepared and even got the name right. Despite not caring whether we would have a boy or girl, we realized how ecstatic we were to have our little Christina.

Four weeks later, we celebrated her christening. It was a sweltering Sunday in July. My old friend, Gerhard, who also had gotten married while in the service and had a little girl as well, was going to be the Godfather. My Aunt Martha, who was visiting from Germany, became Tina's Godmother. Aunt Martha, with whom we had spent our honeymoon, was a great help preparing for the party. Before the war she had lived in the US. She spoke fluent English.

The day was to become an event neither my friends nor my family would ever let me forget. Rushing around in the morning, getting the kids dressed and prepared for the party, we had no time to eat lunch. But all was set and off we went to church for the baptism. It was a sweltering day, and in good long-standing tradition, we were dressed in formal attire. My dad was dressed in a *cut away*, and I wore my double-breasted *Stresemann* suit that I had worn on our wedding.

Coming home from church, hot and with an empty stomach, my dad had to invoke another tradition. He and I had to drink a toast to the little girl and since you cannot stand on one leg, quote unquote, it became two generous glasses of cognac. Well, I am not my dad who could take it—I was drunk. To sober me up, Heide put me in the shower and ran cold water over me but to no avail. All she got was a singing troubadour in the shower. After a while, she gave up and put me to bed.

I never met any of the guests that came for the party, but I understand they had an enjoyable time. My friends still rub it in today; having fun at my expense. To this day I do not understand why Heide did not get mad at me. She only laughed about it. My mom would have been furious if that had happened to my dad.

# Chapter 72

We enjoyed the kids and each other. When our daughter, nicknamed Tina, was about one year old, Heide went with the two children, to visit her parents in Germany.

During the time she was gone, Dad and I worked very hard remodeling our house. I wanted to surprise her by paneling the porch and replacing the old doors with new modern flush ones.

The day before I thought she was coming home, I was sitting in the kitchen having a cigarette and a cup of coffee before putting the finishing touches on our handiwork. Suddenly, I realized that I had the date wrong, she was arriving at JFK in New York that morning; while I was still sitting in Philadelphia unshaven and not showered. I panicked and finished in a hurry—army style. Telling my parents to call the airport and leave a message that I was on my way. I jumped into the car and rushed to New York.

Never in my life have I felt as bad as that morning. After waiting anxiously for them to come home, I had messed up. I was in tears because the love of my live with two little children was sitting in the airport and I was not there to greet them. Again, instead of being furious, all she said is, "It is alright, Honey, don't worry." She always was and still is, a good sport.

All of them looked so beautiful. I realized how much I had missed them.

****

We had made good friends in the neighborhood and enjoyed sitting on the front steps on summer evenings having pizza and beer together. In the wintertime, we would rotate between three different homes.

On January 17, 1966, after another miscarriage, our youngest son, Michael, was born. Since the other two were already older, we thought he was so cute. This time, the christening went off without any misgivings.

I was blessed with a wonderful family, though the money was tight. However interesting my job was, I still needed more income to support my growing family. When I compared my salary, with that of other executives in the apparel field, I realized I was underpaid. Besides the extreme stress in show business, they were making more than double my wages and had less knowledge. I knew that to manufacture regular *street wear*, was far less complicated than the costumes we were making. In addition, every one of our contracts came with a *late delivery clause* that stated if the costumes were not delivered on a certain date and time, we would be penalized and would have to pay for a full house with empty seats.

I began to look for another job and was hired to run a ladies pants factory upstate Pennsylvania. My new salary would be a hefty increase over the pay I had received at Van Horns. After ten years with the company, I gave my notice and accepted the new position. We put our house up for sale and rented an apartment in the small, upstate town.

A couple of weeks into the job, I realized it was not for me. Pushing thousands of the same slacks through the production line every week was as boring as it could get—especially after the exciting and challenging work I had been accustomed to doing. The little *hick-town* was another problem. Being used to city life, even though the area was pretty, we realized that for us small town living was depressing.

294

Heide, being a good trooper, did not complain and I did not want to either, because we needed the money. But she soon knew that something was not right. I could never hide anything from her. Eventually she would notice it. We talked it over and we found that neither of us was happy with the set-up.

Again, I started to look for another job and found one with a uniform company in Philadelphia. Seven months after we had moved to upstate Pennsylvania, we were back home. Fortunately, our house had not sold, which was our luck. God looked out for us in more ways than one. We realized later that had we stayed in that small town, we would have lost everything, including my job. A Hurricane created a big flood that devastated the town after we had left.

I was hired as a designer, which meant pattern making and quality control. An older colleague, by the name of Gus, handled the military uniforms and I the industrial ones. During my career I had many great mentors but this wonderful, warm-hearted friend, was one of the finest. Very quickly he realized I had great technical knowledge but fell short on the mass-production side. Without letting anyone know, he taught me the skills I was lacking. We became close friends. Several years later he died from Parkinson's disease. It shook me up something fierce.

Not long after I started working at the uniform company, I was asked to take over the position as plant manager. However, the company was plagued with internal struggles and nepotism, which created an uncomfortable atmosphere.

Always looking forward to advance and better myself, I saw an advertisement in the trade paper for a working partner. It was a medium-sized contract shop making jackets for boys. Mostly low-end children's apparel. I was given the opportunity to join the company with the promise that I could acquire the company through monthly payments. That sounded like a good deal. *I saw myself already as a Factory Owner.* However, it did not take me long to realize that all the owner wanted was someone with a miracle to fix his quality and output. He had no technical knowledge and no clue of what it takes to make quality garments. Nor did I think he had any real intentions of passing his company on to me, so I went back to the job market.

Again, I was in luck. Two different companies offered me a job. At one company as a designer in a medium-sized menswear company and the other was with a large menswear company as second-in-command of quality control and design.

Heide and I talked about the two choices and tried to weigh them against each other. Each had pros and cons. I liked the people very much in the larger company and it was challenging. But it was a fifty-weeks a year traveling job. In the other company, the owner struck me as a shifty person, but there was no travel involved.

By then I had had my fill of shady characters and was leery about the sincerity of the offer. Being separated all week long and only home on the weekends would be difficult, but the better career move. We went back and forth between the pain of separation and the opportunity to advance my career.

Heide, always the supporting wife, said, "I think you should go with the larger company." Thus, it was that in 1969 I started with the Campus Sweater and Sportswear Company. Again, we saw that the good Lord had looked out for us because less than a year later the other company went bankrupt.

In my new job I ran into my next mentor. My boss was a very tall man with wide shoulders and an athletic build. We never knew how old he was, but he did not look a year over fifty. Personally, I believed he was closer to seventy. This big man was kind and very compassionate. He knew from his own experience how difficult it was to be away all week from your family and tried to schedule my work, so I could be home an extra night here and there.

With his sponsorship, I was accepted into the International Association of Clothing Designers. My responsibilities included pattern work for the sport coat and suit division as well as the quality control in twenty-seven factories. The territory stretched from Massachusetts in the north to the Florida border in the south, from the east coast, and as far west as Kentucky.

The pay was fair but not necessarily compensatory with the arduous work and travel, but it was a lot more than what we were used to. Now we were able to buy a new car with air-conditioning and could begin to look at single homes in the suburbs. We felt we had moved up in the world.

On one of our Sunday afternoon drives, a year, and a half later, we found a new development in New Jersey. The homes were set into the woods with the trees left intact. That made for a lovely setting. The bug bit us; one of the two-story colonials kept us enthralled. We sat for what seemed like hours in the model home trying to figure out what it would be like to own a house like this, and how we could afford it. It did not take us long to figure it out and we eventually bought one.

# Chapter 73

The heavy amount of travel was both taxing and exciting. Taxing because flying from airport to airport, sometimes a different flight every night, renting cars and getting to the factories in the most remote towns of the country, was difficult and tiring. Sitting alone in a motel room and being away from my family, was painful. Heide, raising the kids by herself, with the added burden of running the house, was tough on her. My telephone bills quite often exceeded the company's allowed minutes. Sometimes, after calling home, I lay on the bed in a lonely motel room weeping. I knew it was no different for Heide. However, we learned to cherish our time when we were together. Since time was so precious, we decided to concentrate on loving each other instead of arguing about nonsensical incidents or things.

Although, I must admit that travel had its exciting moments. Rushing from one end of the country to the other, meeting many different people and solving problems in the process, was new and gave me a feeling of being part of big business. It gave me a taste of corporate life with its challenging meetings. However, corporate politics had its drawbacks.

My boss, mentor, and friend always tried to keep the ugly politics away from his team, so we wouldn't be affected by it. This lesson I tried to emulate during my career as a leader of teams with large corporations. I gained the knowledge from this wise friend that leadership was not giving orders, intimidating, belittling people, or making big meaningless speeches. It was teaching, guiding, and directing people as a team to jointly accomplish a task.

Unfortunately, corporate life had many short-sided, insecure, and big talking executives that surrounded themselves with mediocrity for fear of being bypassed. The Peter Principle was born, and inefficiency became rampant in the corporate world and still is. Top executives are usually interested in looking good and protecting their own hides rather than in the well-being of the company with which they have been entrusted. However, I can fend off corporate politics better than living with nepotism.

Travel also had its funny moments. I remember my first trip to Georgia. After arriving in Atlanta at night, I drove to a small town called Cordele and checked into the Holiday Inn. In the morning I went to the restaurant for breakfast. The waitress' southern drawl was interesting, but the housekeeper's German accent mixed with a southern drawl was comical. I studied the menu and ordered two eggs sunny side up with bacon, toast, orange juice, and coffee. The juice and coffee came at once and after a while, the waitress came with my order. I looked at it and said to her, "I am sorry, but you have the wrong order. This is not mine."

She took out her tab, and said, "You ordered two sunny side up, bacon, toast, juice and coffee, right?"

"Yes, I responded."

"That's what Y'all got," she replied.

Dumbfounded, I looked at her and said, "Then what is that stuff the eggs are laying in?"

"Oh, that's grits. Ya pour the red eye gravy ova it. It's good." (If you are not familiar with southern cooking, red eye gravy is made from coffee.)

I tasted a little of the grits and said, "Please do me a favor and just bring me the eggs without that stuff." That taught me to say "No grits, please," before I ordered breakfast in Georgia.

At dinner that evening, I had another interesting experience. Listed on the menu was brook-trout, which I love. I ordered it with a glass of white wine. The waitress informed me that this was a *dry county*. Not familiar with the southern states, I asked, "What does that mean?"

She looked at me like I had come from the moon, and explained, "Dry county means that it is forbidden to serve alcohol in that county." While I was eating my salad, I was looking forward to my nice broiled trout that I had ordered, or so I thought. When my fish came, it was fried like a rock including the white meat. Another lesson learned, in the south their favorite way to prepare food is to fry it. So much for my nice trout. However, the southern hush puppies were good and later, I learned to order catfish, which I enjoy.

I had stayed in the Holiday Inn in Bremen. The factory I needed to visit, was in a small town called Smithfield. The town was in a rural area about a half hour away from the Holiday Inn. The plant manager met me at the hotel, when I arrived for dinner. He drew me a map showing me the way to the factory from the motel and said it was about a half hour's drive.

The next morning, I left the motel and followed his map. After an hour of driving, I still had not found the factory. If you have ever asked for directions in a rural area, you find out that it is a little bit of a problem. Two hours later, after repeatedly asking for directions and driving around in circles, I finally made it to the plant. When I got into the office, the plant manager said, "I thought you were going to be here at eight o'clock?"

I said, "Yes, so did I. I followed your map. I've been driving around for hours trying to find you here."

"How come?" he asked.

"I don't know," I replied. "I followed your map, but it didn't get me here."

"Let me see the map," he said. After looking at it, he said, "Oh, my god, I drew the map backwards!"

*I started to wonder what kind of manager he was.*

On another occasion, I was with a group of colleagues, staying in a different hotel. We were there for an important meeting. The next morning, we were all ready to leave for the office but one of our colleagues, who was notoriously late, had not shown up yet. As we were waiting, a businessman with his luggage and obviously in a hurry, came charging into the lobby and checked out.

After he had hurriedly left, a lady appeared in the lobby, looked around, and approached the clerk behind the desk. She shook her head mumbling to herself and nervously paced back and forth. We were all thinking, *oh boy, whoever was supposed to pick her up must be late.*

About ten minutes later, the man who had been in such a hurry, stormed into the lobby, saying to the women that was pacing back and forth, "Oh my God! I forgot you were with me." He was in such a hurry to get wherever it he was going, he had taken off and left his wife in the hotel room.

We used to attend sales meetings in Cleveland, which always finished with an elaborate banquet at a country club. Hors d'oeuvres with shrimp and oysters Rockefeller, as well as other delicacies, were plentiful. The food was more important to us than the drinks, especially for Ernie, my boss and friend. He was known to be a hardy eater. We filled ourselves with hors d'oeuvres and then to top it off, we had a big prime rib entrée. One of the fellows, sitting opposite from Ernie, was a light eater. He only ate half of his steak and took the other half with him, planning to eat it for breakfast.

We took a taxi back to the hotel, but had the driver drop us off a couple of miles before the hotel so we could walk a bit. As soon as the cab pulled away, the colleague with the steak remembered that he had left it in the taxi. He ran as hard as he could after the cab for two blocks until he caught up with him at a red light. That is what I call dedication or determination.

Shortly before we arrived at our hotel, we passed by a McDonald's. After all the eating we had done, Ernie said, "I am hungry. Let's have a burger." We busted out laughing, but went in with him, and watched him polish off a Big Mack. This man could really eat.

Not all my travels were pleasant. I remember a couple of scary flights. We were taking off from the Roanoke Airport in Virginia. While rolling down the active runway, I looked out the window and saw a plane landing on a cross runway coming straight at us. Fortunately, our pilot, already at full throttle, he made it past the incoming plane before it could hit us. That certainly counted as a *near miss*.

Another time, a colleague and I were coming home from a trip. Our plane was on a direct approach to the Newark Airport when suddenly I was awakened by a big disturbance. With an ashen face my colleague asked, "Do you know what just happened?"

"I assume we hit an air pocket," I said.

He replied, "No, there was a little plane coming from out of nowhere and almost hit us. The captain pulled the nose up and barely passed over him. We almost collided with the plane." That was a narrow miss. I was glad I had not seen it.

On a flight into Dallas-Fort Worth Airport, our flight encountered heavy winds. I knew this airport was known for its wind sheers. I could feel the pilot leaning into the cross wind. We were already very low to the ground and not far from the runway. Looking out the window, I saw the plane suddenly dip to the right side. The wingtip was no more than three feet from the ground. The wind had suddenly shifted. However, the pilot managed to pull the plane up and then literally dropped it on the runway. That was the hardest landing I have ever experienced. Visibly shaken, I had a few drinks before I continued to the hotel.

# Chapter 74

After I had been with the company two years, my friend Ernie retired. The division I served in was split into two and I became the head of design and quality control for the tailored clothing division. I was sorry to see Ernie leave, but was happy for the promotion. The responsibility was all mine now and I intended to follow the wise teaching of my mentor.

The division got a new VP and grew rapidly. However, six years of traveling took its toll. Our oldest son became difficult to handle and Heide really needed help. Somehow, I had to stop this heavy traveling.

Word had it, that a new position was in the making. The opening would be for a director of manufacturing. I felt qualified and thought I should be considered for it since I had done a good job and had paid my dues. If I got the position, it would mean a considerable cut back on travel. However, corporate politics did not see it that way and picked the plant manager who had drawn the backwards map for this position. I felt he was not qualified for other reasons than the map. Also, I felt the VP that had taken over the division, was not quality conscious. He was trying to increase profits at the cost of quality.

Hurt, and my ego bruised, problems with our son because of my constant travel, I changed jobs. I guess I was correct; the two managed to ruin the division within one year. The clothing division was dissolved and combined with the outerwear division.

# Chapter 75

I took a position as Product Manager for a medium-sized leather and sportswear company that manufactured menswear. Two partners privately owned it. I enjoyed being home again in the evenings and the pay was a lot better. However, after having been on the road for so long, it made me a little claustrophobic. The commute to work was about an hour, which was a long drive.

I really liked the one partner who was my immediate boss. We had a lot in common and saw the business very much along the same lines. But the two owners did not see eye to eye, which created somewhat of a problem.

When the company started to manufacture garments in Korea, they needed someone to go over and teach them how to produce quality garments. This was right up my alley, but I was worried about having to leave Heide alone with the kids again. But Heide, still my biggest fan and supporter, believed in my ability to conquer any obstacle and to achieve new heights, was excited and said, "This is a wonderful opportunity for you. I will manage."

Her confidence in my ability scared the wits out of me many times. But it also gave me the strength to go on and try. With her unwavering trust in my capabilities, which I really thought was overstated, I could not let her down and therefore had to succeed in all my endeavors.

Armed with my passport and the tools I needed in my luggage, I set out for my long journey to Seoul, Korea. This was January, circa 1977 when Korea was still very much a third world country, and the Boeing 747 planes had not been invented. I boarded a Pan Am 707, which had six seats across, three on each side. I was the lucky winner of a narrow center seat. I squeezed myself into it, flanked by large men on my right and left.

The flight time was fourteen hours to Tokyo, with a refueling stop in Anchorage. In Tokyo we stayed overnight and flew the next day at noon on to Kimpo Airport in Seoul, which was another six-hour flight.

In my anticipation to see other countries and experiencing their cultures, I was too excited to sleep and passed my time reading up on Korea culture. Heide and I had long been fascinated with the mystique of the orient. She had read many of Pearl Buck's books and now I was to see the real McCoy. Though I was uncomfortable in my seat, squeezed between my two snoring companions, I finally fell asleep only to be awakened by the flight attendant's announcement of preparation for the landing in Anchorage.

It was between one or two o'clock in the morning. Sleep deprived and incoherent, we all got off the plane and went into the waiting area of the airport. The stores were all closed but I saw interesting Eskimo dolls and other toys that would have been nice for the kids. There was also a beautiful sweater I thought would have been great for Heide. I told myself to remember them and buy it on the way back.

After roaming around for about an hour in the airport, we once again boarded the plane for the second leg of our trip to Tokyo. By now I was so tired that I fell asleep at once and did not wake up until lunch, which was served shortly before the landing at Haneda International Airport. At that time, Haneda Airport was the only airport in Tokyo. Narita Airport was not yet planned, much less built.

We were all bussed to the airport hotel where we stayed overnight, complements of Pan Am Airlines. The old planes did not have the range to fly nonstop and at that time of day, there were no connecting flights to Seoul. In fact, the next flight to Korea was not until the next day at noon on a Pan Am flight coming from Hong Kong.

On the bus ride to the hotel, I looked out the window and was fascinated by the oriental architecture I saw. My room at the hotel was small but clean. When we checked in, we were given meal vouchers from the airline for dinner.

The hotel restaurant was full of business people from all over the world. Experiencing for the first time an international business atmosphere was awesome. I heard languages from around the world: English, Russian, German, Hindi, Japanese Korean, Chinese, Italian etc.—all nationalities were present. But, English was the universal language. However, speaking a second language, like German, did come in handy at times.

A couple of trips later I found out that these so-called international gurus were not at all what they were cracked up to be. Since I was a novice in international business, I had assumed they were experts. I found that the corporate world and the political hierarchy, were sending out employees and emissaries who did not have a clue of the culture and customs of the countries with whom they were dealing. The Americans, who walked around like elephants in a glass menagerie, and the Germans, who acted as if they owned the world, were some of the worst trained business people operating in the Far East.

Being adventurous, that first night I ordered for dinner, sashimi as an appetizer, tempura for the main course, and sake to accompany the meal. I got a surprised look from the waitress, astonished that an American was ordering raw fish, which, in the early seventies was unheard of. As far as I was concerned, raw fish was no different than raw meat, and I loved Beef Tartar.

The meal was delicious. Then I went up to my room and called home, after which I went to bed. With the twelve hours' time difference, I woke up at three o'clock in the morning, famished and unable to go back to sleep. Lying in bed, looking at the TV without understanding a word, I was glad when six o'clock came around, so I could get ready and go for breakfast.

Again, the atmosphere was international. I felt like I had arrived on the big stage with the *Makers and Shakers*. There was a big spread of various cuisines for breakfast. There were the typical American and European breakfasts, however, what interested me most was the Japanese spread. I pigged out on dumplings, rice with eel, and other Japanese delights. But Japanese green tea just would not do it in the morning. For that, I needed a strong wake up brew. Luckily, the hotel, accustomed to Europeans, had good strong German coffee.

At noon we boarded another 707. Again, I was the lucky guy with the center seat. On the approach to Kimpo Airport in Seoul, we were ordered to close all window shades for security reasons. Picture-taking from the air was forbidden. It would be punished with a fine and confiscation of the film. At that time, Korea was still governed by marshal law and did not have a true democracy. It was autocratically governed. There was a twelve o'clock curfew in effect and if the police caught a foreigner outside after midnight, they would bring him or her to the hotel in their jeep and fine them fifty dollars. Korean nationals were just simply put into jail for a couple of days.

I learned that Korea is very chauvinistic and extremely protective of their culture. A lot of that goes back to the constant threat and occupation over the centuries by Japan. To avoid their men looking too western, they had a law about hair length —it could not touch their collar. If the police caught a Korean male with his hair touching the shirt collar, they would take him to the closest barber, give him a short military haircut and a fine.

Koreans were and are extremely hard working, proud people, and tough negotiators. Their unwritten motto was, *we must work hard to create a better life for our children*, and that they did.

I remember an incident that occurred while we were driving through the city. A man was about to step into the street when a car came at high speed and blew his horn. He was startled, stopped dead in his tracks, and threw his hands behind his back as if he was hiding something. Puzzled, I asked my Korean companion what the man was doing. I was told that he was protecting his hands because if he got killed that was one thing, but if his hands were damaged he would not be able to work and provide for his family.

Work came first and foremost during the developing years in Korea. Sometimes it took long hours to negotiate, but they never went back on a deal once you shook hands on it. I have a lot of respect for their tough but honorable business dealings.

Established over many generations, the Koreans had two obvious traditions ingrained into their ethnicity. One, when a woman got married she became the property of her husband and not an equal partner. Two, they were extremely race conscious with Eurasians or Amerasians (Children of European and Asians, or, Americans and Asian) becoming outcasts. I believe this to be a survival mechanism to protect their culture and heritage, threatened by two thousand years of invasions from the Japanese, the Manchus, the Chinese, the Mongols, and the Russians. These ethnic customs were very prevalent during the early years of modern Korea.

Because of the many years of foreign occupation, many older Koreans spoke Japanese and could read the Chinese characters used in many of the far eastern countries. However, Korea has its own alphabet called Hangul. There are twenty-seven characters in the Hangul alphabet, it is very easy to learn. It was during the Choson Dynasty, in the year 1446, under the Emperor King Sejong, that the alphabet was invented. It was originally called Hunmin Ching–Um. The emperor was a scholar who realized there were too many Chinese characters in the old writings, and it was too difficult to comprehend. Since most of his people were illiterate, it prompted him to invent new written symbols. There was no illiteracy in Korea on my first trip and many people spoke English.

We landed in the evening. Since Seoul was surrounded by mountains, nightfall came early during the Korean winters. Before I had left, I was told, I would not need a Visa for only a fourteen-day business trip. Immigration at the airport would take care of it. Though this was true, my Korean official still went through my passport several times saying, *Visa. Visa.*

I told him, "I don't have one."

"How long?" was the response.

"Fourteen days," I said, which was already on my landing card. After shaking his head several times and making the famous hissing sound, he finally gave me his *Chop* (stamp). Now, I had to go through Korean Customs, which was well known for its thoroughness. The white-gloved customs official went through every piece of luggage I had. Everything was taken out and turned over several times and with a *"Hey?"* would question what it was.

After a very agonizing encounter at customs, I finally got into the waiting area where a Korean stood with a sign that read: *Mr. Lohn.* I approached him and he introduced himself as Mr. Kwak. The driver grabbed my luggage and Mr. Kwak ushered me into the car. He spoke a heavy accented English. Since I was not accustomed to the sound, I had a difficult time understanding him. I understood that we were going to the Chosun Hotel. At the time, it was the only western hotel in Seoul. He checked me in and told me that he would pick me up at nine o'clock in the morning. It took only a few minutes to check in. He said, "Goodbye, see you in morning," and left. Since it was already dark, I had seen my contact only for about fifteen minutes in a lighted place.

The bellhop took me to my room. It was nice and quiet. In fact, that hotel, for its time, was a four-star accommodation.

After calling home, I settled in. I was so tired and fell asleep in about two seconds flat. The telephone aroused me from a deep, unconscious slumber. The caller identified himself as Mr. Kwak. *Gee I just left him a couple minutes ago. I wonder what he wants now?* I thought to myself. "Can I see you tomorrow morning?" said the caller.

Puzzled I said, "Yes, of course. At nine o'clock, right?" I replied.

"Okay, I see you then," said the caller and hung up. I figured he wanted to make sure I had understood him correctly, or so I thought, and went back to sleep.

Being a stickler on punctuality, I was in the lobby at five minutes before nine in the morning, ready to go to work. At quarter after nine, when no one had showed up, I remembered reading about their culture. Being late was normal and not an insult. So, I figured he would show up soon.

Nine-thirty came and went, and no Mr. Kwak was in sight. In the meantime, I kept looking at everyone coming through the lobby doors. No one approached me and since I had only seen Mr. Kwak for a couple of minutes the night before, I was not sure what he looked like anymore. To me, all the Koreans streaming into the lobby looked familiar, and yet unfamiliar at the same time.

After waiting an hour, strenuously trying to identify every Korean businessman, they all started to look alike. The uniform of the day was dark banker's suits, ties, and no overcoats or gloves despite the cold temperatures outside. I saw the clock in the lobby showed ten-thirty. However, there still was no Mr. Kwak. I felt that he was carrying the customary lateness a little too far, especially since he had called my room the night before to confirm the time.

Ten-forty-five came and went, and still no Mr. Kwak, I was about ready to give up on him and go back to my room when he stormed through the door at eleven o'clock and said, "Good morning Mr. Lohn, shall we go."

I was flabbergasted. No apology or explanation for his lateness, just a mere *shall we go*. He behaved as if *I* was the one that was late. *Oh well, when in Rome do as the Roman's do*, I told myself and off we went to his office.

On the way, I politely inquired about his phone call the night before. I was informed that he had not made a call to my room. "But the caller identified himself as Mr. Kwak," I insisted. Then I got my first lesson about Korean business practices. A) Half of the people's names were either Kwak or Kim, he informed me. B) Every foreign businessman that entered Seoul is listed by name, company, date of arrival, and hotel of residence in the local trade paper. C) Savvy Korean sales people called the incoming foreigners to see whether they can drum up some business.

# Chapter 76

On the way to the office, traffic was very heavy. My contact informed me that the driver would try to take a shortcut. Over the years I had learned that all the company drivers unsuccessfully tried this. Company drivers were held in high regards in Korea. They were not to be messed with since when you were in *their* car, they held your life in their hands. I guess, driving the car gave them ownership.

When we arrived at the office of Samdo, I was shown into an office. The room was furnished with a cabinet full of china and trophies, a low rectangular coffee table with six heavy leather armchairs, four facing each other across the table, and one on each end. Each chair had a lace doily over the top. On one wall was a large picture of a man with two Korean flags, flanked by smaller picture of two men, one on each side.

Later, I found out that the man in the center was the president of the country and the two flanking him were the president and the chairman of Samdo, the company I was dealing with. It reminded me a little of Nazi Germany where you couldn't go anywhere without looking at Hitler's face.

Before arriving in Korea, I had read that before you could start doing business, you had to endure the ceremonial coffee. I was seated at one end of the table, which meant the Honor Chair. Someone of higher rank than Mr. Kwak still had to join us, since he and three underlings, sat on the side chairs. Directly next to the open chair on the right sat Mr. Kwak, and across from him his number two man.

"Coffee?" asked Mr. Kwak, or as they say in their Korean-English *cobby*.

"Please," I said. A young lady appeared with a tray. Coffee was served in fine china cups from an exquisite porcelain pot with a matching creamer and sugar-bowl; and cookies on a matching serving plate. As soon as the coffee was served, including a cup in front of the empty chair, the door opened, and a distinguished gentleman entered the room. They all jumped up and bowed. It was interesting to see the difference in the way they bowed. Mr. Kwak, who was the head of the department, made a minor bow. The second in command bowed lower. And the lowest ranking ones bowed so low that they almost hit the table with their foreheads. I was then introduced to the President of Samdo. To be greeted by the top-ranking executive was a high honor.

We sat for two hours and drank coffee while he talked about Samdo's achievements and growth. This was followed by an earful of propaganda about the great Republic of Korea. Then I was asked many questions about the company's business that I represented. After the president had exhausted his well-rehearsed speech, he excused himself, said goodbye, and wished me a pleasant stay in Korea and a successful business trip.

I thought, *all right, now we finally can get to work.* Not so.

Mr. Kwak said, "Let's have lunch."

Well another lesson learned: Only two things a Korean must do in his life, all others are optional. A) He must eat three meals a day and if possible, routinely at the same time each day. B) He knows he must die, even though he knows not when.

I was treated to a bulgogi lunch and what a wonderful lunch it was. If you are not familiar with Korean cuisine, bulgogi is a thinly sliced, marinated steak. It gets cooked along with whole cloves of garlic on an iron grill, sitting in the middle of the table on top of a pot full of hot coal. The meat is accompanied with salad leaves, sauces, and many variations of kimchi (very garlicky marinated cabbage and vegetables), rice, and cold noodles in a broth. From what I understand, the smell of garlic is very strong and everywhere, including in the clothes of the Koreans. But since I have no sense of smell, I can't verify this. One thing I know, it did not bother me one bit, and it tasted wonderful. My Korean friends all had beer with the meal, but I wisely declined.

At last we were ready to go to the factory, which was the reason for my visit. With a full stomach, I fell asleep on the way to the industrial area, which was on the outskirts of Seoul. Beautiful mountains surrounded Seoul and the Han Dong (The River Han) now running through the center of the city. However, in the seventies, the river flowed at the edge of the existing city. Across the river were fields of rice and vegetables. Since the Olympics, in 1988, the fields have become a booming city as well.

\*\*\*\*

All the big factories in Korea were surrounded by walls or high wrought iron fences with large gates. The structures were usually built in a U shape with a courtyard in the middle. The gates were staffed and opened by guards in crisp military uniforms, with side-arms on their belts.

As we drove through the gate, the guards saluted smartly; which made me feel like I was back in the army and had been promoted to a general. The first factory that I visited was an old building. In the center of the courtyard were fabrics stored on pallets and covered by waterproof tarps. *Oh boy, what have I gotten myself into?* I thought as we walked into the cold and freezing building. Then I got to know firsthand about Korean service elevators.

Up on the third floor was the cutting room. Throughout the staircase were young girls forming a chain, passing the rolls of fabric from one to the other until the rolls ended up from the pallets in the courtyard, to the cutting room. Labor was a lot cheaper than putting in an elevator. Besides, getting one would take a year and with the constant blackouts, was impractical. Telephones took months to acquire, a boiler a year and a half and so forth.

When we got to the office, I was introduced to Tiger Kim, the owner of the factory. He was a short, stocky, muscular man. Koreans are fanatically protective of their masculine reputations. The Korean males had nicknames that underlined their strength, such as *Tiger Kim*. And what a tiger he was.

This was especially true in the early years in Korea. Mr. Kim did not speak English, so everything had to be interpreted. Again, we went for an hour through the ceremonial coffee. Doing business in Korea in the earlier days, you had to be able to stomach a lot of coffee and had to have a lot of patience. Saving face and having patience, are two important traits to observe when dealing throughout the Far East.

Finally, it was time to see the factory. As I just mentioned, the cutting room was on the third floor. There, I got a glimpse of Korean ingenuity and automation. Where we had spreading machines laying up fabric automatically, run by one person, they had a young man sitting cross-legged on each end of the table holding down the material. Another young man was holding a round steel rod up in the air with a roll of fabric and ran along the table like the devil was chasing him. Well, slowing him down would be a pleasure for the Cutters Union in the states.

The cutters were at work on another table. They were crouching barefooted on the table, operating tall eight-inch cutting knifes. Instead of paper markers (blueprints to lay on top of fabric for cutting) they used the old method of lightweight felt markers. Soon, I found out why. To save fabric, they would chalk the pattern onto the felt, and then they soaked the markers in water, so they would shrink. The shrinking did wonders for the size of the garments. Size 40 became a 39, 42 a 40, and so on.

Immediately, I instituted rule number one: No wetting down of markers on Al's garments.

From there we went to the next floor, the sewing room. Instead of a bundle system, where you pass a bundle of x number of garments from operator to operator, they passed single garments from operator to operator set apart at equal minute values. There was an advantage to this. They had little inventory in the line. Within a brief time of starting a new style, finished garments came off the line. The disadvantage of this arrangement was, if one operator had a problem, the whole line was dead. That meant, all the rest of the operators would be sitting idle. For that reason, I realized, it was vitally important to think each operation thoroughly through before teaching the method to the operator. Once the line was started, it was impossible to change the way they were making the garments. In fact, the Koreans wouldn't change anything once a style got into the line because they did not want to lose the time and money that a stop on a line would create.

The next stop was the pressing room. Here I got another surprise. Water leaked from the pressing machines like they were faucets. The pressing pads were water-soaked and made the garments look as if they were washed instead of pressed. Through the interpreter, I let Tiger Kim know that he had a big problem and really had no pressing capability for the garments.

He wanted to know why? I explained that to press properly, the machines needed to be supplied with dry steam from a boiler that had enough capacity.

He said that to get a bigger boiler or additional boilers to increase the steam output would take at least eight to nine months even with paying bribes or *Documentation Fees* as they called them. In the seventies, bribes were a way of life in Korea; since you needed government authorization for everything. Red tape slowed down any process since the military and the heavy industry, had priority status. Big enough bribes could cut down the process by thirty to forty percent. However, in this case, it would still mean the garments could not be delivered on time and would be of no use to us.

Tiger Kim let me know there was, "no problem," and then said something to his foreman.

Then, Mr. Kwak said, "Let's go to office."

We had more coffee and I had to sit and listen while the whole group chatted away in Korean. As far as I could make out, it was a heated conversation with an occasional embarrassed laughter accompanied by the shaking of the head. I heard a lot of hissing sounds, which was made by sucking air through the teeth. This was a typical Korean habit. Sitting there listening to the foreign sounds like a dummy, I kept on drinking coffee. I also noticed that his secretary came in and plugged in an electric heater. The temperature had dropped a few degrees in the office.

While I was waiting, I assessed my precarious situation:

• A) The building was dark and dingy not conducive to detect quality problems easily, especially shading.

• B) The pressing was a huge problem.

• C) From what I could gather, none of the materials were in the country yet, because Korea had an import law that stated, "*Imported fabrics and trims must be manufactured within 120 days and exported, or they will be taxed at a 100% of their value.*" All our fabric and accessories came from Japan. Therefore, the material would not arrive early enough for me to set up production before I had to leave the country. My temporary visa was only good for fourteen days.

While I was still thinking how to overcome these handicaps, Mr. Kwak said, "Let's go," and off we went to the pressing room again. The operators were sitting on the machines in the cold sewing room shivering. They were dressed now in snow jackets

320

and fingerless gloves. When we got to the pressing machines, to my surprise, they had plenty of steam. Tiger Kim had solved the problem at the cost of the freezing employees by shutting off the steam to the heating elements. Smiling from ear to ear, Tiger Kim said, "Okay," the only comment he could make in English.

I threw up my hands. What can you say to something like that?

Mr. Kwak then said, "I will bring you back to the hotel where you can rest for a couple of hours. Mr. Kim has invited us to dinner. I will pick you up at 7:00 PM, okay?"

I said, "All right. But when will we be able to start working on the samples?"

"Soon. Not to worry" was his answer.

"But I must leave Korea soon," I replied.

His answer was, "No problem."

I was tired and rather than going out to dinner, I would have loved to go to sleep. However, I could not offend them. So, I set my alarm clock for 6:45 PM and took a nap.

# Chapter 77

Contrary to the morning's tardiness, he called from the lobby at precisely 7:00 PM. We got into the car and drove to the restaurant. On the way I was informed that Tiger Kim was throwing a *Kisaeng Party* in my honor. I had heard of that and was warned not to choose hard liquor when asked, "What would you like to drink?" I was told that they were all heavy drinkers, one could easily get plastered if you tried to keep up with them.

When we arrived at the restaurant, I was asked to take off my shoes, which stayed outside in the cold. A young lady, dressed in the traditional Korean Kimono, escorted us to a room no larger than the size of a small hotel room. Our host, with several people from the factory and office, was already seated. They sat on cushions around a low rectangular table. Against the wall was a brocaded upholstered seat with armrests, like a child's potty-chair. This, I found out, was for the honored guest, yours truly.

Everybody jumped to their feet, bowed and did the traditional Korean double-hands, handshake. Then I was ushered to the honor seat where I tried to get my legs situated using the old cross-legged Indian position.

The Koreans chatted for a few minutes. I supposed they were figuring out the menu and the agenda. Tiger Kim then clapped his hands together and called out something in Korean. A hostess, who must have been waiting outside of the door for this signal, appeared at once. She bowed in greeting.

Mr. Kwak turned to me and asked, "What would you like to drink?"

Forewarned, I said, "Some wine would be fine."

"You sure you would not like something a little stronger?" he let me know.

"No, thank you, I can't. I have a problem with my stomach," I explained. Fortunately, I knew that health issues were an acceptable reason to reject an offer without offending the host.

Soon I was to find out why my friend had forewarned me about the choice of drink. In came the waitresses, also dressed in a traditional kimono, set down enough bottles of Korean rice wine to intoxicate an army. Then she placed small china cups with gold dragons painted on them in front of everyone.

I did not understand why they put two of the same cups in front of each seat, but I did not have to wait long to find out. The door opened, and a group of young girls dressed in kimonos entered. They bowed and extended greetings in Korean. Tiger Kim directed a girl to sit on the right side of each guest. Then Tiger Kim made a toast to a good future business venture; and all drank, bottoms up.

Then Mr. Kwak did the same and now it was my turn, but it did not stop there. I got reminded again why I was given the warning. Everyone started to toast the honorable guest who had to continue to drink bottoms up. The real game started when they toasted you and did not drink but passed the cup to you, you got it and it was bottoms up. The rice wine was easy to take. If that would have been hard liquor, I would have been out already.

Well, I figured two could play that game. So, I started out very quickly to toast around the table, so I could pass on the cup without having to drink. I noticed another trick these wise guys were playing. When they got the cup passed to them, they would only take a sip and then pass it to the girl next to them who drank it. Yours truly was no dummy. I copied that custom real fast.

My legs started to fall asleep and my knees hurt. When I tried to straighten them out a bit, the girl next to me began massaging my legs at once, to the laughter of the Koreans. I do not know whether they laughed because my legs cramped, or at my obvious embarrassment.

Finally, the food arrived. It was a pleasant diversion from the drinking. I had never seen so many different dishes on one table. Meats, fish, vegetables, rice, noodles in various forms, don't ask what it was that I ate, I do not know. One thing I do know, it was good even if they had dog meat among it.

The young lady next to me took my chopsticks and put food on my plate. I thought I was going to be in trouble because I had never used chopsticks before. Besides, these were long, ivory ones that were a lot harder to handle than the short ones. But, that turned out not to be a problem; my pleasant young lady fed me with a smile. All I had to do was open my mouth and chew.

Everything was delicious and according to Korean tradition, enough food was left over after we had eaten our dinner. This assured that the guests were no longer hungry and there were some leftovers for the poor. Except for the rice wine, the table was cleared, and tea was served. Then the door opened and in marched five musicians. Now the time had come for what the Koreans call, *serious drinking*. Soon, it got very noisy in that little room especially with the addition of a five-piece band that was *not* playing Brahms.

Most Koreans are born entertainers. My host got up and performed with the band while the rest of us watched and drank rice wine. Despite believing I could deal with the rice wine, it did finally start to get to me. Then, horror of horrors, they wanted me to get up and perform. Since that is not something I am comfortable doing, I waved them off. But no such luck. They dragged me up front and asked what tune the band should play. By that time, I was too far-gone, I can't remember what I told them. But it doesn't matter; I don't know the words to any songs. Egged on with shouting and clapping I remember that I ended up jumping around and singing *La, la, la, la...* to whatever tune they were playing.

With everyone feeling no pain, the party finally ended. I thanked our host, said goodbye and stepped into my shoes. Boy, did that sober me up fast! It felt as if I had just stuck my feet into a bucket of ice.

My host dropped me off at the hotel with the comment, "I pick you up at ten o'clock tomorrow."

Before I went to sleep that night, I promised myself never to get caught in a *Kisaeng Party* again.

The next couple of days, Mr. Kwak dragged me from one factory to another with the comment, "For future business."

However, when I would ask, "When can we start on the samples?" the answer was always the same, "Soon, not to worry."

Well, I was getting worried because I had come to do a job and was unable to do it.

# Chapter 78

When the weekend came, Mr. Kwak took me sightseeing and that was amazing. First, we went to the Chanddeokgung Palace in the center of Seoul. The palace is a marvel of Korean history and very well preserved. Next, we went up to the Namsan Park with its TV transmitting/observation tower. However, in the seventies, for security reasons, the tower was closed to the public and occupied by antiaircraft guns. But the view from the top of the mountain was spectacular.

Korea is a beautiful country with mountains and its unique evergreen trees. The park was full of both young and old people dressed in their colorful traditional garb. During the week you rarely saw anyone dressed other than in western clothes, but on weekends, the traditions were alive and well exhibited. I also found out why they were not cold when they only wore a suit and no overcoat. They wore several layers of heavy undergarments beneath their suits.

In the evening we had dinner at the well-known Walker Hill hotel. It was in this hotel where a big scandal involving some American politicians had taken place. The hotel had rooms, a casino, and a dinner theater with a traditional Korean folklore show. The food was excellent and the show colorful and interesting. Many of the dances and songs looked and sounded like Russian derivatives. Of special interest to me were the costumes because of my professional background.

Sunday morning, I attended mass at the Cathedral. It was an interesting experience to attend a mass in Korean. Afterwards,

Mr. Kwak picked me up for another day of sightseeing. On the way to the Namsangol Hanok Maeul, the Korean Folk Village, we visited the Admiral Yi shrine. Admiral Yi was famous for giving the Japanese a run for their money during the Choson Dynasty. Also, he was the first one in the world to use an ironclad warship.

The Korean Folk Village was fascinating. Little towns were set up, styled of all the Korean provinces, including North Korea. Just like our historical sights, the attending towns-people were dressed in their different local historic garb. Some dated back to the old dynasty, as did the cottages. Different dishes of food from the various cuisines were there to sample.

I learned about three important historical pieces of information, or at least according to my Korean friend. He explained to me that: 1) Genghis Khan, the famous Mongol leader, was of Korean descent. (Of course, if you speak to the Chinese, they will vehemently deny this) 2) All Mongol baby girls have a little rose tattooed on their behind, just as the North Koreans do. Which was his proof that the Mongols were of Korean descent. (Again, I am sure the Chinese and the Russians will deny that too) 3) According to Mr. Kwak, Korea invented radiant floor heating.

Now that one might be true. The heating systems in the old historical houses did indeed have a form of radiant floor heating. The floors were leveled clay, covered, and bonded with paper and then highly polished so that they looked like polished epoxy. Under the floor were channels leading from side to side. On one side of the house was a fire pit, and on the other side the channels ended into chimneys. Fires were lit in the pits, and the chimneys would pull the hot air through the shafts under the clay foundation warming the rooms. It was wonderful walking around on the warm floor in socks. That was an ingenious method considering everyone else, during the Choson Dynasty, was still heating their homes with open fire pits.

Korea had four-thousand years of recorded history, which is second only to China.

After returning to the hotel, from a very enlightened day, I had a quiet dinner at the hotel's restaurant. I treated myself to a delicious meal in the French dining room. The wonderful red wine went well with the soft violin music. The food could match any fine French Restaurant in New York City. What was missing, was Heide. When I thought of how much she would enjoy this, I felt guilty and homesick.

# Chapter 79

The following days went by much like the others. I had two more days left before I had to fly out of the country and re-enter Korea to get another fourteen-day visa. Naturally, I had kept my boss apprised of the situation and was told, "Do what you have to. Use your judgment."

When I conferred with Mr. Kwak, he informed me that the fabric and trims had arrived at the port in Puson. I commented, "I will not have enough time to get the samples done and the line started before I must leave the country."

He at once came back with his favorite sentence, "No problem. I will pick you up tomorrow morning."

After dinner that night, I went to the bar and had a drink. I had it! No matter what I tried, I could not get that show on the road. Sitting in a booth with my scotch and soda, I watched another American hammering away at a Korean. He looked as disgusted as I felt. After what seemed to be a hot and heavy discussion, the Korean got up, bowed, said goodbye and left.

The American shook his head, mumbled something that I am sure was not for sensitive ears and slammed his fist on the table. When he looked up, our eyes met, "A rough day?" I said.

He picked up his drink and came over to my table, sat down and said, "You will not believe what I went through today with these guys."

"Oh, I believe it. I had one of those days all week long," I replied.

We introduced ourselves, and then cried into each other's drink about the difficulties dealing with the Koreans. We agreed that no one would believe, or understand it, unless they had also experienced it.

My new friend said to me, "I wish I could get one darn piece that works properly."

Being sure that *the rag business I was in, had to be the worst*, I asked, "What business are you in?"

Here came the kicker, "I buy Pacemakers."

"Wow!" I said. "Give me the name of those pacemakers. Should I ever need one I want to be sure that I don't get one of yours!"

Despite the seriousness, we broke out laughing about the irony, had another drink and then parted to go our separate ways; I went to bed.

Mr. Kwak picked me up in the morning and said, "We need to go to the airport. Do you have your passport?"

I always took my papers and passport with me everywhere I went, I confirmed that I had it with me. Tiger Kim met us at the airport. He asked, via Mr. Kwak, for my passport. Giving someone my credentials was not something I did lightly, but Mr. Kwak assured me it was okay.

Tiger Kim took my passport, put something into it, and disappeared into another room. 15 minutes later he came out, gave me my passport back and said the most often spoken words in Korea, "Okay, no problem."

When I opened my passport, there was another fourteen-day visa in it. I found out that even laws could be overturned for the right fee.

Three items were on the national *hot* list: Businesses that brought in dollars, military readiness in case the north would start another war, and arduous work to create a better life for their future generations. Consequently, the bureaucrats would always yield to *business*. Military readiness was apparent everywhere. All young men served in the military reserve indefinitely. Every civilian pilot was also a military pilot. The main roadways were extremely wide and perfectly straight to be used for landing strips in case of war. The possibility of war was a daily companion to the Korean people. It was not unusual to have your Korean contact disappear into the army for fourteen-days without notice. Twice a month the sirens would go off unannounced for an air-raid drill. During the drill, all traffic stopped and everyone had to get off the street and into an air raid shelter.

# Chapter 80

After two agonizing weeks, we were finally ready to start work. The fabrics, trims, and linings were to be delivered the next day and surprisingly, they were. I had them pull several rolls of fabric, lining, and samples of trim for inspection. I wanted to make sure that the colors, and quality was up to specs. Worried about the fabrics that were being stored in the courtyard under tarps, I managed to convince them to store the materials on the cutting room floor. The fabrics and trims all checked out okay. This was Saturday and on Monday we would start the tedious work of teaching them to make the difficult and tricky jacket.

Saturday afternoon and Sunday, I was at last on my own. I had looked forward to that. I took it easy on Saturday, recharging my batteries as it were, and had a leisurely dinner in the hotel.

After mass on Sunday morning, I had intended to explore the local stores. Unbeknownst to me, the Korean workers had one Sunday a month off. Otherwise, they worked seven days a week. It was my luck that on that Sunday, the city was packed with shoppers. I was pushed and shuffled around but managed to buy some presents to take home.

Coming out of a smaller store, I noticed a department store across the street. I wanted to see what it was like and started to climb up the steps of the walkway overpass. Before I knew it, I was caught among a group of Korean women who were jogging across the overpass. I had no choice but to do the same. It must have been a hilarious sight for the locals, seeing me all dressed up, and jogging along amid a group of short Korean women.

After my shopping spree, I went into the hotel lobby and had coffee and cake. While sitting at my table, a man walked in and obviously was looking for a place to sit down. The chairs in the lobby were mostly occupied, so I motioned for him to sit down with me. It turned out that he was the head administrator of the Danish State Adoption Agency. His English was superb. We had a delightful afternoon, which we finished with dinner and quite a few drinks.

During our conversation, we compared notes on the difficulties of working in Korea. I found out that he was trying to arrange the adoptions of Korean babies for Danish couples. He told me that there were many fine couples ready to adopt, but the South Korean government would not let him have any of the many orphans, because the North Koreans were accusing the South Koreans of selling their babies. It was a shame that these poor little babies, especially the Amerasians and Eurasians that were shunned, living in orphanages under less than ideal circumstances, could not be given to loving parents with fine homes.

# Chapter 81

When we got to the factory on Monday I was astonished by the obvious eagerness to learn. Tiger Kim had each section surrounding me and watching every move I made, even if they were not involved in my merchandise. Starting with checking the full set of patterns to making sure nothing got lost or distorted; to the cutting of a dozen garments for samples. Then I went through the process of setting up each operation. That is how my nickname *The Professor* originated and later it spread to other countries in Asia.

I was surprised that it was easier than I had expected. Then I wanted to see how the supervisors would train their people. The samples came out nice. I was pleased that I could approve them for production.

However, now it was my time for me to learn something. The sewing supervisors gathered in a group and started a lively pow-wow. At the end of the discussion, each supervisor took cut parts for one jacket and went to a sewing machine to make a garment. That was smart I thought, only none of them did it the way I had taught them. I said to Mr. Kwak, "No, stop them! That is not the way you can make this jacket!"

He calmed me down and said, "Let's go have lunch."

At that point, I didn't know enough about their culture. Before accepting my way, they had to prove to themselves that there was no other way, or better way to make the jacket. When we got back from lunch, I saw several abortions of the jacket lying on a table. The floor manager was smiling, and said to Mr. Kwak,

"Tell Mr. Lohn, his way-good way," and with that, we started the line to produce the jackets.

While I had taught the supervisors and gone to lunch, the cutting room had cut the first lot. It was amazing to see how skillful the supervisors taught the operators each operation and within hours the first finished garments were coming off the line.

All this time it was cold in the factory. Tiger Kim never turned the heat on again as long I was there.

My trip had taken a little longer than it was supposed to, but it turned out to be an immense success.

# Chapter 82

After receiving quality merchandise from Korea, the following year the owner of the company decided to make some leather jackets in Korea. Naked leather, a process in which leather is drum-died instead of painted, was in style. Painted skins can have an appearance of plastic while the drum-died ones, sealed or unsealed, have a luxurious natural look with a depth to it. Since leather is a skin, just like human skin, each skin tans differently. Depending on the size of the animal, more or fewer hides were needed to make a garment. Therefore, it was critical to blend the same color skins into a bundle for each coat. With the Koreans just starting to make leather garments for the finicky American market, I knew I was in for another breath-holding trip.

This time my contact was a Mr. Jeong. He picked me up and deposited me at the Chosun Hotel. By now I considered myself a veteran Korean traveler, or so I thought. This time I stayed in my room until he called me from downstairs. He was only forty minutes tardy.

Again, we went through the usual office routine of the coffee ceremonies, company propaganda, and before I knew it, two days had gone by with salesroom visitations of things in which I was and was not interested. Two more days were spent visiting factories of small contract shops that did a decent job. I thought this might be easier than the first time; wrong again. I inquired, "Which one of the factories will be making my garments, and when can we start making some samples?"

I was confronted with a surprise. I was told, "None of the factories we have visited."

It seemed, the garments were going to be made in a factory in Puson, and again, I heard the old familiar words, "Not to worry. The quality will be the same as what you have seen here."

"Sorry, not good enough," I said. "I must see the factory and work out all the manufacturing details with the management."

Well, that obviously had not been in the plan. After Mr. Jeong, the merchandise manager, conferred in a lengthy debate with the director of the department and his underlings, I was told that there was a problem. I thought to myself, *what else is new?*

I was told that they could take me to the factory in Puson, which was about a two-hour flight. However, Mr. Jeong could not accompany me because he had to report for military duty. They assured me that they would have an interpreter accompany me. They wanted to know if that was all right.

Since this trip was for technical purposes, Mr. Jeong would be of no real help anyway. Therefore, an interpreter would be all I needed. I told them it was, "Okay."

The next morning, with my bags packed, I waited for my pick-up call. When it came, I went downstairs where a young man of about twenty-two introduced himself as my traveling companion and interpreter.

Off we went to the airport. On the way, he informed me, "I am student of Shin Wang. I work for Samdo." Later I found out, that these were the only two fluent sentences my official interpreter knew how to say.

You could always identify the college they had attended by the way they started out their sentences. Graduates from one university would start every sentence with, "Frankly speaking." Others had different idioms. But at least my young friend knew his way around the airport and got us checked in.

We still had time before boarding, so we went to the counter for a snack. I was thirsty and wanted a glass of milk. I turned to my interpreter and asked him to order me a glass of milk. He mumbled something, and said, shrugging his shoulders, "Sorry." There was no doubt about it; he did not know what I had said. Turning to a waitress behind the counter, I said, "Milk please?"

She looked at me for a moment, and then said, "Fresh milk?"

"I don't care fresh or pasteurized," I replied.

She again said, "Fresh milk?"

To make it easy, I said, "Yes." I got my milk and all was fine.

My interpreter reminded me again, "I am student of Shin Wang. I work for Samdo."

Oh well, I guessed I had hit the jackpot with my English-speaking friend. I was still thirsty and wanted another glass of milk. This time I figured it would be best to ask the waitress that had understood me before and so I did. To simplify it, I said in Pigeon English, "Another glass of milk?"

She looked at me, laughed, and walked away. I called after her, "Please!"

Coming back again I asked, "Another milk?" Again, she laughed and walked off. I thought I would try it on my Korean interpreter. So, I told him the same thing. He also laughed and shrugged his shoulders. Not intending to give up so easily, I took my glass, held it up, and said to the waitress, "Milk?"

Back came, "Fresh milk?"

"Yes," I said and with that I got my thirst quencher. Later I found out from a friend, who was an experienced traveler in Korea, that the word another had thrown them for a loop. And, *Fresh Milk* meant real milk instead of powdered milk.

Furthermore, they were embarrassed that they didn't understand and when they were embarrassed, they laughed.

Before boarding, we had to go through customs where everything was taken out of my bag again. But this time, they put it all back into the suitcase, which they did not do with some of the oriental businessmen. Also, I noticed that when they were frisking westerners, they would bow and say "sorry," and then frisk them. While with some Orientals they would just search and others were treated a little rough. Puzzled by what I had seen, I later asked my world-traveling friend, "How come?"

He told me that the Koreans really despise the Japanese. Every time they saw a Japanese coming through custom, they treated them disrespectfully and man-handled them just short of roughing them up. Another lesson learned.

Which reminds me of another trick that I learned by accident. When I flew back from Puson, I switched planes in Soul to go on to the US. Since this was the end of my trip, I had plenty of dirty clothes in my suitcase. When I got to customs at check in, the official opened my suitcase, looked at my dirty clothes and without checking anything, closed it, and sent me through. From then on, I always put some dirty clothes on top of the clean ones, separated by a plastic bag. I never had a problem again with the custom inspectors taking any of my items out of my suitcase.

\*\*\*\*

Back to my flight to Puson. The flight was uneventful except that the airport had no radar. Landing in foggy conditions, was a bit scary. *The Korean Fighter Jocks*, who flew the planes to Puson, did not get discouraged by fog.

In the early years, Westerners did not often visit Puson and if they did, they stayed at a resort hotel on the beach, of which yours truly was not aware. The Korean company had made the

342

arrangements and reserved a room in a Korean hotel. However, it had a western bed instead of the usual flax mattress on the floor. In those days there were no Western hotels in the city of Puson. The room was small but clean. The interpreter checked me in but did not stay there. My student of Shin Wang made me understand, by holding up nine fingers that he would pick me up at nine in the morning and left.

The hotel had a Chinese restaurant with a great menu. I decided to dine there and ordered Lobster Cantonese, it was one of my favorite dishes. My surprise came when I found out that they were not set up for dumb Americans who did not have the skills to eat with chopsticks. They did not have forks and knifes. Yours truly likes to eat and does not go hungry. I learned very quickly to eat with chopsticks. But for this dinner I had a big problem. The cracked lobster was served with the shell in a heavy but tasty oyster sauce. The silverware consisted of the longest silver chopsticks I had ever seen. Every time I thought I had the slippery lobster in my mouth, it was back on my plate with a splash of sauce on my jacket, shirt, and tie. I was getting hungrier by the minute, I was frustrated to no end. Just after an especially big splash, the waiter came to my rescue. He brought me a big bib to put around my neck, a bowl for the shells, another bowl with water to wash my hands, and best of all, motioned me to use my fingers. He must have been watching me. But I was finally able to feed my starving stomach.

The next morning, we went to the factory. After the usual coffee ceremony and meeting the administrative and technical staff, I went to inspect the shop. The building had very few windows and the lighting was bad. However, the operators were skilled and the stitching in general was good. But because of the poor lighting, I could not tell whether the different pieces on the garments matched or not. That would present a big problem.

343

Shading problems would make the garments unsellable, except as seconds.

The cutting was done European style, with short knives on a glass tables (In the states the cutting was done on butcher blocks). I preferred the glass tables because they are bigger and therefore eliminated distortions that can happen on smaller butcher blocks. But the matching of the skins was a big problem. Procedurally, they matched the skins properly. However, when I took them outside into the daylight, they were as mismatched as a checkerboard. I took a couple of coats outside, they looked awful. They had appeared to be matched when I viewed them in the sewing room's bad light.

A gentleman had entered the factory and was introduced to me as the technical factory manager. As luck would have it, he was German. My communication difficulty was solved. We went through the standards that I had set up for the quality of my garments and worked on solving the matching problem together. We found an area outside under an overhang that faced north. The north light is considered the true daylight and is best for the blending of hides.

After a table was set up, we were in business. But we still needed to find a solution for the times when the weather was bad. There was one window with good northern light in the office. Koreans, known for their ingenuity, had no problem rearranging the office and turning the area in front of the window into a prep area for the cutting room.

The problem was solved. After working out the operation for the assorted styles, I went back to Seoul where I was supposed to receive samples for approval before leaving for the USA. In good old Korean fashion, the samples arrived in the last minute before I walked onto the plane. It gave me no time to inspect the garments and no time to remake them if needed.

Of course, Korea has changed over the years. Only those, who were there in the early days, ran into these working conditions. Today, Korea has sophisticated apparel manufacturers thanks to the early American frontiers that showed them the know-how.

# Chapter 83

The company I worked for started to run into financial difficulties. They pressured me to move closer to the factory and took away my company car. Heide and I did not want to move from what we considered our dream house. However, our oldest son became more of a problem. He began to get in and out of trouble. Examining our options, we realized that moving could be a blessing. It would get our son away from the gang he was getting into trouble with. Perhaps, it might be a turnaround for him.

We put the house on the market and started to check out real estate at the shore area. The homes in that area were a lot more expensive, but we found one in Tinton Falls, New Jersey. It needed a lot of work, but it had possibilities; and with that in mind, we moved to the shore.

The company's problems began to get worse. Management's shortsightedness of recognizing the changes that rocked the industry, they became less and less competitive. It was time to find another job. I was about ready to accept a position in Massachusetts, when I got hurt in an accident. My ulna nerve was cut above the elbow of my left arm. This stopped me from accepting the job. But this too became a blessing. One year later, this company went out of business as well.

While recuperating from my accident, a friend in the industry said to me, "Why are you staying in the men's wear business? Get a job in the womenswear industry. The pay is much better. You have an enormous knowledge that few executives can bring to the market. None of them have the technical knowledge, plus the administrative, and business experience you have."

I was flattered by the comment, and since the menswear business was in the dumps anyway, I decided, why not? He knew of a company that made bridge-quality ladies sportswear and suits. They needed someone with my experience. When I went for an interview, I was hired on the spot and became the production manager. The company was privately owned and had a wonderful line of merchandise. My friend was correct. My salary increased by thirty percent and it included a company car. This was a big jump for me.

Now my travels not only took me to Korea, but also to Hong Kong. By then, air travel had also changed. The stretch 707 was able to fly from JFK directly to Tokyo with a connecting flight to Hong Kong. Since I had moved up in the world, I was also entitled to fly first class. What a difference it made in comfort, food, and service. Dinner started with caviar and a choice of entrée accompanied by drinks and wines.

Watching the approach to Hong Kong was mesmerizing. We crossed over a mountain when the plane banked left for the approach to the Kai Tak Airport. A sea of light greeted us. Depending on the direction of the wind, planes would come in on different headings. That day, it was the most interesting approach to the airport. It took us right between the skyscrapers to the runway. It gave me the feeling of landing on the main street of Hong Kong. The sight was amazing.

However, the way Immigration handled the passport checks, was a surprise. With all the high tech, for which Hong Kong was known, each traveler was checked manually against a book that listed all travelers as to their status good or bad, but custom clearance was easy. Hong Kong was a duty-free port.

I was told to look for the sign that announced the transportation to the Shangri-La Hotel. If you have never been to

Hong Kong, you have not experienced the meaning of service. When I approached the position, identified by the sign, I was ushered at once into a Shangri-La Rolls Royce limousine and driven to the hotel. What a hotel it was! One look and I could tell it had Luxury, with a capital L, written all over it. Upon arrival, I was greeted by a young lady and called by my family name. The check-in form was already filled out and after signing it, I was shown to my room. The room was huge, beautifully furnished, and outfitted with all the comforts of a five-star hotel.

The bathroom was tiled in marble, had a shower as well as a Jacuzzi tub, and it was stocked with every amenity from soap to after-shaving lotion, slippers, and a robe.

In the room was a fully stocked bar with wine, liquor, and snacks. A big TV, with channels presenting English programs, CNN world news, and the major European stations. A big picture window covered the back wall. The view overlooked the harbor and the island of Hong Kong with its millions of lights. Ferries crossed the harbor connecting Kowloon with the Hong Kong island. Cruise ships were anchored at the Hong Kong Harbor and the Kowloon Harbor. Chinese junkets bobbed in the water along the shore.

I was in awe looking at the fascinating sight of the shimmering water, reflecting the many lights, with the colorful neon signs and the ocean-going freighters, fishing, and supply junkets, and an old-fashioned Chinese sailboat powered by authentic-looking antique sails. Watching the mesmerizing sight, the doorbell rang.

I wondered, *who could that be? I do not know anyone in the hotel, and it is too late for someone to come from the office.* When I opened the door, a steward welcomed me to the hotel with a tray of tea, cookies, and a bowl of fruit. Contrary to Korea, he spoke a fluent English. Then he turned down my bed and explained all the automated functions on the nightstand console.

I was staying on the Kowloon Peninsula where all the apparel business was conducted. Hong Kong City was the financial and government district. The Peninsula of Kowloon was part of Mainland China. However, at that time it was still under the ninety-nine years lease the British had negotiated with China. Hong Kong and Kowloon were still governed by a British Governor and a Hong Kong administration. Both Kowloon and Hong Kong were big shopping centers for the global market.

Store after store with flashy neon signs lined the streets. Savvy shop owners stood in front of their stores trying to lure tourists and business travelers in. On the waterfront was the Ocean Terminal, where luxury cruise ships berthed. The terminal was a city block long with a three-story building full of stores. Hong Kong was a shopper's paradise and if you had a local friend to take you to legitimate stores, you could buy quality merchandise for very reasonable prices.

Besides the many luxury hotels, all kinds of stores and many restaurants were a sight to explore in the city of Hong Kong. The tram, going up to Victoria Peak, is a must see. It was the highest point on the island. When you reached the peak, the view was magnificent. It overlooked the harbor with its many quays, Kowloon, the Portuguese Island of Macao, and on a clear day mainland China across the South China Sea.

On the way up to the peak, I admired the most luxurious homes of Hong Kong. In the olden days, during the strict British Colonial Rule, the Chinese people were treated as second-class citizens. They were not allowed to own property on Victoria Peak. Only English expatriates could own a house on Victoria Peak. Henceforth, the Chinese developed a dislike for the British and named them *Qilos*, (meaning, white devils).

After World War II life changed. Many wealthy Chinese emerged. At the time of my first visit, it was said that Hong Kong encompassed four hundred square miles and had four hundred and one Rolls Royces. Automobile traffic was a stop and go procedure. It was more a parade of the well to do showing off their fine automobiles, than a means of transportation.

Another tourist attraction was Aberdeen where the *boat people* lived. Aberdeen was a harbor full of Chinese houseboats and fishing junkets. These people were born, lived, and died on their boats. They made their living by fishing. Small boats sold merchandise from groceries to clothes, or anything that they could load onto their boats. The boats were floating stores. They would pull up alongside the houseboats and peddle their wares. It was an unusual but smelly place. Fish markets lined the shore, that were supplied by the boat people.

Near the Chinese border was an old walled-in city. The homes were built in the old architecture and tradition of the last dynasty. The people lived a primitive lifestyle, very much the old-fashion way, yet, TV antennas could be seen on every roof. Also, it was interesting to see how women were cooking in iron pots hanging over open fires in front of the homes, and the laundry was done on washboards down by the river.

Outside the city walls was a gazebo from where you could look across the barbwire border of China. On the China side of the border was a town, which was for show and tell only, no one lived there.

Two old ladies in traditional black dresses, with the typical wide-brimmed straw hats, were smoking long-stemmed white clay pipes. It was a remarkable sight. Like all American tourists, we took a lot of pictures. However, if you took a picture with the old women in it and did not pay them, they would come after you yell and screaming. According to the information that we were given, they believed that if you took a picture of them, they would lose their souls. I guess money would remedy that. They must have had a lot of souls, because every tourist took their picture.

351

The Portuguese Island of Macao was another favored tourist sight. Macao was a tropical island under Portuguese rule. All the buildings were constructed in Portuguese architecture. The main attraction, beside the town itself, was the facade of an old Portuguese church and the gambling casino. The Hong Kong Chinese, known for their addiction to gambling, filled the gaming tables every day of the week.

Some garment manufacturing, in small shops, existed in Macao. These were mostly Hong Kong-owned shops circumventing the quota restrictions of Hong Kong. Otherwise, the island lived off tourism and gambling. Of course, both Hong Kong and Macao have since returned to Chinese rule. Hong Kong on July 1, 1997, and Macao on December 20, 1999. Until then they were under British and Portuguese rule respectively.

# Chapter 84

Not only were the luxury hotels in Hong Kong some of the world's finest but so were the restaurants. The chefs were in competition with each other and outdid themselves by inventing new and exciting dishes every couple of weeks. Any cuisine from around the world could be found and was authentically prepared in Hong Kong. I found the countless varieties of different Chinese cuisines and the fresh seafood prepared to perfection, irresistible.

It has been said, that one can eat a different dish at mealtime for an entire year without exhausting the vast Chinese menu. When you ordered seafood, you were taken to a fish tank where live lobsters, shrimp, grouper, and other fish were still swimming in the water for your selection. One cannot get it any fresher. When I was taken out for dinner, depending on the size of the group, the banquet could include anywhere from eighteen to thirty different dishes. Dining in Hong Kong was a mouthwatering experience.

\*\*\*\*

I was picked up on Monday morning by the agent who handled our affairs in Hong Kong. He was a very refined Chinese gentleman. He took me to his buying office and introduced me to his staff. The agency was on an upper floor in a building that overlooked the harbor. As soon as I walked into the office, I immediately sensed an efficient operation with a highly skilled staff. The rooms were practically furnished and clean, but ice cold.

It was extremely hot and humid outside, but the air conditioner was set so cold that I was freezing. The contrast between the sweltering outside temperature and the frigid airconditioned air, was too extreme.

In our first meeting, I was handed a folder with the factory's bios and their evaluations. Next, I was handed a complete production schedule with the status of each item. Here was sophistication at work, unlike what I had found in Korea.

Another surprise for me was, unlike Korea, everyone had a Christian first name; like Mary, Joe and so forth. Curious, I asked, "How come that everyone has a Christian name instead of a Chinese one?" I was informed that most everybody had gone to the Missionary Schools where the teachers assigned Christian first names to the students on the first day of school. The reason for this was, the nuns could not pronounce the Chinese names.

The factories we visited, were well equipped, well lit, and professionally managed. Hong Kong already had big conglomerates with multiple factories. The ones we used were all privately owned and smaller than the big, publicly owned factories in Korea. However, despite their skill, excellent equipment, and superb managerial leadership, I found that the structured suits and sportswear needed some attention. They were missing some finesse to turn them into tailored garments instead of dressmaker's attire. With some suggestions and teaching, which were much appreciated by the factories, I was able to rectify what was wrong in the sewing area. However, their pressing equipment and technique, needed a total overhaul. In Hong Kong, contrary to Korea, equipment was readily available. After picking out and setting up the pressing machines necessary to do the job, I instructed the pressers in the art of finishing constructed garments. Until then, all pressing had been done with lightweight steam irons, which is fine for dresses and soft garments, but not good enough for suits and tailored sportswear.

Overall, it was a successful and enlightening trip.

Because of the versatile creativity of womenswear, I enjoyed the challenges it presented a lot more than that of menswear. However, the ladies wear industry in the US was also known for its unreliable establishments. The lifespan of companies in general was short. They were here today and gone tomorrow.

A lot of the problems were due to the lack of proper organization and procedures. Due to the experience I had gathered in my previous positions, I was able to establish proper procedures and production control. With a timely information flow and good follow-up, quality merchandise was delivered on time.

All should have been well, but it was not. Within a brief time, I realized that this company was not right for me. The owner, a creative man, had many talents but lacked people-skills. He had created an atmosphere of fear among his employees. Decisions were not made unless it was directly approved by the boss for fear of his wrath, should he not agree with the choice.

After a year, I had made up my mind to find another job. It was time for another Hong Kong trip. I arranged my return flight through Germany where I met Heide at her parent's home. We discussed the situation on our flight home and I decided to start a search as soon as we got back. When we got home, there was a message waiting for me from a recruiter I had known for many years. When I called him, he asked me whether I was interested in a job change. His call could not have come in a timelier manner. We made a date to discuss the position.

# Chapter 85

When I met with my friend, Walter, the executive recruiter, he explained the position he was trying to fill. It was with Liz Claiborne, Inc. It was the fastest growing womenswear company, with one hundred and fifty million dollars in sales per year. They were looking for a VP of Manufacturing for their *Collection Division*. Walter told me that in his research, he had seen noticeable improvement in the quality of the garments since I had joined my present employer. After discussing it with me, Walter made an appointment for an interview with Mr. Boxer, who was the Executive VP in charge of all production.

Punctually, I arrived at the New York office and was met by Leonard Boxer. He was a warmhearted and soft-spoken man, whom I liked from the minute I met him. We had a very relaxed meeting in which I explained my background and my goals. About fifteen minutes into the conversation, he excused himself and left the room. Shortly thereafter, he returned and introduced me to Mr. Art Ortenberg, the chairman of the corporation and who was also the husband of Liz Claiborne.

I repeated what I had already told Leonard. After asking some questions and telling me about Liz Claiborne, Inc., their company's philosophy, and plans, he excused himself, left, and came back with Liz Claiborne. Very quickly we were into shoptalk. Art, realizing that our interests in quality merchandise were the same, he went out and came back with Gerry Chazen, the Vice-chairman of the company who handled marketing and sales.

I could tell it was a talented team; a fantastic consumer-oriented designer, brilliant tactician in all operations, an excellent marketing and sales genius, and a very hard-working production man who had opened the international supply market. No wonder this corporation was growing rapidly.

Listening to Liz and me chatting away, with the others asking a question here and there, Art took one after the other outside and then came back in with them. After Liz and I had chatted for some time, Art looked at her, and I saw Liz nodding her head. He then said, "Al, we want you to join us. We will put together a package that we think is fair. Leonard will call you on Saturday with our offer."

Saturday came, and Leonard made me an offer. It was fair and a much greater package than I ever had before. I accepted and after the customary notice to my present employer I started my position at Liz Claiborne. When walked into the Secaucus office in 1982, I got a glimpse of a world-class corporation.

Liz Claiborne, Inc. was founded in 1976 by Liz Claiborne, Art Ortenberg, Jerome Chazen, and Leonard Boxer. Through hard work, talent, and ingenuity, they had built the company into a 150,000,000 dollar publicly owned company. None of the four founders were afraid of work, no matter how menial it seemed to someone else.

Many times, I heard stories of their difficult beginnings. One that emphasized the spirit of the company was told to me right after I began working there. In the early years a salesman came to the office and saw a woman scrubbing the floor. He was looking for Liz Claiborne and asked the woman where he could find her. The woman, scrubbing the floor, got up and said, "I am Liz." I do not think there is any need to explain the determination and resolve upon which the company was built.

The fast growth had surpassed the company's structure and ability to continue to grow further without some new procedures and a fast restructuring of the manufacturing organization. Analyzing the need of the company to grow further, I realized I had to address the fundamentals, fit, quality, timely-production details, low-cost production, and on-time delivery of finished merchandise.

That was where my vast background came in handy. Having worked with designers in show business, I had learned how to see garments through the eyes of a designer. Therefore, under Liz's capable guidance, I had no problem creating garments with a consistent fit and without losing the look Liz had envisioned.

I set standards for quality that were not to be compromised under any circumstance and staffed the organization with capable quality control engineers to control and monitor the garments in process. Getting pre-production details going, was a matter of proper procedures, capable staff, and follow up.

I always prided myself of being a good negotiator, controlling dollars and cents to assure low-cost manufacturing. Delivering sportswear groups complete onto the sales floor, is always tricky. Our groups had as many as twenty to thirty-five different styled garments made in multiple countries. They could not be shipped unless all the styles were in stock. Good procedures for tracking and follow-up took care of that.

A year later, I was asked to take over the Sports Division as well, which had grown rapidly. We split the sports division into two, creating Liz Wear and Liz Sport. I was promoted to Senior Vice President in charge of Liz Collection, Liz Sport, and Liz Wear. After Leonard Boxer retired, I became responsible for all woven products covering all divisions.

359

# Chapter 86

During my tenure with the company, several new divisions were created: Claiborne Men's, Liz Girls, Liz Claiborne Petite, Liz Claiborne Women, and Dana Buchman. The company grew year after year in the high double digits until it was a 1.4 billion dollar a year business in 1989. Despite the enormous growth, we managed not to lose control of quality, fit, or on-time delivery, nor our ten percent after tax profits. Liz Claiborne, Inc. was the most admired growing company in the US and the darling of Wall Street. It was a joy and an honor to be part of the team. The company rewarded all its employees with generous monetary packages. It was a marriage made in heaven.

Art was the most brilliant, visionary executive I have ever met in my entire career. His saying was always, "Let's think long term. Do not worry about Wall Street's quarterly figures. If we do everything correctly, the figures will be there and propel us forwards," and so they did. Through his guidance and leadership, I learned to manage my responsibilities worthy of a world-class business not equaled by any other company in the apparel industry.

Liz was the most talented, smart, and personable lady I have ever met in this business. Her designs were always practical, smart, and colorful. And most of all, she looked out for her customers to receive quality garments for affordable prices. Working with her was an absolute pleasure. The years with the company were the most memorable ones of my career.

****

International business travel during my tenor with Liz Claiborne took me all over the world. We manufactured in almost all the Far Eastern countries, plus India, Nepal, Israel, Hungary, Italy, Mexico, Brazil, Costa Rica, Guatemala, and the Caribbean Islands. Most of the time I did not get to admire the sites. I was too busy trying to cover as much ground in as short a time as possible. The exceptions were when Heide accompanied me, which she did once a year. Then I would take off weekends to go sightseeing. We also traveled heavily during vacation times making up for the sightseeing that I had missed on my business trips. I enjoyed the beauty and charm of the vastly different countries and their amazing cultures. We explored the countries from the relatively new, to the ancient cultures of the Americas, to the thousands and thousands of years old Asian and Israeli cultures.

It was intriguing and of great interest to me dealing with the diverse cultures and their vastly different thinking. I became addicted to studying how to deal with the subtleties and traditions around the world. The staff under me had to listen to my preaching, "Any good coach of a professional ball team will study the opposing team, their strategies, and their ball parks. It is no different when you are in business. When you travel for the first time to a country, study the cultures and know the dos and don'ts." To this day it does not cease to amaze me that the government and the corporate world, have not grasped the importance of training their people in the cultures and traditions of the nations they service before they send them out to negotiate or to do business. Untrained klutzes are still walking around like elephants in a glass menagerie trying to negotiate with cultures they don't understand.

It is plain ignorance to think that all Asian's negotiate the same way. Only people with lack of knowledge and understanding think that it is all right to conduct business in the same manner as if they were doing business in New York.

I found during my career that saving face was the only common denominator among the cultures of the Far East. While the Koreans were tough negotiators who honored their commitments at all cost, I found the Japanese to be slick and always trying to find better deals and sometimes reneged on agreements. The Chinese are very honorable partners who dealt in a mild, laid-back manner, and to the letter honored every agreement I negotiated with them. They were also the most sensitive to, *face saving,* of all the Far Eastern countries. They were also the most difficult to read due to their indirect ways of communicating. While New Yorkers are known for falling into the house with the door, the Chinese will convey a problem by saying, *"perhaps there might be problem."* When you hear that, a seasoned negotiator dealing in China knows that it is not *"it might be,"* but is rather a *"big"* problem.

I observed a typical example of the lack of understanding the culture. After working all day, I was relaxing with a glass of beer at the lounge on the twenty-sixth floor of the Shangri-La Hotel. While I overlooked the harbor, admiring the lights of Hong Kong, I became aware of a young, loudmouthed, New York retail buyer trying to negotiate with a Chinese merchant. The buyer appeared to be just out of college and untrained in the ways of Chinese negotiators. He was apparently ignorant of the going prices and quota charges. He was also arrogantly obnoxious in his dealings with the merchant. He was waving a garment around in the air, hammering away at the merchant in an unnecessary, aggressive manner. He tried to get fifteen cents off the price. I realized that the price the merchant had quoted, was a fair price. I would have accepted it without hesitation.

As I listened, the Chinese merchant very calmly and patiently tried to explain to the young buyer why he had to charge the price he had quoted. Then, without regard for the etiquette of negotiation in a Chinese country or understanding the importance of leaving a way for the merchant to save face, the brash young man continued in his arrogant way and only became louder and more obnoxious. Finally, the Chinese merchant gave in and lowered his price by the fifteen cents that the buyer had demanded. But then, the merchant informed the young buyer that he needed to add $1.50 per item for quota, a charge he could not control.

The loudmouthed, misguided buyer smiled from ear to ear gloating over his fifteen-cent victory. However, he was unaware that he had been royally taken because, the going quota price was only fifty cents. Had he been professionally trained in the etiquette of negotiating and had he informed himself of the going quota prices, as well as what a fair price was for his garment, this would not have happened. If he really needed to get a few cents off the price, he should have very nicely asked for help and offered a couple of cents more on a garment where he could afford it, he would have gotten the reduction without overpaying on the quota. This is a typical example of how corporate America sends out untrained kids to do a grown-up's job.

It is no different with the politicians and government negotiators. Both parties, when they in the majority, send unprepared politicians around the world.

Some senators and congressmen that were on a fact-finding mission, stood on the pier in Hong Kong and pointed at a freighter saying, "There goes the illegally circumvented quota merchandise with fraudulent country of origin, and counterfeit designer labels." They had no evidence to support this comment, but it shows the ignorance of our elected officials.

Child labor is another one of my bones of contention. As much as I like to see every child well fed, happily playing, and being educated to the fullest like my lovely grandchildren.

However, we must understand the culture and the state of affairs of the country we want to deal in. Only seventy years ago we had no qualms about child labor in our own country, and when I grew up in the 40s and 50s, Germany had none either.

There are many countries that are at least one hundred years behind us in their development. They are struggling to build a productive, industrial country with decent living standards. But it takes time. Trying to force our standards onto them is neither productive, nor appropriate.

I remember when the labor unions paraded a young lady from Honduras around the USA during Labor Secretary Reich's reign. They stressed the point that the unfortunate young lady had to start working when she was thirteen-years-old to support herself. Mr. Reich supported this charade. Not mentioned was the fact that the young lady was an orphan; nor what would have happened to this thirteen-year-old young girl in a country plagued with prostitution, had she not gone to work.

Don't get me wrong. I am not a proponent of child labor. However, unless we can turn a country like Honduras into a world-class industrial state, we should be realistic and accept their local work system. Under the same administration, while I was part of the advisory committee on trade for the Retail Federation, I had a lively discussion with Mr. Reich's second-in-command about Burma, or as it is now known, Myanmar. I fully agree with the statement that this country's governing Junta has no regard for human rights. But it escapes my humble mind how putting an embargo on manufacturing in Burma helps the Burmese people. The Labor Department's representative gave a speech about the human rights violations in Burma, its corrupt rulers, and how we cannot allow their merchandise to enter our country. I tried to explain my experiences to him and about the havoc our government's restrictions caused the people of Burma.

At the time, we at Liz Claiborne, were doing business with a very reputable Chinese gentleman from Hong Kong, later from Singapore, who operated factories all through the Far East. My friend operated the finest factories, was a most reliable businessman, and he took care of his employees. He had started and operated a factory in Burma. The unemployment rate in Burma at the time was around seventy-five percent.

To operate any business in Burma, you were required to have the government in on the action as a partner. Yes, a lousy idea but not avoidable in that country. With his own money, he bought another building and turned it into a hospital. He employed doctors and imported medical supplies including an ambulance. We had a big need for merchandise and provided him with plenty of work for his people. His generosity put people to work, fed many families, and provided much needed medical care.

But what did the US Government do? It came and put an embargo on the merchandise from Burma, putting not only our company in a bind, but took the food out of the mouths of the needy people in Burma.

He had to struggle and almost went bankrupt because of the *Humanitarian Efforts* of our politicians. When I asked our famous Labor Department's representative what they had accomplished by stopping us from sending work to Burma? His only answer was, "We must stop the human rights violations." Really? Good job Mr. Representative. Let's take some more food out of people's mouths and we can stop the violations by starving them to death.

Improving the living conditions in third and fourth world countries can only be achieved by putting people to work so they can feed their families. That includes teaching children a trade. Forcing *our* labor standards onto other countries does not spare children the agony of being deliberately crippled by their parents. I have seen the beggar's children in Bangladesh crawling around on all fours like animals to arouse more sympathy when begging. I have seen them hang around the fences at the hotels with blank stares looking at the lucky foreigners who have it all. If you have seen the disparity of hungry children without hope, it will make you weep. Heide and I wiped away the moisture that welled up in our eyes when we observed those children.

Give a person a fish and he eat once, teach him how to fish and he eats for a lifetime; but do not tell the countries who can fish and who can't.

# Chapter 87

Here are some of the encounters that taught me the art of negotiating in Asia. On my first trip to Mainland China after trade agreements were established during the Nixon years, I had the pleasure of having Mrs. Chow, an elderly lady from Hong Kong accompanying me as my advisor. She had been born in Shanghai and was an expert in how to get around and negotiate business with the government officials. At the time, all negotiations were conducted with the government, as there were no privately-owned factories in China. Having quite a bit of experience in conducting business with Chinese merchants in Hong Kong and Taiwan, I thought the only difference would be dealing in a bureaucratic, military-controlled environment. But when I arrived in Shanghai, I noticed the absence of armed guards, armed police, or rifle toting soldiers. Taiwan had military guards standing everywhere at parade-rest with bayoneted rifles and a very strict passport control, which Hong Kong also had.

My first surprise came at the airport. Getting through immigration and customs was a breeze. Within minutes we were out of the airport, unlike the cumbersome process in Taiwan and Hong Kong. The uniformed personnel at the airport did not carry any sidearms nor did most of the police in Shanghai. Interestingly, the baggage went on a belt through a plywood tunnel that was supposed to be a scanner. Looking through it from the other side, I realized it was only an empty box without any monitoring equipment.

The drive to the hotel in Shanghai was quite interesting. The cars on the streets were rare. But millions of bicycles slowed down traffic. Besides the Chinese architecture, in the Chinese quarters of the city, many of the European countries had left their mark in Shanghai. Due to the trading interests of the Europeans during and before the last emperor's dynasty, a large part of the city is divided into British, French, and German architectural homes and business buildings.

In the mid-eighties, there were only two hotels where a westerner could stay, the *Friendship Hotel,* an old dumpy and dirty place, and the *Jing An* also old, but clean and had an excellent restaurant.

Women and men on the street were dressed in only gray and navy-colored *Mao jackets and caps.* Only two types of stores existed, the Friendship stores, where only foreigners could buy and the regular government stores, where only Chinese could buy. Westerners at that time were a novelty. They were treated by the curious locals like celebrities. When we stopped at gates, it was not unusual that a crowd of people would surround the car, push their faces close to the windows, and stare inside to get a glimpse of the strangers.

In the early days of trading in Shanghai, it was not unusual to be informed in the morning that you had to check out from the hotel, despite having a guaranteed reservation for another couple of days. That meant, if you had to stay longer, you had to bunk with one of your business companions.

The morning after we arrived in Shanghai, we went to the office of China Silk. It was the official trading entity for silk fabrics and silk garment production. I wanted to place with them a considerable order. It would have kept one of their factories busy for three months, with more to follow; providing their quality was up to my standards. I had planned to commit our company to an ongoing program.

We were shown into a plain and simple office. A few minutes later, three gentlemen walked in and Mrs. Chow introduced me to the head of Shanghai Silk, Mr. Liang, his second-in-command, and the interpreter. After the traditional tea ceremony with the usual small talk, how was your flight etc., I explained the history, the methodology, and operation of our company and the program I wanted to place with China Silk.

Of course, all of this was communicated through the interpreter and Mrs. Chow, my adviser. This process lasted about an hour and a half. Mr. Liang listened very politely and then informed me that he could not take my business. I was disappointed and said to Mrs. Chow, "I guess we struck out and have to try another time."

"No," she said, "keep on talking."

"Talk about what?" I asked.

"Anything," she replied.

I am not known for lack of conversational topics. So, I ignored his rejection and continued the conversation. After another hour had gone by, Mr. Liang offered to take part of the order. Now we were getting somewhere. Mrs. Chow again said, "Keep talking. You are doing fine." The conversation continued and by noontime he agreed to take the whole program.

Mrs. Chow then advised me, "Request factory-X, and workroom-B. They have the most skilled sewers."

When I made my request, Mr. Liang informed me through the interpreter that this would be impossible. Because he needed to fill open production wherever it was available. After more conversation and negotiating, he agreed to accommodate me with the factory I had requested, if I would keep the workroom busy all year around.

Through the interpreter, I informed him that would not be a problem providing we got quality garments and they were shipped on time. However, he informed me that if I wanted the factory to adhere to my quality standards, he would need to update the pressing equipment, but he did not have the dollars to buy the machines in Hong Kong. I then offered to buy the equipment as a present to the factory, which he graciously accepted. I figured the price of the equipment into the cost of the garments and knew we would still make an excellent profit.

When we visited the factory, I had to agree that the workers were highly skilled. But he was correct, the factory needed to upgrade the pressing equipment. After we had inspected the factory, it was evening and time to go to dinner. We invited Mr. Liang, his second in command, and the interpreter to dinner. At the dinner I found out Mr. Liang spoke perfect English and had no need for an interpreter. I can't blame him for being smart and buying time to formulate responses. But boy that was sly. It was a wonderful evening and the beginning of a very successful business relationship.

However, that day had been a big puzzle to me. I needed to get it clarified. On the way back to the hotel, I asked Mrs. Chow, "Can you explain to me what went on in today's negotiation?"

Mrs. Chow smiled and said, "You have to understand the Chinese mind. Since he had to deal with you, he was more interested in you than your company. To study you, he needed time; therefore, the lengthy negotiation. But, I can tell you that you have gained a partner that will not disappoint you."

She was correct. Mr. Liang became our most accommodating business partner in China. We set up an office in Shanghai with all the capabilities necessary to follow up the production and provide technical expertise to the factory. This successful business venture would not have been possible, had I not had the advice of an expert in Chinese negotiations. With this, I like to stress again, how important it is to know and understand the culture of the country you want to deal in.

The Shanghai venture was very lucrative and the amount of business turned into large shipments. Our office grew and was run as a sub-office of Hong Kong, the regional base for the Far East.

You can imagine our surprise when a call and fax came saying, "The office is in disarray, the manager flipped out, the staff is in hiding. The regional manager flew to Shanghai to assess the problem. But she went into hiding under her maiden name and is incommunicado!"

To us, it sounded like a mystery novel, but unfortunately it was real. For several days we were in the dark and did not know what was going on in Shanghai. Two weeks later, after the dust had settled, we found out what had happened. The office manager had a mental break down. She collected all the passports of the young Hong Kong employees, who were all Chinese, opened bottles of whiskey, and made them drink. She then threatened them with arrest by the police if they left.

The staff, mostly young ladies, went into hiding and somehow got word to Hong Kong about their predicament. At the news, the regional manager, an American lady that spoke fluent Chinese, flew to Shanghai to resolve the dilemma. After speaking with the staff, she realized that they were indeed in danger. Because of the lies the Shanghai office manager had fed to the police, if caught, they would have been arrested.

The regional company manager, in hiding under her maiden name, got in contact with a lawyer in Shanghai. Eventually he straightened out the problems. But, the staff was so scared that they left Shanghai and never returned.

# Chapter 88

The company sent a young German woman to Shanghai from Hong Kong to rebuild the office, which she expertly did. She staffed the office with other young ladies from Hong Kong who were all new to Shanghai.

On Christmas Eve, the young ladies, being entirely of the Buddhist faith, wanted to go dancing in a disco. As they walked around the city, they noticed a large building with a crowd of people waiting out front. Curious, they went to see what was going on. A policeman, controlling the crowd, checked their passports. He noticed that they were Hong Kong citizens. Showing them special courtesy, he made way for the young ladies and guided them into the building. To their surprise, it was not a disco but a Catholic Church that was about to start their midnight mass. Instead of dancing, they ended up being trapped for several hours in a midnight mass on Christmas Eve.

\*\*\*\*

Two years later, on a follow-up trip to Shanghai, I was advised that Mr. Liang needed to see me. By now I was an old hand at Chinese negotiations and had become very friendly with Mr. Liang. We met at ten in the morning and spoke for nearly two hours without touching on any subject of importance. I knew he wanted to talk about a matter of importance. However, all he talked about was trivial. Then, without warning, but with an apology, he advised me that they could not take any further business from our company for the rest of the year.

I was shocked but did not show it. Instead of going on a rampage and saying, "You can't do this to me!" I said very politely, "Did we do anything improper?"

"Oh no," said Mr. Liang, without elaborating.

I continued, "Is there anything we can do to overcome the problem?"

"Yes," he said again without explanations.

"How can we solve the problem?" I asked.

He said, "We can continue to work if you agree to make a present to the factory in the amount of what the work is worth, and we will make your garments without charge."

I agreed, since I knew we could still invoice the shipment without violating the custom regulations. The situation was puzzling to me, but I knew better than to ask Mr. Liang why. He knew I was dying to know the story behind this but appreciated that I did not put him on the spot by asking why. Later, in the day, he took me aside and privately solved the puzzle for me. He explained, "The workers in your factory made a lot more money than in the other factories, which under our system is not allowed."

Now I had the answer. Again, I became a little bit wiser in the art of negotiation. Patience and subtlety go a long way in China. Push and shove get you nothing.

\*\*\*\*

Life treated Heide and me very well. We were able to buy what we wanted, remodeled our home, put a pool in the backyard, and increased the value of our house up to four times the purchase price. Traveling became a favorite form of recreation for us, both traveling for business and for pleasure. We stayed at the best hotels and ate at the best restaurants in the world.

We took a picture-taking safari trip to Kenya during my vacation. Exploring the national parks of Africa, became one of our most enjoyable trips. Watching exotic animals in the wild from close-up, was truly amazing. The lions and cheetahs nursing their young was a remarkable sight, as was watching the lions in a pack stalking the wildebeests for their next meal.

We experienced firsthand the speed of a cheetah, while she hunted down an antelope that she had first separated from the herd. A cheetah can run up to seventy miles per hour. They are considered the fastest animal on land.

When we flew to our first destination, the Amboseli National Park, we had an interesting encounter with a little primate. The vans that took us into the parks had kind of a sun roof. It enabled us to stand up, look out, watch the animals, and take pictures. After exiting the DC-4, we boarded our van. As we watched and admired the zebras, antelopes, and wildebeest grazing near the runway, a small monkey jumped into the vehicle, grabbed a lady's handbag, and rummaged through the bag until it found the chewing gum. With the chewing gum in hand, the little critter jumped back into the tree, unwrapped the gum, and leisurely ate it while she watched us.

Visiting a village on the Masai Mara reserve and meeting the people, was a wonderful experience. And so was a hot air balloon ride over the plains. We started just before sunrise. As we rose up above the trees, the sun rose on the horizon, and flooded the untouched plains of the vast African wilderness. Herds of wildebeests, gazelles, and zebras, grazing their way towards the Tanzania's Serengeti was an unforgettable sight. After drifting over the reserve for three hours, we came in for a landing in the middle of the huge wildlife park. The crew served Champagne and cooked breakfast, using the propane fuel tanks from the balloons to cook.

# Chapter 89

On another trip we got to see the museum in Taipei with its vast treasures, the seaside resort of Kaohsiung, the temples of Taipei and Snake Alley. On an evening after dinner, our host asked us whether we were interested in seeing an active, old Buddhist temple. We were excited, it was a real treasure. Afterwards, he asked us whether we were interested in seeing something *different* like Snake Alley. Adventurous as the two of us were, we went to Snake Alley. We did not know what to expect, but what we saw was a very narrow street with stands on each side selling live chickens, chicken parts, snakes, snake blood, and snake soup. There were all kinds of snakes. Shopkeepers sliced open the snakes, squeezed out the blood, and sold it to the Chinese who drank it as an elixir for good health.

If you are not squeamish, you must see it. Several times I had snake soup in restaurants. Each time the soup was prepared differently. All of them tasted very well. The meat tasted like chicken.

****

Singapore, one of the cleanest cities in the world by far, with luxurious hotels including the old restored Raffles Hotel with its original Long Bar, we experienced the crème de la crème of High Tea, and luxury accommodations at unreasonable prices. If you like luxury and do not mind paying for it, try the Raffles in Singapore.

With their cleanliness came also laws; like the ban on chewing gum. Personally, I hate chewing gum with a passion especially stepping or sitting in it. That was no problem in Singapore. If you get caught with gum, you get slapped with a heavy fine. But, it is a beautiful place to recuperate after spending a couple of days in Bangladesh or India.

****

The metropolitan cities in India have Four-Star hotels. However, the infrastructure and the apparel industry were of third world standards. Streets in the big cities were lined with makeshift tents made from cardboard. Families lived in them along the heavily traveled roads. The children and grownups were subjected to the exhausts from vehicles. They had no means of washing themselves, or access to clean drinking water, not to mention food. Because of the unclean environment, most all the garments manufactured in India needed to be washed or dry cleaned when they were finished. There were some modern factories, and more of the industry were in the process of being upgraded. However, the infrastructure still left a lot to be desired. *Chai Pani* (bribes), or as the Indian officials like to call it, *Documentation Fees*, was a way of life. If you wanted anything done, you paid documentation fees and hoped you paid the right person.

The flights into New Deli usually arrive in the middle of the night. On one of my trips, after clearing the lengthy immigration process, I looked for the car that was supposed to pick me up and drive me to the hotel. However, no one was there. It was two o'clock in the morning. I took my suitcases and headed for the exit to look for a cab. When I came out of the door, I saw people sleeping on the ground everywhere. As I stepped over them, they all came alive and got up. They converged on me and said something I could not understand. It was eerie; I hurried back into the terminal where I found an English-speaking shopkeeper who helped me get a taxi.

The drive to the hotel was another experience. I don't think he knew which side of the road he was supposed to be on. Nor did he think he needed to be concerned about running over people.

After I had checked into the hotel and gone to my room, I got a phone call. "Mr. Lohn, where are you? I am at the airport waiting for you." Well if that was the case, he was only about two hours late.

On another trip to India, they lost my luggage on the way from Bombay to Deli. During my five days stay, every night I gave my underwear, shirt, slacks, and socks to the valet to clean so that in the morning I would have something clean to wear. After a lot of effort on the part of the local agent, my luggage turned up at the airport when I was checking in my flight to London.

I know there were many interesting sights to see in India, but it seemed I never allowed enough time to see them. Heide has visited the Taj Mahal, which she described as unbelievably beautiful. She said, that the transparency of the stones made them look alive. Too bad she had to pay for it with the Indian version of Montezuma's revenge. She ate some rice in a questionable establishment, which I had warned her about.

****

India's neighbor, Nepal, is one of the places we loved very much. The country is poor. However, families take care of each other. There are no beggars on the streets like in India or Bangladesh. The country is very colorful and is surrounded by unbelievable natural beauty. Outside of Katmandu, the supply and meeting place for the Mt. Everest climbing teams, are wonderful valleys with terraced farmlands. The route most often used to climb Mount Everest, starts in Nepal. But most enjoyable was the view of the snowcapped mountains of the Himalayas. We marveled over them as we ate lunch at an outdoors restaurant, above the terrace farmland.

Nepal has many temples with exquisite woodcarvings. We enjoyed a little city outside of Katmandu that took us back into biblical times. In some of the active temples, animals were still offered up as sacrifices. In the middle of the town was an ancient square that was surrounded by small stores where shopkeepers sat cross-legged in tiny spaces with low ceilings. If you wanted to purchase anything, you had to tell the merchant what you wanted. There was not enough space to enter the store.

In the center of the square, was a well that supplied the townspeople with water and a place to bath. The women would come and fill their pottery vessels with water and then carry them back on their head to their homes. A woman, in colorful garb, was in the square husking the grain. The grain had been laid out to dry in the market-square.

At the edge of the well sat a beautiful young woman with her newborn baby and an older girl. The young mother was dressed in a purple wrap. An elderly woman rubbed the baby and mom down with linseed oil. We found out that according to the local custom, after the birth of a child, the young mother is cared for the first eight weeks by her family' and then by her husband's parents for the second eight weeks. Every day, mother and baby were treated to a linseed oil rubdown to smooth and nourish their skin. The little girl and the baby were as beautiful as the mother. Indeed, it was a biblical scene.

On another trip we arrived at the Oberoy Hotel in Katmandu. The desk clerk informed us with a sincere apology that all the rooms were taken. Guests that were to have left, had stayed longer. But not to worry, they would put us into a suite in an adjacent building. What a treat that turned out to be. The building had been built to house the heads of states for the Asian Conference. Our suite consisted of a big living and dining room, a master bedroom suit with an elaborate bathroom, three guest bedrooms, and a fully stocked kitchen. Since one of my technical engineers was with us, he had his pick of the guest bedrooms.

Being too tired to go to the restaurant and eat, we wanted to order room service. But when I called, I was told someone would be right over. We thought they would send a waiter over with a menu, since there were none in the room. Surprise! A chef came over and asked what he could cook for us. That was a service I had not expected.

****

Another spot in the world we liked very much, was the island of Bali in Indonesia. Whenever Heide accompanied me on one of my business trips, I always tried to schedule a long weekend in Bali; of course, at our expense. Bali was located between Singapore and Jakarta. My agenda, when I had to go to that region, would always bring me from Singapore to Jakarta, which made Bali a convenient stopover. On the second time that Heide was with me, we stayed at the Four Seasons.

The hotel was built on the slopes of a mountain in a jungle-like forest overlooking the Bali Sea. It was unique. A main building, built in a classical Indonesian architecture, housed several restaurants, reception, administration, offices, and stores etc. Adjacent to the building were several pools, an outdoor restaurant, and a bar.

The rest of the hotel was built like an ancient town. The individual guestrooms were walled-in Villas surrounding a central house for the village elder, who took care of housekeeping, room service and served as concierge. Teak wood and weathered ancient-looking quarry stones, were the materials used for the house, walls, and villas. Built onto the jungle slope, it looked like the settlement of an ancient civilization. Each compound had a main building that housed the air-conditioned bedroom and bathroom with all the comforts of a five-star hotel and then some. The living-dining room was an open-air building with a straw roof, and up-and-down bamboo shades to keep out the rain. It was furnished with comfortable teak furniture and a well-stocked refrigerator with liquor, wine, and treats.

In the courtyard of each villa was an ancient statue of a Hindu God. Every morning, the village elder prayed and placed an offering of flowers and food in front of the statue. The walls stretched around three sides of the courtyard and were open facing east towards the ocean. A six by fifteen-foot pool faced the open side of the wall. Cooling off in the pool, we admired the shore and the waves of the ocean rolling in on the shore. The pool was in front of a steep cliff that led down to the water.

On the last morning of our stay, we finally made it out of bed at five o'clock to watch the sunrise. It was a spectacular sight. First, a shimmer of golden yellow appeared over the water on the horizon. The shimmer kept growing from moment to moment until the entire sky on the horizon was glowing golden yellow. The blazing sky reflected on the gentle waves of the ocean. We watched in awe the natural spectacle of the sun appearing like a big, red fireball. It changed the mix of color from golden yellow to blood red. Illuminated by the light, the peaceful glittering waves were bathed in the new colors. This was a phenomenon that one must have experienced when in Bali.

At the beach, just before the incoming tide, local men dug holes in the sand and in ceremonial fashion covered themselves with a mixture of sand and water. They waited for the incoming tide to wash them clean. We guessed that it was a religious ceremony. However, we don't really know.

We explored the local life. The natives were wonderful, gentle, and mild-mannered people. They are very imaginative in the art of carving, handicrafts, and woodblock printing. We bought some exquisite woodcarvings, Batik-printed scarves, and beach covers.

On another occasion we visited the Monkey Forest in Bali. Besides eighteen-inch bats hanging from tree branches there were gazillions of cute little monkeys.

Inside the forest, is the Temple of the Dead. It is solely inhabited by monkeys and bats. These monkeys are not tame and can get nasty. It is not a game reserve, but a regular jungle inhabited by animals. There is a big sign exclaiming: '*Do not feed the animals*' before you enter the forest. But right under the sign sat a vender selling bananas and bags of peanuts. Of course, all the visitors including us ignored the sign and bought food for the monkeys.

While we were enjoying passing out nuts, a little baby monkey walked up to Heide, pulled on her skirt, and held out its hand chattering. The message was clear, "*Here I am, give me some nuts.*" As Heide fed it, we heard the grunt of an old-timer. All the monkeys made room for the distinguished aged adult male strutting in a commanding mode up to Heide. He examined her with his eyes from top to bottom. Then, with a quick motion of his hand, he grabbed the bag with nuts and gave Heide what looked like a dirty look. Without hurrying, he strutted back to a rock and sat on it. He looked at Heide as he opened the bag and ate nut after nut. He was the *Ruler of the Apes*. None of the other members of the tribe contested his action. The scene said, "*Do you not know the rules of the jungle? Bring homage to the king first, and then mingle with the clan.*"

# Chapter 90

Other countries, like Sri Lanka, were not my choice to travel to. However, for a while, we did some successful business there. In the beginning years, the hotels were of inferior quality and were nothing like the ones the Far East had to offer, but later they improved.

Since I was not familiar with the country, the local factory had made my reservation on my first trip. The accommodations were in the Browns Beach Hotel. It was located right on the ocean and convenient to the industrial area, a free-trade zone. It sounded all right until I got there. Oh, it was on the beach and the location was lovely, however, as I told my wife when I called her, "Everything that is supposed to be in the water or the woods, is crawling up the walls in my room."

She said, "Oh my god, what are you going to do?"

I replied, "I am going to shut the light off, keep my socks on, and go to sleep." After all, I had been in the army and had slept in many god-forsaken places.

Civil war and terrorist attacks in Sri Lanka, made it difficult to produce merchandise. We never knew whether the garments would be delivered or delivered on time. To control the quality, I had technical engineers stationed throughout the worldwide supply net including in Colombo, Sri Lanka.

Collin, a technical engineer from Scotland, his wife and baby, were living in a house on a street with many Embassies. During a flare-up of hostilities, bombings, and shootings, we could not reach Collin and were extremely worried.

After a couple of weeks, we finally got through to him. I told him to take the next plane out of Sri Lanka regardless where the plane was going. I said, "Just get yourself and your family out of that country. They had lived for two weeks in the basement while shooting was going on night and day in front of their house. We didn't want our people exposed to this kind of environment. We immediately ceased to do business in Sri Lanka.

****

Unfortunately, Heide did not get to see the Philippines. Manila is a pretty city and full of history, especially the World War II kind. My experience in Manila dates to the days when Marcos was in power. They had *jeepees* as taxis. The locals called them jeepees. They were leftover jeeps from World War II that the locals had cut apart, lengthened, and turned into mini buses or taxis. How they kept them running all these years is beyond my understanding.

With the help from our local office, the factories turned out quality merchandise. We used facilities in Manila's metro area, as well as in Bataan. Bataan is known for the *Bataan Death March*. Thousands of our soldiers suffered and died after General King surrendered Bataan on April 12, 1942.

During the time that I went there, there were three ways to go to Bataan from Manila. A) By hydrofoil across the Manila Bay. B) By helicopter from a heliport on the roof of the Peninsular Hotel. C) By car. By car was the long way and it was dangerous. The road led through forested areas. The traveling time to the factories was too long to return before dark. Bandits and Guerilla Fighters would ambush the vehicles and rob the passengers of their possessions; especially in the dark.

I always took a chopper, it was the fastest way. En route we would pass a group of stalagmite-type rocks that generated an updraft, which would cause the chopper to bob up and down.

One of my colleagues, who shall stay nameless, was very gullible. He had heard of the bandits in the woods. Some wise guys had told him that these rebels would sometimes shoot at the chopper. To make matters worse, they told him a Philippine worker, dressed in dirty work clothes washing the chopper, was the pilot. After that, the poor guy was a nervous wreck. But he boarded the chopper anyway. When they got to the rock formation, the chopper hit the usual turbulence. He cried out, "Oh my God! We got hit!"

Everyone started to laugh and began to calm down the jittery executive that was about to lose it. It took some time to convince him that they had been pulling his leg. Well, he did not know whether he should get angry or be relieved, but, being the gentle person that he was, he took it calmly with the words, "That was not nice." I happen to agree with him, but it became part of the travel repertoire in Claiborne.

I arrived in Manila during the turbulent times and was rushed out of the airport because of a bomb scare. At another time, when I called home in the night, Heide was worried. She had seen pictures of riots in a square of Manila on the TV. I asked her at what time this was supposed to have happened. When she told me the time, I said, "No way! I was in that square at that time, if they threw anything, it was flowers."

Later, one of the locals told me that some smart US reporter had paid some kids to throw smoke canisters in the street to stage a *riot*. As you can understand, I am skeptical as to the reliability of our news media.

****

391

As I mentioned earlier, Heide never had the pleasure of traveling to Manila. We were in Singapore with our suitcases packed and ready to fly there. After a good breakfast, we were ready to call the Bellhop to pick up our suitcases, when the phone rang. The office manager from Manila was on the line and informed us that it was unsafe to come to the Philippines. The rebels had tried to take over the VIP lounge at the airport during the night. I was not a glutton for punishment and cancelled our trip. Too bad, Heide never got to see Imelda's shoes. Some years later I got back to Manila. I found that not much had changed. Bribes were still being paid only to different officials.

****

Central America and the Caribbean islands, became an attractive market because of the Caribbean Trade Initiative. Costa Rica, a beautiful country with an above average educated workforce, turned out to be a good marriage.

Guatemala was marginal. All the factories there were owned and operated by the Koreans. The Koreans wanted to use Korean raw materials, which excluded the merchandise from the 809 provisions. This provision exempted the merchandise from duty on raw materials providing the garments were cut in the US, from US fabric.

However, the Dominican Republic became an important Market. Initially, Gulf and Western Corp. developed the country with large sugar cane plantations and processing facilities. By the time I made my first trip to the Dominican, it had been sold to a private Cuban businessman.

The free-trade zone in La Romano had good factories. With technical help from us, they were able to produce quality garments. Since the factories were too far away from any city, I stayed at Campo De Casa, a resort located next to the free-trade zone. It was a first-class vacation resort with villas, beaches, several golf courses, polo ground, an airstrip, and all the luxuries of home.

On an exploratory trip to Haiti, during the reign of Papa Doc, Heide and I took a private plane from La Romano to Port-au-Prince in Haiti. The plane seated four, had twin engines, and only one pilot aboard. The trip turned out to be unproductive. However, the same plane, the same pilot, crashed fourteen days later in the mountains between La Romano and Port-au-Prince. It still gives me the shivers when I think about it. It could have happened on our flight.

I made another trip to check out some factories in the Santiago Free-trade Zone. To go from La Romano by car, the trip would take six hours over a dilapidated road. The factory manager in La Romano suggested I take a private plane to a military airfield in Santiago, which would save me several hours of traveling.

He made the arrangements, and in the evening, he took me to the La Romano Airstrip. The plane was a single engine, two-seater Cessna, with just the pilot and me aboard. After we got into the air, I discovered that he did not speak English and I did not speak Spanish. Consequently, we had a problem communicating.

Twenty minutes into the flight, he pointed at some dark clouds ahead of us and said something I did not understand. Since he banked to the right, I surmised he was informing me that he would fly around the front. A while later, I realized that he was not flying around the front but was circling in a holding pattern.

*Well*, I thought to myself, *we have a problem here.*

Fifteen minutes went by, when he started to chat franticly. Shaking his head, he pointed at the black cloud that was getting larger and was coming closer. I did not have a clue as to what he was trying to tell me, but I just hoped he had a full tank of gas. A couple of minutes later, he again was shaking his head and waved his hand, pointing at the dark front which started to look more fearsome by the minute. When I heard the words Santiago and Puerto Plata, and saw his gestures, I figured he was telling me that he could not land in Santiago and had to divert to Puerto Plata.

By then it was evening. Dusk set in, and it was getting dark. I wanted to land somewhere. So, I said, "Puerto Plata okay?"

"Si," he replied and off we went to land at the Puerto Plata Airport. He must have known the airport well, because the runway was not lit. The airport had no tower, nor air controllers. But he landed the plane safely. There was a small building serving as the terminal, but it was dark and for all intent and purpose, the greater airport of Puerto Plata was closed.

There I was, dressed in a suit and tie with my luggage at a deserted airport. The airport was not in walking distance to any town. The only people at the airport were a couple of kids who had seen the plane come in. They curiously jabbered away, "Senor? Senor money?"

I heard the word *taxi*. When the pilot said something to me. I replied, "Yes," hoping that he meant whether I wanted a taxi. He gave some instructions to the children. They ran off and a while later a car arrived. The car, driven by a big huge Dominican, was banged up, rusted through in many spots, and had a ripped-up interior with springs poking through the upholstery. Besides all of that, the car was dirty and had been hotwired. Otherwise, everything was fine, I had transportation; *Yea, right, you would think.*

Just like the pilot, my driver did not speak English. I had difficulty making him understand where in Santiago I wanted to go. At about that time a young boy, about ten-years-old, came running up and in Pigeon English said, "Senor, please take me. I interpreter."

Well, that turned out to be the best investment that I had made in a long time. His English was good enough to get me where I was going. "Okay I pay you. Hop in the car," I said to the young boy and off we went toward Santiago. It was an extremely hot and humid night. All I could think of was to get out of my perspiration-soaked clothes and into a shower. I could not wait to get there.

The drive to Santiago took several hours on a winding, poorly maintained road. The situation reminded me of an old movie where this guy in a suit, tie, and a bowler hat sat on the back of a chicken truck with a suitcase in his lap blowing chicken feathers from his nose. I must have resembled this fellow in some way.

My young friend served me well and my giant driver was as gentle a man as they come. Twenty minutes into our trip, it started to rain. I wanted to roll up the window, but my young friend explained, "No window."

When it started to really pour, I thought, *Great, with no windows on the car I will get soaked to boot.*

But my ingenious driver pulled over, grabbed some plastic from under his seat, and closed the open holes with plastic. The heat and humidity in the car rose a few degrees, but at least we were not getting wet.

We continued our trip, and after a couple of hours, we arrived at the outskirts of Santiago. It was pouring cats and dogs. The cars were coming from all directions and blinding us inside the dilapidated car because of the opaque plastic. Now I was wondering whether we would make it to the hotel without getting into an accident. However, we arrived safely at the hotel. I paid the driver and my valuable interpreter. I thanked them and went inside to check in. I could not wait to get my clothes off and take a shower.

Inside, the lobby was dimly lit which made me suspicious. From behind the desk the clerk apologized for the inconvenience of having no water and no lights until the morning. There went my dream of a shower and air-conditioning. Also, the restaurants were closed. Sweaty and dirty, I survived the one-star hotel in this third world country without the comforts of home, and on a couple of crackers and a warm soda.

# Chapter 91

The Dominican Republic is an interesting country, as two people from my staff can attest. My quality control manager, for domestic merchandise, was a very capable Vietnamese lady, seasoned by a difficult past through the war years. Temporarily, I attached a technical engineer to her for training into the methodology of the company. I felt it was vital for him to understand the standards of the company before he could make effective decisions, once he was stationed in the Far East.

The QC manager took the new tech engineer with her to the Dominican Republic, rented a car, and after finishing the job in La Romano, headed for Santiago. While they drove through a forest on a deserted road, a group of soldiers dressed in fatigue uniforms with automatic weapons emerged from the woods and stopped the car. The QC manager thought it was a passport control, or checkpoint. Instead, they demanded their money and valuables. They were not soldiers, but common bandits.

The blood seemed to drain out of the English fellow's face and visibly shaken, he started to remove his wallet. But the Vietnamese lady, toughened by her wartime experiences, said, "What, my money? You got to be nuts. She floored the car and made the bandits jump out of the way and drove off."

As fate would have it, the next month they went to the Dominican again. That time I got a phone call at night at home. She told me that they were in jail, and could I get them out? They did not know why they were arrested since the police spoke no English.

I immediately called the plant manager, woke him up, and asked whether he could help. Without hesitation, he made his way into town where they were being held. After parleying with the police, he found out that they were arrested for driving an unregistered car. He negotiated and paid a five hundred dollar fine, but the car was impounded. The QC manager had rented a legitimate car from Avis at the Puerto Plata Airport. But the local rental agencies were operating several cars on one registration, the double headed cow syndrome. With an apology and reimbursement of the fine, the agency brought out a new car saying it was all a misunderstanding. I am sure it was a misunderstanding, Dominican style.

****

Business led me to Israel as well. Besides it being a beautiful and exotic country, the sights of Old Jerusalem, still a true biblical city with its history of Christian, Jewish, and Islamic holy sites, was overwhelming. There are too many to list, but the Via Dolorosa, the Mount of Olives, the Church of the Holy Sepulcher, the Western Wall of the Temple Mount, also called The Wailing Wall, the Dome of the Rock an Islamic, Jewish, and Christian sacred site, and the archeological excavations are just some of the awesome highlights in Israel.

Heide and I stayed at the King David Hotel, a palatial Middle Eastern structure from where you can overlook the wall surrounding Old Jerusalem. In the night, we could see the illuminated wall with the Jaffa Gate from our window.

Another extraordinary sight was the Masada, built by King Herod as a sanctuary against attacks from Cleopatra and local dissidents. In its time, it was truly an impenetrable fortress; complete with years of provisions, and cisterns hacked into the rock to collect the rainwater. This citadel sat 430 meters above the

Dead Sea. It was built on a boat-shaped craggy mountain and could be defended against a siege for years.

During the Jewish rebellion in the year 66 AD of the first century, a group of Zealots seized the fortress from the Romans. In the year 70 AD, after the fall and destruction of Jerusalem, the surviving Israelites from the city, joined the Zealots and harassed the Romans. The zealots were using Masada as their base citadel. The last resisting group against the Romans in Palestine grew to 960 men, women, and children. In 72 AD. The Tenth Roman Legion, under the command of the Roman Governor Flavius Silva, attacked the fortress. Knowing that the fortress was unconquerable, he used captured Israelis to build a ramp up to the fortress, knowing that the zealots would not kill their own brethren. However, before the Romans could capture the Zealots, they committed suicide.

As history tells it, the leader of the defenders, Eleazar Ben Ya'ir implored, "Let our wives die before they are abused, and our children, before they have tasted slavery. After we have slain them, let us bestow that glorious benefit upon one another mutually and preserve ourselves in freedom, as an excellent funeral moment for us."

To witness and touch a part of a two-thousand-year-old history, was so remarkable that it gave me the chills.

****

The Dead Sea is another phenomenon of nature not to be missed when in Israel. Because the water is so saturated with salt and minerals that nothing can live within it. Therefore, it was given the name, Dead Sea. However, it is said that the unique chemical composition of chloride, bicarbonate, sulphate, sodium, potassium, calcium, and magnesium, endows the Dead Sea with considerable curative properties. Thus, mud bath treatments can be enjoyed at its shores to help heal several ailments.

After overcoming the fear of drowning and with Heide urging me on, I had the pleasure of floating in the Dead Sea without the ability to swim. It is the heavy salt and mineral saturated water that keeps you afloat. One funny sight was seeing a man floating in the water while reading a newspaper. However, I do not suggest getting the water into your eyes as it burns terribly. According to an Israeli lady, the only remedy is to look straight into the sun and let the tears wash out the salt.

Getting upright, after floating, became a problem for me. Heide had to come and help me up from my floating position by pushing my legs down.

Despite great factories, our business in Israel was sporadic, mostly due to high prices that were not competitive with the Far East. I traveled to Israel from 1984 to 1989, at which time I observed a harmonious coexistence between the Arabs and Israelis in Israel. They took me to Arab owned factories supplying Israeli businesses with merchandise. Arabs and Jews lived side by side. If only the world could harness the militants on both sides, life would be peaceful in this wonderful historic country.

It was amazing to see how the Israelis had accomplished successful farming in the desert. They grew vegetables, fruits on farms and orchards by cultivating infertile soil by ingeniously fertilizing and watering the desert.

Restaurants with Middle Eastern cuisines were terrific. We especially enjoyed an open-air restaurant in an olive grove on top of a hill on the outskirts of Tel Aviv. I can still taste the stuffed grapes, the rolled grape leaves, and the wonderful goat cheese sauces.

When I visited a factory outside of Jerusalem with my host, a factory owned by an elderly Arab gentleman, we were served Turkish Coffee. It was without doubt the best Turkish coffee I have ever tasted, and I have had the pleasure of drinking good Turkish coffee in Turkey.

One day, after we had inspected several factories, my Israeli friends took me for lunch at a steak house in Jerusalem. It was an extremely sweltering day and I was very thirsty. Not thinking, I asked the waitress for an ice-cold glass of milk. My Israeli friends busted out laughing, but, the waitress gave me the dirtiest look. Being Catholic, I forgot to remember the Kosher Laws, consume no dairy products with meat.

# Chapter 92

Europe was not a market for us; except for some sweaters from Italy and a few garments from Hungary. At the time, Hungary was still behind the iron curtain. It was an eerie feeling when I had to surrender my passport to the hotel clerk at check in. As an American citizen, I was not comfortable moving about the country without a passport, but that was the rule.

Budapest is a beautiful city, full of rich history. The Danube divides the city into Buda on one side and Pest on the other.

The factories were located between vineyards in the Takaji Wine Region outside the city. I had the pleasure of the factory manager taking me to a folksy restaurant for dinner. A true Gypsy band accompanied dancers, playing, and singing beautiful songs.

During the reign of the communists in Hungary it was difficult to do business. Raw materials were hard to get, and the understanding of matching colors between fabric and lining, or other trims was non-existent. The wheelers and dealers were government officials who had no knowledge of the apparel industry. When I pointed out that the lining color did not match the fabric, I was asked, "What is your problem? Both are red." That the two were different shades of red, did not concern them.

My nickname for the company director, a stern lady walking around in boots, was *The Commissar*. She did not comprehend or did not want to understand, that not all shades of red match or even blend. The business venture was short-lived.

\*\*\*\*

Heide and I made a point to vacation in Europe for at least two weeks a year. One week we would spend with Heide's Parents, and the other week, exploring different parts of Europe. The breathtaking mountains of Bavaria, Austria, and the Swiss Alps, became familiar. Quaint cities and towns like Luzerne, Salzburg, Innsbruck, Heiligenblut, Heidelberg, and Rothenburg auf der Tauber, were charming. Other metropolitan cities like Paris, London, Cologne, Munich, Hamburg, Straßburg, Rome, Florence, Naples, Venice, and Vienna, fascinated us with their architectural and cultural richness.

Two trips stand out in my memory and for different reasons, one, because of its uniqueness, and the other, for the comedy of errors.

Having enjoyed the hot air balloon in Africa, we signed up with Buddy Bombard Balloon Vacation in the Loire Valley of France. It was a unique experience. During the day, we went Château hopping and admired the grandiose estates of kings, queens, and other nobility of the past. In the evening, when the thermals died down, we lifted off in balloons, piloted by Buddy Bombard, and one by his lady pilot. It was a very serene experience floating over the green landscape, laced with trees and flowers, the river snaking along through the valley and no distraction from roadway noise. When we landed the minibuses that had been in contact with the pilots by cell phones, would collect us, and take us to a restaurant for dinner, but not before we had a champagne toast with the local farmers celebrating a successful flight.

On one night, we had a memorable dinner in a five hundred-year-old castle watchtower, complete with armors, swords, and lances.

Another night was memorable for a different reason. We were in the air with two balloons, ours being piloted by the

Number Two pilot, a young lady from England. Hot air balloons are steered by the direction of the wind. The pilot can only set the balloon on a different course by finding another wind direction. This is achieved by lifting or lowering the balloon. Firing the burner controls the lift and descent; heating lifts the balloon, and cooling drops it. The burners are fueled by propane gas. Each tank holds between ten to twenty gallons of gas, and the fuel consumption is about fifteen gallons per hour.

Dusk was fast approaching. It was time to land before it became too dark. Ahead of us we saw a small meadow on the border of a forest. It was to be our landing pad. If we did not make this one, the next landing pad would be a long way behind the forest.

The landing would be tricky, as we needed to clear a farmhouse just before the meadow and then drop down rather quick.

As luck would have it, the basket was about to clear the roof, when the wind angled the balloon and dropped the back ridge of the basket about ten inches. The edge of the basket took off a piece of the roof, but we still landed safely in the meadow. The young lady was embarrassed and apologized profusely to the farmers, who came running out. By the looks of the roof, the farmer was fortunate. The roof was in disrepair and needed to be replaced. Now Buddy's insurance would pay to replace it.

Speaking fluent French, the lady pilot assured the farmer that the insurance would cover the damage. The farmers were extremely nice people and told Buddy not to worry. In fact, they helped to secure the balloons and store them and the accessories into the trucks. Buddy broke out the champagne and soon we had a fun party going. We wished we could have been able to speak the language to converse with these friendly farmers.

****

This memorable trip brought to my mind the comedy of errors on a trip to Italy. We flew into Rome and rented a car. That was our first mistake. The car was a spanking new silver-gray BMW. After loading our luggage into the car, we headed from the airport to the Excelsior Hotel in the wonderful city of Rome.

Thirty minutes is all the drive should have taken us, but after driving around for two hours in the city, we still had not found the hotel. In fact, we could not find the street signs and we were unable to speak Italian. For the umpteenth time, I stopped and asked a policeman by just pointing at my reservation notice. He looked at it, turned, and laughingly pointed at the building behind him. We were standing at the side entrance of the hotel. We had passed it a dozen times. It was then that we saw that the street signs were part of the buildings. They were painted on the stucco of the buildings and not like ours or the German signs.

We finally checked in. However, when we went to our room, we found it unacceptable. For the price of the rooms and the reputation the hotel supposedly had, we expected better. After we complained to the manager, we were shown another room, equally unacceptable. It took five rooms before we found one that came close to what one would expect from a *Five-Star* hotel.

Our five-day stay was exciting, but still too short for all the sights that were there to see. Wonderful restaurants were everywhere. I can especially recommend a small restaurant called the *Piccolo Mondo;* providing it still exists. The food was superb. After each course, we told the Maître D how much we enjoyed it. He in turn, brought us a tasting of every dish on the menu, *after* we had finished our dinner. We walked out stuffed and could hardly move. We ate it all because we did not want to offend our friendly host; besides all of it was delicious.

Our next destination was Florence. We left the hotel in the morning and stopped on the way in Pisa and a walled city on top of a mountain. Both stops were enjoyable. However, it delayed our arrival in Florence. It was already dark when we got to the outskirts of the city. We had the same problem again; we could not find the hotel. One person would send us in one direction and another in a different direction. After running around in circles for ever, I asked a bus driver who had just unloaded his passengers in front of a hotel. We showed him our hotel reservation, and using sign language, he let us know to follow him, that he would take us there.

When he stopped at a street crossing, he pointed down the street. We thanked him and arrived within minutes at the Excelsior Hotel in Florence. We had a guaranteed reservation for three nights. However, at the check-in desk we were told, "So sorry, but we gave your room away because you did not call us before six pm."

Despite having a *guaranteed* reservation, we had no room. We were told the famous three words, *not to worry*. They arranged accommodations at the Villa Medici for two nights. But for the third night, we needed to come back to the Excelsior. The Villa Medici was only a block down the street, and no, we did not get lost.

Our room turned out to be a beautiful suite. We had left the car and keys with the doorman, who was going to park it for us. Ten minutes after we had settled in, we got a call from him. His question was, "How do I shut the alarm off on the car?"

"There is a little key on the key ring for the alarm," I replied.

"No," he said. "No little key."

I went downstairs to show him. The alarm was blaring away, but there was no little key. Nothing we tried would stop the noise, but after a while, the alarm shut itself off. Now the car was stuck in front of the door. Because the anti-theft device had disabled the car. It was also too late to do anything about it, Avis was closed. The next morning, I called Avis. They came out and fixed the alarm, so we could drive the car.

Okay, we solved another roadblock in our trip. Since we could only stay two nights at the Villa Medici, we had to check into the Excelsior for the last night. At check in, the doorman asked whether we would like the car parked in the garage or left in front of the door. After he assured us that it was safe, we chose the latter since we were leaving early in the morning for Portofino.

The next morning, after a hardy breakfast, we checked out and waited for the doorman to bring the car to the door. We waited fifteen minutes, but no car. The bellhop assured us it would be there soon. Another twenty minutes went by and still no car. Now it was no longer funny. Annoyed, I inquired again and was told, with an embarrassed look, that they could not find our car.

I went into the garage but did not find the car there either. Upon looking outside, I saw a silver-gray BMW, but it was not mine. Then it dawned on me, I asked, "Could it be possible that you gave my car to someone else?"

Yes, they had! Lucky for us, we had taken everything out of the car, including the rental papers. Our car had nothing in it except some non-essential papers. *What to do?* was the question. So, we went again to Avis and explained the situation. In typical leisurely fashion, the desk clerk took my papers, changed the car registration on my contract and told me, "Don't say anything when you turn the car in at the Milan airport. Just turn it in." Only in Italy is anything like that possible. I do not know how the person with no rental papers managed to turn in my car.

To finish off the comedy of errors, when we were supposed to fly home from Milan, the airport was on strike. Of course, that was nothing new in Italy. We were told they would fly us out from Turin. I told the lady from the airlines, "Okay, we will drive there and check in at the Turin airport."

"That is not possible," I was told. "You must check in at Milan, from there we will bus you to Turin." That made no sense, since the distance was the same from Portofino to Milan as it was to Turin. Well, just another Italian comedy of errors.

# Chapter 93

We enjoyed life to the fullest, lived in the fast lane, traveled the world in first class, and enjoyed the best cars, clothes, and food. Liz Claiborne, Inc. had grown from a one hundred fifty-million-dollar business in 1982, to 1.4 billion dollars by 1989, and with it my financial independence grew. We bought property in Beaver Creek Colorado, a winter resort, where we enjoyed skiing. We went on a Caribbean Cruise and soaked up the sun. We also enjoyed concerts and the opera in style.

However, in 1989, Liz Claiborne and her husband decided to retire. It was hard for me to deal with that situation. The company had lost the *Heart and Soul*. With my ego bruised for not being elevated into a controlling position, afraid that the remaining management would not be as quality conscious, and therefore would no longer uphold all that had made the company great, I decided it was time for me to leave.

We cashed in my options and traveled all over Europe for a month. Upon returning, I took a position with Jones of New York, for a year. Again, I was approached by my old friend Walter, who was recruiting someone to start up a manufacturing division for Spiegel Inc. in Chicago.

\*\*\*\*

When my friend contacted me about the position with Spiegel, I had no intention of moving to Chicago. Although the position sounded interesting, I wanted to stay in New Jersey where my family was located and retire within three years. I thought I was playing a joke on Heide when I asked her, "What do you think about moving to Chicago?"

To my surprise, instead of saying that is crazy, she said, "Do you think the position might be challenging? What would you do if it were in New York or Philadelphia?"

My answer was, "I would love to set up a division from scratch. If it would be in New York, I would seriously consider it. It would be great to prove to myself that I could be successful a second time."

We had been in Chicago, for a convention. Heide had fallen in love with the city. So, her reply was, "Why don't you check into it?"

So, I did. After a meeting with the VP of Merchandising in New York, I was asked to go to Chicago for an interview. I was to meet the top management of Spiegel, Inc. If they wanted me, my intention was to set up the division, stay for three years, and then retire on the east coast.

I asked Heide to go with me and explore the housing situation. I wanted her to check whether there was something we could rent. We flew in on a Thursday night and had dinner with the Corporate VP of Human Resources. The next day I met with the CEO and Chairman of the Spiegel Group, and the CFO. I was asked to consider staying there at least five years. My response was, "I will take it under consideration."

In the evening, Heide and I compared notes. She had found a house that she fell in love with, but it was not for rent. It was in a gated community and still in the building stage. I mentioned to her that I liked the people in management and that I was sure I could work with them. However, they would like me to take the job for at least five years. The next day, a Saturday, Heide took me to see the model homes. What I found was a beautiful area with town houses that had imagination and superior quality. We picked

412

out the model we desired and a lot that overlooked the immaculately landscaped community. Should I be offered the position, we decided to proceed and buy it.

Within a couple of days, I was offered the position as Corporate Vice President of Manufacturing for the Spiegel Group. The Spiegel Group consisted of, the Spiegel Catalogue Co, the Eddy Bauer Co, the FCNB Bank, and later we acquired the Newport News Catalogue Co.

After accepting their offer, we took a month off to travel in Europe.

On June 1, 1990, I started at Spiegel Inc. We moved to the western suburbs of Chicago and stayed for four months in a company paid furnished apartment until our house in Burr Ridge was finished. It was a lovely area surrounded by quaint little towns and was only thirty minutes away from the most beautiful city in the country, Chicago. For those who may not know, Chicago has lakefront parks, sensational shopping and restaurant areas, fantastic cultural events, it is a dream city. If we could have been able to get our children to move closer, we would still be living there.

My office was conveniently located and only twenty-five minutes away from our house. On the first day of my new job, after I had gotten the lay of the land and had been introduced to the staff, the CEO handed me a piece of chalk, and a blackboard, and said, "That is all there is. Have fun."

With that, I began to formulate what needed to be done and created a budget. A new building was planned and the groundbreaking took place shortly after my arrival. However, no provisions had been made to house the manufacturing division. Therefore, the company rented a 54,000 square foot building within five minutes walking distance of the new headquarters building. My task was to structure the division, find and hire a competent staff, procure the latest computer equipment to serve both the technical and administrative functions of the new division. Because of my experience at Liz Claiborne Inc., I was able to create a very sophisticated manufacturing unit. In fact, if it were not for the interaction with other departments and suppliers, the entire unit could have functioned paperless.

Spiegel was a publicly held company controlled by Dr. Otto of Otto Versand in Germany. Dr. Otto held all the voting stock. All of his holdings, including the Spiegel Group, were retail entities.

This was the first time for me dealing directly in a retail environment. I soon realized the company had an ingrained culture, controlled by foreigners that were ignorant of the US market, its peculiarities, and laws. Though, wholeheartedly supported by the CEO and CFO, my job soon became an uphill battle. Instead of customer, fashion, and sales-oriented merchandisers, the culture was ruled by the mentality, *the buyer is the king and has absolute power*. It was so ingrained, that it was almost impossible from them to relinquish the control over the making of the merchandise.

It turned out that the power-hungry buyers, afraid of losing control, worked against the manufacturing staff rather than becoming partners and supporters. There was not much help from Germany. They had the same mentality and were not convinced that there was a need for a manufacturing division.

Despite the roadblocks, I did manage to improve the quality and the on-time delivery, which was horrendous before the manufacturing division got involved. The backorder cancellations had been out-of-control. It was difficult to make the young, inexperienced buyers understand that there is a difference between cheap merchandise and value merchandise. My motto has always been, a $10.00 garment has a value as well as an $8,000.00 garment. A customer, who can only afford to spend $10.00, will examine the merchandise closer than a lady buying an

$8,000.00 dress. When the $8,000.00 customer sees another person wearing the same dress at an affair, it automatically becomes *worthless* in her eyes. Not so with the lady that made sure she got her money's worth when she bought the $10.00 garment.

During my tenure at Spiegel, Heide and I enjoyed the new life in Chicago, especially the arts. We got involved in the Chicago Symphony Association, the Lyric Opera Association, the local Newcomers Club, and traveled; we lived a very busy life.

We took our daughter and son on a Mediterranean Cruise with stops at Delphi, Myconos, Nice, Corsica, Malta, and Naples, the exciting city of Pompeii, Florence, and an extended stay in Venice. We sailed during the night and saw the sights during the day. Every evening we enjoyed a concert, entertainment, and dancing. The vastly variable sights made it an exciting cruise.

# Chapter 94

My business travel continued to countries I was already familiar with. However, after the iron curtain had vanished, I made some exploratory trips to the Eastern Bloc countries and Vietnam. The first trip was to Macedonia, the Czech Republic, and the Ukraine.

Prague is a charming city full of history and rich architecture. As far as business was concerned, I could not get to first base. Overpriced and outdated communist inflexibility made it impossible.

In Macedonia, I found good factories making quality merchandise, but no one was set up and ready to deal with the many styles and the few units per style. The countryside was spectacular though.

However, I arrived at a time when the city was overrun with convention visitors. My reservation was at a small hotel. Since I was only staying two nights, I did not care. When I checked in, they told me the only room they had was a small one and it was on the fifth floor. "Okay, no problem," I said.

After registering, I asked where the elevator was. The clerk informed me, "There is none."

Since I had been traveling for a couple of weeks, I had a heavy bag and a heavy attaché case. "Do you have a bellhop?" I inquired.

"No sir," was the answer again.

After schlepping my luggage five long flights up, I entered my room out of breath. The room was not much bigger than a walk-in closet, with a slanted ceiling and a dormer facing the street. The linens, blankets, and pillows were neatly stacked on the bed. Evidently, making the bed did not come with the room, nor was the bed made the next day. However, it was clean, and I was tired.

In all my years of traveling; the bugs in Sri Lanka, the straw mattress on the floor in Japan, the communal bath in the nude in Japan, and an early eviction from my room, this was a first.

****

My trip to Kiev, in the Ukraine, was very enlightening. In front of immigration were long lines. I had been told at home that I did not need a visa. When I finally got to the immigration official, he went back and forth through my passport and asked, "Visa?"

I said, "No visa."

He sent me to another line and when I got to that official, he kept saying, "Letter? Letter?"

I guess he wanted to see a letter of invitation, which I didn't have. Going through my attaché case I found a copy of a fax I had sent to Hungary, which had no bearing on this trip. He saw me reading the fax and said, "Okay." He pulled it out of my hand, stapled it to my landing papers, and said "Go." He was unable to read anything that was written in a western alphabet.

A Hungarian lady, that we had picked to represent our interest in the Ukraine, *should* we decide to do business there, waited outside the customs office. She had a car and chauffer waiting to drive us to the hotel. The chauffer was dressed in a three-quarter-length leather coat and the car was a Russian-made Moskovich. The Hungarian young lady was a very capable agent, whom I knew from working in Hungary. She spoke fluent Russian, as well as English.

After a while of getting reacquainted, the young lady asked, "Do you know who this man is?" pointing at the driver.

"I assume that is your driver," I replied.

"No," she said, "he is the ex-KGB chief of Kiev. We try to hire him because he has access to all the factories and knows everybody. It is hard to get into the factories without a local contact, but do not worry. He does not understand, nor speak, English."

I said, "Are you certain he does not understand English?" She shook her head saying, "Yes I am certain."

I inquired, "I thought the communist regime was dead, and the KGB no longer had any influence."

She grinned and said, "You would think so."

I was still concerned about our conversation being overheard, but she reassured me that he spoke no English...maybe.

The hotel was an old classic Inn. It was spotless, with highly polished parquet hardwood floors, beautiful Persian carpets, and furnished with antiques. However, the restaurant had an extremely limited menu, and the prices were listed in rubles with enough digits to be telephone numbers. I had invited both the agent and the driver, or maybe my KGB watchdog, for dinner. When I found out they were not excepting credit cards, I worried whether I had enough cash to pay for the meal. When the bill came, I had the agent convert the telephone number into dollars for me. The whole meal came to about $6.50. Well, it was not the greatest meal, but the price was dirt cheap, even for a Mc Donald's it would have been.

The next day we went to inspect factories outside the city. Our route took us past the famous Chernobyl Power Plant. The homes in that area were abandoned.

All the factories we saw, were well equipped with the newest machines. The operators were highly skilled, and the quality was superb. However, the factories were set up for large quantities, and the rigid management was incapable of service to the capitalistic world, which made it impossible to produce garments in the Ukraine. However, the biggest obstacle was the monetary restrictions. All the fabrics and trims needed to be imported since the local ones were of inferior quality. The factories had no foreign currency, and our suppliers, nor the European suppliers, would accept rubles. Therefore, the raw materials would have had to be bought by us, exported into the Ukraine, and then exported in garment form to the USA. It would have been a cumbersome, complex process, and a loss of control on wastage. Although it was an interesting trip, it was unfruitful.

****

My third exploratory trip was to Russia. Heide accompanied me on this trip. When we landed, Heide's long-forgotten fear and despise of the Russians, suddenly resurfaced with a vengeance. Heide was visibly shaken. It took her a while to overcome her feelings and calm down.

Our first stop was St. Petersburg, an ancient city with a long history. Unfortunately, the famous Hermitage Museum was closed on the Sunday when we were there. However, we did get to see Catherine the Great's Palace of Tsarskoye Selo, which was the summer palace of the Tsars. The palace had been destroyed during World War II, but the Soviets had restored it. During the war, it had served as headquarters for the invading German army. During that time, the Nazis had plundered most of the art objects.

The palace was like a history lesson; it projected the life and culture of the Tsars and their reign.

The factories that we saw were clean, well-equipped, and made quality merchandise. But again, the same problems existed as in the Ukraine. Had I not known any better, I would have surely surmised that the communists were still in power. Despite needing work and US dollars, the management was arrogant and had no

420

managerial skills to run a modern business. I asked for samples to take back and a price to manufacture the garments, which is a normal procedure before you get into actual business. The reply was, "Give me an order and I give you a sample and price." They could not comprehend how global business works. It was a wasted trip.

From there we flew to Moscow on a Tupolov. After that excursion, I swore never, ever to fly on a Russian airplane again. I thought the rattling contraption, called an airplane by the Russians, was going to fall apart any minute. Not even the worst planes in China could compete with that piece of scrap metal.

Prior to our trip, we had heard how rampant crime raged in Russia, and that anything you did not hold onto, would be stolen.

After our plane parked at a remote gate, we were picked up in minibuses. I don't think any of the gangways were operational. While we were waiting for the bus to pull out, Heide noticed a guard walking around the bus holding up a travel valet. She said, "Isn't that yours?"

Looking, I replied, "Yes, it is." I had left it on the plane. In it were our passports and flight tickets. So much for crime in Russia. Not everyone stole everything that was not nailed down.

While we were driven to the gate, I noticed a fleet of MIGS parked across the tarmac. But most of them seemed to have parts missing. They looked more like a *mothball fleet* than anything formidable, or of use.

Our guide for Moscow and Kursk, our next stop, was a Russian that lived in the US. He had advised us to stay in a Russian hotel instead of the Metropol Moscow, where most Americans stayed. Taking his advice, he made reservations in a hotel that was run by a Swiss company and had a fantastic French restaurant. I enjoyed the delicious caviar and the great Siberian smoked salmon.

Later, we found out that our Russian friend had valuable information. Armed bandits had held up the guests in the Metropol Hotel. Fortunately, the police apprehended them within a few minutes. A week after we had been there, a Russian businessman was killed from a pipe-bomb in his car.

As for doing business in Moscow, it turned out that it was the same as the rest of Russia—good factories, but arrogant incapable management.

We went to see the famous Red Square with the Kremlin, St. Basil's Cathedral, and the Lenin Mausoleum. The Red Square, which I remembered from the May Day parades on TV, was unimpressive and much smaller than I had imagined. Our Russian friend explained that the troops, tanks, mobile missile launchers etc., had marched repeatedly past the cameras to give the appearance of a much larger troop strength.

The Lenin Mausoleum, on which the Kremlin rulers reviewed the parade, was also much smaller than it had appeared on TV. Since we were there, we went into the mausoleum to see the embalmed Lenin. The atmosphere was hush-hush with stern-looking military guards standing at attention. When I tried to say something to Heide, an officer of the guard shushed me. I guess communism was not all together dead. By now, Lenin should have become an outlaw. However, the Kremlin did look impressive, but was closed to the public.

St. Basils Cathedral was beautiful on the outside and invoked pictures in our minds of the Tsarist winters. Inside, it was plain and cramped.

Next to the Red Square was a galleria with expensive French and Italian designer shops, art galleries, and jewelry stores. Sales were brisk, the mall was crowded.

Since we had refused to fly on another Russian airplane, our host arranged a sleeper reservation on the train from Moscow to Kursk. It would be an eight-hour trip. Before we settled in, our host gave us a wooden matchbox and showed us how to insert it into the lock of the door. With the matchbox in place, it would prevent anyone from getting into our compartment. He explained that there had been incidents of robberies when people were asleep. During one incident, the people on the train had been knocked out with gas during the night and all their belongings had been stolen. At that point, we did not know which was more dangerous, the falling apart Tupolov, or the train robberies.

The compartments were a far cry from our Pullman Sleeper. This Russian sleeper car had two regular wooden benches with feather bedding on it. It seemed that every time I went to sleep the train made a jerky stop almost throwing me off the bench.

However, we arrived in Kursk without incident and were greeted by a tall, blond-haired young muscular man, by the name of Misha. He spoke perfect English and picked up our heavy suitcases as if they were empty.

After checking into the hotel, we had a meeting with the management staff of the factory. This time, there was no arrogance, just friendly people wanting to do business. The factory was a large, old, knitting mill without the sophistication of the Moscow and St. Petersburg factories. But to our disappointment, once again, their requirement for minimum lots were too large for us.

They invited us into the factory's executive dining room, where we had a delicious business lunch complete with caviar and vodka. These people were sincere. The toasting to friendship, and good business relations, between the US and Russia went on for some time.

After lunch, we were asked if we would like to see the town, which we happily accepted. Misha was designated as our tour guide and showed us around. When we went to the beautiful local Byzantine Church we observed a Russian Orthodox wedding. It was a very colorful ceremony, performed with great splendor.

Upon asking Misha how strong the participation in the church was, after the years of communism, he explained that religion had always been alive. But the churches had become empty since the KGB had watched who went to church and took their names. Participants in religious activities had been discriminated against in many ways. They were barred from better schools, colleges, and jobs etc.

The town was well known for the Battle of Kursk during World War II, or as the Germans called it, Operation Zitadelle. It was one of the fiercest tank battles on the Eastern Front. The battle stopped the German offense in July 1943 and changed the outcome of the war. It turned the Soviets from a defensive force into an offensive army.

While Misha was telling us about the history of Kursk and showing us the World War II monument, he also explained that there were no monuments honoring the soldiers that had fought and died in Afghanistan. He explained that the action in Afghanistan was not talked about or acknowledged during the years of the Soviet reign. Misha had been part of the Russian Special Forces; the Spetsnaz, fighting in Afghanistan and knew what he was talking about. After a battle, he had awakened in a field hospital, one of only two survivors from his entire company. As a result, he suffered a mental breakdown and nightmares destroyed his marriage. It left lasting scars. What made matters worse, after his return to Russia, he was debriefed and told never to say or admit that he had been in Afghanistan, not even to his wife or parents. Consequently, his army papers made no mention of it and therefore, he was refused any medical help or treatment by the government.

Ten years later, his family still did not know about any of this. He told us his reason for not saying anything, was, "It would serve no purpose now." His attitude was that governments start wars and the young men, women, and children pay the price.

# Chapter 95

On October 1, 1996, our little granddaughter was born. Christen Briann was the most beautiful baby we had ever seen, but then all grandparents say that. We were ecstatic, and Heide was no longer interested in stores unless they had children's clothes. As I have often said, "Had I known grandchildren are so precious, I would have skipped the children and had grandchildren instead." I am only kidding. We love our children very much. However, there is something special about grandchildren.

Every six to eight weeks we made a trip from Chicago to the east coast to see our little princess. We began to realize how much we were missing, living eight hundred miles away. We struggled and were torn between our love for our family and the love for the city of Chicago and all it had to offer. Soon, I began to think about retirement especially considering the internal politics at work.

Two years prior to my retirement, I started a new business for Spiegel, selling premium items to corporations for use in marketing as incentives. In the second year, we already had sales of twenty-five million dollars. The business had a potential of three hundred million dollars and would have been a perfect companion to the manufacturing division.

In the meantime, I was getting tired of the political games and the power struggles that were going on. Any problems in the company were blamed by the merchandising staff on the expenses of the manufacturing division. Shortsightedness and inept foreign management did not recognize, nor face the real problems the company had. There was a lack of understanding their costumers and potential markets. The top line was pushed through with easy credit from the Spiegel-owned bank, attracting customers that would default on their outstanding balance. That problem was never addressed.

On January 1, 1998, after a year of semi-retirement, I fully retired. The manufacturing division was dismantled under the auspices of saving money, and later the premium business, *as incompatible with the company goals.* It became evident five years later, that the expense of operating a manufacturing division, was not the reason Spiegel could not move forwards. Corporate ignorance drove the company into Chapter Eleven five years after the manufacturing division. Thus, proving that the problems had not been the cost of operating a manufacturing division.

# Chapter 96

Finally, I had arrived at the stage of my life for which I had worked for all these years. I retired. Heide and I had to learn how to deal with the pleasures of retirement. At first, it was hard to live with no more deadlines to meet and tomorrow was another day. We both had to learn that when I asked, "What are you up to today?" That it did not mean I was trying to interfere with Heide's routine. Fortunately, we quickly learned to enjoy life together without losing our individual interests.

So many retired couples get into each other's way because they did not develop interests to pursue after retirement. Or they had been too busy making a living and raising their children to keep their love alive. Such was not the case with us.

My hobby was the computer, reading, and writing. I am now the author of eight published books. While I was working, I did not have the time or the patience to spend on those activities.

We loved traveling, especially through the US, and exploring places in Europe we had not yet seen and resumed contact with old childhood friends from Germany. Together we traveled to the natural wonders of our beautiful country, the USA. The four-week trip took us to the Painted Desert, Grand Canyon, Yellowstone Park, the Badlands, and on to Niagara Falls and the seashore. Our friends admired the sights and were in awe of it all. Besides that trip, more memorable trips were to Alaska, the Galapagos Islands, and Peru.

Alaska, with its glaciers, wildlife, interesting culture, and history, was fascinating. Together, with our friends, we embarked on an inside passage cruise starting in Ketchikan and ending in Juneau, the capital of Alaska. On the way we explored the towns and the Eskimo museums of Sitka, Haines, and Skagway.

With only eighty passengers aboard, the ship was ideal for getting into the small inlets and sounds. The itinerary was less regimented than on a large cruise vessel. Anytime we encountered whales, seals, or sea lions, the captain stopped the ship and allowed for enough time to enjoy nature's wonderful creatures. It was marvelous to watch the seals bathing and playing on the transparent blue icebergs. We were able to get close enough to the calving glaciers to watch them crash into the water with a loud thundering noise.

On our way to Denali Park, we stopped over in Fairbanks. It was there that we became aware of the long days and short nights. Sitting outside at midnight felt like four o'clock in the afternoon. From Fairbanks, we went by bus into the park. The lodge we stayed at was owned and operated by an Eskimo tribe. It was the furthermost inside quarters of the Denali National Park. The six million acres of sub-arctic tundra, with the rich wild life of bears, caribous, musk oxen etc., and the mountains including Mt. McKinley, were extraordinary.

****

In the year 2000 we flew with a group of sixteen to Lima Peru, and on to Cuzco, and then to the Galapagos Islands. In Lima we admired the park along the waterfront with its beautiful flowers and trees, the Gold Museum with the intricate Inca gold artwork, and the Anthropology Museum with its extensive prehistoric exhibits of Peru.

Cuzco, the old Inca capital is a colorful city with a wealth of history and is laid out in the shape of a Puma. The great plaza is surrounded with beautiful architecture and is illuminated in the evening. The archways are filled with colorfully dressed Inca street vendors, peddling their merchandise. Many of the buildings and churches in the city have been erected on the foundations of old Inca ruins.

We learned that in 1650, a devastating earthquake destroyed nearly all the buildings in Cuzco, except the old Inca structures. It had withstood the earthquake without the slightest bit of damage. The descendants of the Incas proudly pointed out the masterful stonework of their ancestors, and the quote, unquote, crude, work of the Spaniards. It is astonishing how the builders of the ancient Inca nation were able to cut huge rocks, sometimes with ten to fifteen surfaces, and fit them together with no space between them. Not even a knife could be inserted between the stones. They were not bonded together by cement. Only the weight and the ingenious craftsmanship of cutting and fitting, made the structures earthquake proof.

The city is in the midrange of the Andes at an altitude of 11,150 feet. There is a scarcity of oxygen to which I can attest. The Coco Leaf Tea was the best medicine for altitude sickness. We heard so much about the chewing of coco leaves by the mountain people, we wanted to know what it tasted like. After dinner, we had a drink in the beautiful lobby of a hotel that had been converted from a monastery. Since we were all curious, we tried a piece of coco leaf. To me, it did not have much of a taste, nor did it have any effect on me. Neither did it affect any of the others in the group, except for my lovely wife. In all our married life, I had never seen Heide as giddy as that evening after she had tasted a little piece of coco leaf. All of us had fun at her expense. She is still being ribbed by our friends.

When we visited Pula Pukara outside of Cuzco, we had the pleasure of attending a Shaman service. This colorful ceremony emphasized the close bond between the Inca Indians and nature.

Despite the strong influence of Catholicism, these rituals are alive and well to this day.

The trip would not have been complete without exploring Machu Picchu. This old Inca City is located about 112 km from Cuzco, on the lower part of the Machu Picchu Mountain at an altitude of 2,300 meters. It was connected by the old Inca trail to Cuzco. Majestic mountains surround the ruins and the view was breathtaking. The buildings were connected by a serious of 1,000 stairs. Aqueducts fed the Citadel with spring water and irrigated the agricultural terraces. To describe the many structures, built with the same craftsmanship as the ones in Cuzco, would take an entire book by itself.

Throughout the region, we saw women in colorful Indian garb herding lamas and selling gorgeous hand-woven blankets. Heide became the top negotiator. She showed us her talent in haggling for a fair price.

On a hot and rainy day, as we were walking past the many street vendors in the town of Machu Picchu, to the amusement of the locals and my friends, the snaps on my waterproof pants popped open and dropped down to my ankles. No, it was not as bad as you think, I did have another pair of pants underneath.

\*\*\*\*

After Peru, we boarded a sailboat in Puerto Baquarizo Moreno, on the far most eastern island of San Cristobal. The ship was an eight-cabin schooner with a crew of six and service second to none. The island with its beaches and coves, surrounded by blue and green shimmering waters, was breathtaking. We learned how Darwin developed his theory of the origin of the species. Exploring the Galapagos Islands is where he developed his theory. It is a naturalist's paradise with the many land, sea, and bird species.

What was interesting were the three types of colorful Iguanas. The Marine Iguana is the only sea-going lizard. The giant tortoises, weighing up to 500 pounds, live for more than a hundred years. There are many species of birds like the red-footed Boobies, the masked Boobies, and the blue-footed Boobies. Also, the thirteen species of Darwin Finches and the Frigate birds. They are best known for their bright red sacks beneath the beaks on the males. The Waved Albatross is only found on the island of Espanola and nowhere else in the world. With his streamlined body, the Flightless Cormorant, is an excellent swimmer and diver, but cannot fly. The thirty-five centimeters tall Galapagos Penguin is the smallest penguin in the world.

Marine life there is full of endemic species from the red, blue, and orange Sally Lightfoot Crabs, to the Golden Rays; and from the Scalloped Hammerhead Shark, to the Baleen Whales, dolphins, seals, and sea lions.

On the return trip to San Cristobal, cruising the waters on a schooner and watching the wildlife undisturbed on the islands, was a pleasure unequaled. Lying on the deck with a drink in our hands we enjoyed one of the most glorious sunsets. It was as if the Galapagos Islands were putting on a special farewell extravaganza just for us. The wind in the sails, sliding over the glistening waves with the deck slightly swaying, and no sound disturbing God's majestic creation, was an experience to behold.

****

Heide and I took another trip through the plains of the good old US of A. We went from Chicago to Victoria in Canada, via Seattle and Vancouver, then continued along the west coast via Route 101 through the Redwood Forest and on down to San Diego. From there we visited friends in the hills outside of San Diego in a town called Ramona. It was there that we witnessed the great tragedy of 9/11. We will never forget where we were on that day full of grief and tears. Our friends and us were unable to move away from the television. We were watching the reports of the horror as it unfolded.

Our return trip through Nevada, Utah, and Colorado towards home, was a somber one. In hotels, restaurants and rest stops, the conversation revolved only around the horror of the unprovoked attack on the World Trade Center, the Pentagon, and the downed plane in the fields of Pennsylvania. With tears in their eyes, people would confide in strangers about the latest news they had heard. Stories of heroism from firefighters, policemen, and ordinary citizens, were told and retold throughout the country. Our nation became alive with patriotism that united us in pain, grief, and resolve. Strangers became friends and political enemies united. Born, out of a national tragedy, a national unity emerged that we should cherish and nurture. If only this *United We Stand* could be bottled, and when necessary be permeated throughout the country, corporate greed would harness itself; politician's behavior and misdirected decisions, governed by the lust for power, would turn to actions taken for the good of the country.

\*\*\*\*

In the meantime, our status as grandparents became the highlight of our lives. Christen, the beautiful little baby started to grow into an adorable little girl. Until our little grandson was born, it was hard to envision that one could love another grandbaby with the same intensity. On June 14, 1998, Joseph came into our lives and we realized that God had given us enough love to share with as many of his creations as we wished to, and the more we shared, the fuller our cup of love became.

Then, on April 16, 2002, we were blessed with another little granddaughter by the lovely name of Alexandra. This adorable little girl can bring a smile to your face day or night. After her birth, we realized that it was time for us to move back to the east coast. We realized that we were missing too many precious moments in our children and grandchildren's lives.

We sold our house and returned to New Jersey. It was a pleasure watching our little *munchkins* growing up. Christen is now a beautiful twenty-one-year-old young lady of immense talents. She is going to start her senior year in college. She has her goal set for the medical field.

Handsome Joseph, the computer game genius, has finished his freshman year at the Monmouth University. His eye is also set on the medical field.

The littlest of the *munchkins;* Alexandra, now sixteen years old, is a natural athlete. She is one of three freshmen on the track and field varsity team and excels playing field-hockey. She wants to major in pre-med as well.

Life is much simpler now. Life in the fast lane cannot compete with the pleasure of grand-parenting. Love, faith, and mutual respect bore the fruit of an enjoyable life's autumn.

\*\*\*\*

Through the years, Heide and I lost both sets of parents. My dad died in 1982 of cancer. With his passing we lost a loving father, a great teacher, a mentor, a hero to emulate, but most of all, a loving friend. We miss his jokes and mischievous smile, his sound advice and his generous heart, his support and his undying love. He loved his children and grandchildren with all his heart, but unfortunately, did not live long enough to see his great-grandchildren.

Heide's father died in 1991from a heart attack. We lost another wise and loving friend. Like my own, he was a loving father to me. We miss his wicked grin when he told the stories about his youth, we miss listening to his hunting stories, we miss his kindness and his love, and we miss his presence when we visited. Part of our home and family in Europe is no more. He experienced hardships in his life but was spared the pain of witnessing the death of his favorite grandson.

Eight years later in 1999, Heide's mom died a couple of weeks before Christmas, also from a heart attack. She would have been ninety-years-old the following July. All of us had looked forward to celebrating her 90th birthday. She did not get to see Joseph and did not know about Alexandra before the Lord took her home. Mom loved all her babies. Next to Heide, she was my greatest admirer and supporter. I loved her like my own mom.

After her death, we lost the heart of the family and the home abroad. We miss her love and devotion. We enjoy how she used to laugh at herself, her hustling and bustling around the house, reading her romance books with her glasses on the tip of her nose, her sitting on the couch engrossed in her favorite detective story with cookies on the table, but most of all we miss her. The home abroad we cherished so much, is no longer but the memories of her, will always be in our hearts.

The next year, in November of 2000, my mom died from the ravages of Alzheimer's. Remembering her sharp mind and creative talents in handicrafts, it was painful to watch her broken body and mind shuffling around without aim or purpose. I remember how her love, during the war years tried to make my life bearable. The many sacrifices she and Dad made for us children and the values she instilled in us. She was energetic and always in a hurry. Dad often joked about the way she would collide with things due to her hastiness. One of her talents was that she had the ability to enjoy the smallest of pleasures and simplest of meals. We miss her love and her presence. The door is closed, the home is gone, and the loving face is no more.

With both sets of our parents gone, the old guard is no more. The home that was once the cradle of safety, the bastion of love, the cradle of strength, and the basket of wisdom, has been passed on to us. Will we be worthy of the trust? How will we pass it on to our children? Will their cup be full or empty?

I often wondered what the meaning of life was all about. Writing this book, and looking back on the ups and downs, the pleasures and pain, the achievements and disappointments, and the love and faith in one another and God, I now realize, those are the tools for growth.

****

We are taller now than when we were born
We are wiser and smarter than when we were born
We are older than when we were born
We have laughed, and we have cried
We have danced, and we have rested
We have risen, and we have fallen
We had gains and we had losses
We had help and we gave help
We learned, and we taught
We had mentors and we mentored
We had ancestors and we have descendants

# Chapter 97

The family's baton from our ancestors, made of faith, love, charity, honor, wisdom, and resolve has been passed on to us by our parents. Have we accepted the challenge that came with it? Have we maintained the integrity built into it? When the time comes, will we be able to pass the baton on with all its beauty and spirit intact? During our journey in this world, we are given the opportunity to grow and mature in wisdom. Is this the incubator and proving ground for humans to grow and become adults, worthy to enter eternal life? Is the purpose of being born to create and groom descendants for a higher existence? Will we ever know whether, or when, we touched someone and left a positive mark? We only know those who have touched us with love and kindness. May God bless them!

To my children, grandchildren, and their descendants I say, "This I wrote down, so you may know your ancestors and what they stood for. Accept the challenge and pick up the baton your ancestors passed on. Cherish it, bring honor to it, and when the time comes, pass it on with its beauty and spirit intact. My love and that of your family will always be with you."

**Author Al Lohn** was born in 1934 on the outskirts of Cologne Germany and educated in the art of apparel manufacturing. He worked until 1956 in his father's business. In November 1956, he immigrated to the USA with his parents and younger brother. Drafted thirteen months later, he served in the US Army for two years, two years in the Army Reserve, and two years on stand- by. While stationed in Germany he met his wife.

After his discharge from the Army, he became the manager of Brooks-Van Horn's manufacturing department in Philadelphia, a Theatrical costume company serving the entertainment industry. During his ten year-tenure, he worked on many challenging projects such as 'Holiday on Ice', 'Hello Dolly', the Philadelphia Mummers, historical reproductions for the Marine Corps, the Smithsonian Institute and wax museums.

During his fifty-year career, he served as Corporate Senior Vice President for Liz Claiborne Inc and retired as Corporate Vice President from the Spiegel Group in 1998.

His extensive travel during his 50-year career took him around the world to all five continents. His travels gained him a deep understanding of the world's cultures as well as their trials and tribulations. This, combined with his experience growing up in a war-torn country during World War II, and his military service, compelled him to turn to writing after his retirement.

He resides in New Jersey with his wife of fifty-seven years were they enjoy their children and three grandchildren. Now he writes and is the author of eight published books.

439

CPSIA information can be obtained
at www.ICGtesting.com
Printed in the USA
LVHW021932021122
732211LV00001B/43